3

ST. BRENDANS COMMUNITY SCHOOL
BIRR, CO. OFFALY

New GALAXY 1

GW00482733

Junior
Certificate
ENGLISH

Editor: John Moriarty

MENTOR PUBLICATIONS

© Copyright: - Mentor Publications 1995
All Rights Reserved

Text and Adaptations by: John Moriarty
Nuala Lavin

Illustrations: Ann O'Connell
Anne Sheppard

Typesetting: Maria O'Reilly

Published by: Mentor Publications,
43 Furze Road,
Sandyford Industrial Estate,
Dublin 18.

ISBN No. 0 947548 10 6

Cover

The cover was designed and painted by Ann O'Connell

Printed in Ireland
by
COLOUR BOOKS LTD.

Contents

I — Short Stories

II — Poetry

III — Writing Skills 1

IV — Drama

Contents

V — Writing Skills 2

VI — Reading & Media Studies

Acknowledgements

For permission to reproduce copyright material, the publishers and authors wish to thank the following: The Blackstaff Press for *A Rat and Some Renovations* from "Secrets and Other Stories" by Bernard MacLaverty; Sam McAughtry for *Tired of Life*; John Murray (Publishers) Ltd. for *You, the Jury* from "Six Plays for Today" by Paul Groves and Nigel Grimshaw; Faber and Faber Ltd. and Ted Hughes for the play *The Coming of the Kings*; The Society of Authors on behalf of the copyright owner, Mrs Iris Wise for *Check* by James Stephens; James Kirkup for *The Caged Bird in Springtime*; Jan Mark and Penguin Books Ltd. for *William's Version* from "Nothing to be Afraid of"; Faber and Faber Ltd. and Seamus Heaney for an extract from the poem *When all the Others*; Reed Consumer Books Ltd. for *My Ship* from "Come Softly to my Wake" by Christy Brown, published by Martin Secker & Warburg Ltd.; D. J. Enright and Chatto & Windus Ltd. for *Better Be Kind to Them Now*; Bloodaxe Books for *Lightning* from "A Time for Voices" by Brendan Kennelly; McGraw-Hill Book Company, Europe and Mrs E. M. Hanson for *The Sandpiper* and *Stopping by Woods on a Snowy Evening*; Erna Naughton for *Spit Nolan* and *The Goalkeeper's Revenge* from "The Goalkeeper's Revenge and Other Stories" by Bill Naughton published by Heinemann New Windmills; Patrick Gilligan for *Conán Maol and the Head-Hunter*; Irish Times Ltd., D'Olier Street, Dublin 2 for various extracts; Independent Newspapers Ltd. and the Sunday Independent, Middle Abbey Street, Dublin 1 for various extracts; Evening Herald, Middle Abbey Street, Dublin 1 for various extracts; Irish Press Ltd and The Sunday Press, Tara Street, Dublin 2; Lakeside Publishing Co. Chicago, for selected extracts; Mr Barry Kenny; Iarnród Éireann for photographic material; International Newsprint Limited, Paris, for selected extracts; European Photographic Library, Bonn, Germany; Office of the European Commission, Brussels, Belgium; American Library of Congress, Washington D.C. Delta Publications Limited, Houston, Texas, USA for selected extracts and use of photographic material.

The publishers have made every effort to trace the sources of copyright material and acknowledge the holders of copyright material included in this publication. In the event of any copyright holders having been overlooked, the publishers will be pleased to come to a suitable arrangement at the earliest opportunity.

I - Short Stories

Introduction

• Storytelling is probably the oldest art of all. In the past, stories were passed down from generation to generation by word of mouth. It is only in the last few hundred years or so that stories have been printed.

• Short stories hold a respected place in literature. Practically all the greatest writers in English have tried their hand at this particular form of storytelling. The successful short story writer must use special skills to be able to capture the imagination and entertain the reader in a few short pages. The selection of short stories given here have been chosen to illustrate the short story at its best.

A RAT AND SOME RENOVATIONS

Almost everyone in Ireland must have experienced American visitors or, as we called them, 'The Yanks'. Just before we were visited for the first time, my mother decided to have the working kitchen modernised. We lived in a terrace of dilapidated Victorian houses whose front gardens measured two feet by the breadth of the house. The scullery, separated from the kitchen by a wall, was the same size as the garden, and just as arable. When we pulled out the vegetable cupboard we found three or four potatoes which had fallen down behind and taken root. Ma said, 'God, if the Yanks had seen that.'

She engaged the workmen early so the job would be finished and the newness worn off by the time the Yanks arrived. She said she wouldn't like them to think that she got it done up just for them.

The first day the workmen arrived they demolished the wall, ripped up the floor and left the cold water tap hanging four feet above a bucket. We didn't see them again for three weeks. Grandma kept trying to make excuses for them, saying that it was very strenuous work. My mother however managed to get them back and they worked for three days, erecting a sink unit and leaving a hole for the outlet pipe. It must have been through this hole that the rat got in.

The first signs were discovered by Ma in the drawer of the new unit. She called me and said, 'What's those?' I looked and saw six hard brown ovals trundling about the drawer.

'Rat droppings,' I said. Ma backed disbelievingly away, her hands over her mouth, repeating, 'It's mouse, it's mouse, it must be mouse.'

The man from next door, a Mr Frank Twoomey, who had lived most of his life in the country, was called - he said from the size of them, it could well be a horse. At this my mother took her nightdress and toothbrush and moved in with an aunt across the street, leaving the brother and myself with the problem. Armed with a hatchet and shovel we banged and rattled the cupboards, then when we felt sure it was gone we blocked the hole with hardboard and sent word to Ma to return, that all was well.

It was after two days safety that she discovered the small brown bombs again. I met her with her nightdress under her arm, in the path. She just said, 'I found more,' and headed for her sister's.

That evening it was Grandma's suggestion that we should borrow the Grimleys' cat. The brother was sent and had to pull it from beneath the side-board because it was very shy of strangers. He carried it across the road and the rat-killer was so terrified of the traffic and Peter squeezing it that it peed all down his front. By this time Ma's curiosity had got the better of her and she ventured from her sister's to stand pale and nervous in our path. The brother set the cat down and turned to look for a cloth to wipe himself. The cat shot past him down the hall, past Ma who screamed, 'Jesus, the rat', and leapt into the hedge. The cat ran until a bus stopped it with a thud. The Grimleys haven't spoken to us since.

Ma had begun to despair. 'What age do rats live to?' she asked. 'And what'll we do if it's still here when the Yanks come?' Peter said that they loved pigs in the kitchen.

The next day we bought stuff, pungent like phosphorus and spread it on cubes of bread. The idea of this stuff was to roast the rat inside when he ate it so that he would drink himself to death.

'Just like Uncle Matt,' said Peter. He tactlessly read out the instructions to Grandma who then came out in sympathy with the rat. Ma thought it may have gone outside, so to make sure, we littered the yard with pieces of bread as well. In case it didn't work Ma decided to do a novena of masses so she got up the next morning and on the driveway to the chapel which runs along the back of our house she noticed six birds with their feet in the air, stone dead.

Later that day the rat was found in the same condition on the kitchen floor. It was quickly buried in the dust-bin using the shovel as a hearse. The next day the workmen came, finished the job, and the Yanks arrived just as the paint was drying.

They looked strangely out of place with their brown, leathery faces, rimless glasses and hat brims flamboyantly large, as we met them at the boat . . . Too summery by half, against the dripping eaves of the sheds at the dock-yard. At home by a roaring fire on a July day, after having laughed a little at the quaintness of the taxi, they exchanged greetings, talked about family likenesses, jobs, and then dried up. For the next half hour the conversation had to be manufactured, except for a comparison of education systems which was confusing and therefore lasted longer. Then everything stopped.

The brother said, 'I wouldn't call this an embarrassing silence.'

They all laughed, nervously dispelling the silence but not the embarrassment.

Ma tried to cover up. 'Would yous like another cup of cawfee?' Already she had begun to pick up the accent. They agreed and the oldish one with the blue hair followed her out to the kitchen.

'Gee, isn't this madern,' she said.

Ma, untacking her hand from the paint on the drawer, said, 'Yeah, we done it up last year.'

— *Bernard MacLaverty*

? Questions and Assignments

1. Why did the narrator's mother decide to have the kitchen renovated?

2. What is your opinion of
   (i)   the workmen?
   (ii) Frank Twoomey?

3. Describe the episode with the cat.

4. What signs were there that the rat poison worked?

5. (i)   Describe the 'Yanks' visit in your own words.
   (ii) Do you think it was worth doing up the kitchen for the 'Yanks'? Give reasons for your answer.

6. Give your impression of the character of
   (i)   the narrator,
   (ii) his mother.

7. What parts of the story did you find particularly funny?

8. Write about an event which caused panic in your home.

9. Imagine that you are a judge in a short story competition. Mark the story out of ten and explain briefly why you marked it as you did. (See page 18 for guidelines on how to do this.)

WP   **Word Power**

Find the words in the story which have similar meanings to each of the words and phrases below. The number in brackets after each one indicates the number of letters in the *answer*. The words appear in the story in the same order as the meanings given below.

1. shabby; in bad repair (11)

2. tiring and difficult (9)

3. putting together; building up (8)

4. rolling (9)

5. found (10)

6. an idea put forward (10)

7. timid in the presence of others (3)

8. very frightened (9)

9. went with caution (8)

10. strong-smelling (7)

11. very noticeably; colourfully (12)

12. chat; talk (12)

13. getting rid of (10)

14. way of talking (6)

☞ Points to Note

A person who writes a story is called an *author*. An author can make up a story entirely from his or her imagination and can base a story on things which actually happened without having to stick to the facts.

The author of the story you have just read, *'A Rat and Some Renovations'*, is Bernard MacLaverty. However the events in the story may or may not have happened to him when he was a boy. He may have used his imagination to make up the whole story or it may have happened to his family. It is also possible that something similar might have happened to somebody he knew, and he then invented a few more details to make it more enjoyable.

The author chose to let a character in the story - the son of the household - tell the story. This character is called the *narrator*. The author could have chosen the mother to tell the story instead. If he had done so we would probably have a slightly different version of the story.

TIRED OF LIFE

In the spring of 1929 I decided to run away from home. I was eight years of age. It must have been spring because the grass was damp during running away hours, and the reason I know the grass was damp is that I had resolved to sit on the damp grass on purpose, after running away, get the cold and sicken and die, and teach my mother a thorough-going lesson for what she had done to me. Which was as follows:

I was standing at the door of our house in Cosgrave street when Davy McAuley and Frankie Pattison walked past.

'Where are you going?' I asked them.

'We're going to Joe's,' they said, 'are you coming?'

They meant the picture house owned by a man called Joe McKibbin. A pleasure palace where, for a penny, you could occupy twelve inches of wooden form, breathe in concentrated disinfectant, and scream at the antics of Charlie Chaplin, or Buster Keaton, or a hundred other heroes.

But I hadn't any pennies. In the circumstances Plan X was indicated.

'I'm not going to the pictures,' I shouted at the top of my voice. 'I've no money, and my mother won't give me a penny.'

The plan worked perfectly at the start. Before I had even closed my mouth the kitchen door was flung open, a soapy hand came out, and I was hauled inside the house, coming to rest by the washtub where mother spent most of her waking hours. I tensed myself for the sudsy slap across the back of the leg. Sure enough it arrived. Then Plan X allowed for a tongue-lashing for showing mother up in front of the neighbours, and this, too, arrived on schedule. The last part of the calculation foresaw a penny being crammed into my hand and myself being hurled back outside again, to set off with my mates to the pictures.

Not so. All I got was hurled outside. No penny. No nothing. I made up my mind to run away.

Up Cosgrave Street, up the Limestone Road, and into Alexandra Park. There I sat deliberately on the damp grass in order to kill myself.

After about three minutes I was beginning to think it wasn't the greatest way to go. I rose, pulled my trousers away from the skin, and decided instead to climb up and touch the screen the next time I went to the pictures. Everybody knew the screen was full of electricity. I could shout at the horrified audience: 'This is my mother's fault,' and then touch the screen.

I was interrupted in my planning by a voice, calling me: 'D'ye want to see a bird's nest?'

It was a boy from the Limestone Road district. He beckoned me over to a hawthorn bush. Sure enough there was a nest, round and snug. But it was empty.

'Don't touch it,' the boy warned me, 'or they won't come back to it. They can smell if you touch it.'

We stared at it for a bit and then wandered down to the almost deserted swings, occupying one each.

'What school do you go to?' the other asked.

'Barney's,' I told him, giving him the nickname of St Barnabas'.

'I go to the Star of the Sea,' he said.

I looked at him with interest. 'What's it like?' I wanted to know.

'Rotten,' he replied, 'you get hit with the tawse for nothing.'

'We get hit with the cane for nothing,' I said. 'Last week I got six slaps just for climbing up a spout. Barney's is stinking,' I told him, with feeling. But there was something I wanted this fellow to clear up. 'Tell me this,' I asked him, 'do you have to drink holy water in the Star of the Sea?'

My companion turned round on his swing and looked at me as if I was ready to be certified. 'You don't drink holy water,' he said patiently, 'are you stupid or something?'

Before I could pursue the matter any further the other boy jumped off his swing and, giving himself a two-length start, challenged me to a race over to the river.

The river was actually a narrow stream. It was full of minnows. Off came our slippers to be shoved in our pockets, and we began to co-operate in the catching of minnows. Working as a skilled team we surrounded and scooped up a good dozen minnows, letting them off again because we had no jampot to keep them in. As the afternoon wore on we gradually worked our way upstream until we had reached the point where it emerged in Alexandra Park after its journey under the Antrim Road from the Corporation Waterworks. When we were too cold to stand it any longer we rubbed each other's toes with grass to warm them up, then we put our canvas slippers back on again.

'I go home this way,' the boy from the Limestone Road said, pointing to a hole in the boundary hedge where thousands of boys before him had punched an entrance to the Antrim Road. He turned back to me before he left: 'Will you be here tomorrow?' he asked.

'I don't know,' I told him. 'I might kill myself. But if I don't,' I finished, 'I'll see you beside the bird's nest after school.'

Then I went on my way home. The family were all sitting up to the tea when I walked in. Without interrupting their eating they moved up to make room for me.

I couldn't help thinking whenever I sat down at the table that not one of them had even noticed that I had run away and returned again. I decided to run away properly the next day. Either that or deliberately choke myself to death with bread and butter.

— Sam McAughtry

? **Questions and Assignments**

1. What do you find in the opening paragraph which makes you curious to read the rest of the story?

2. What do we learn about the picture house from the story?

3. Describe clearly what would have happened if Plan X had worked perfectly.

4. At what stage did Plan X go wrong?

5. How do we know that the narrator did not understand how a cinema projector worked?

6. Why do you think that the boys went to different schools?

7. Do you think that they had an enjoyable afternoon? Give reasons for your answer.

8. Describe an occasion when you were young and felt like running away from home.

9. Imagine that somebody asked you - 'Who was tired of life?' Write out your reply.

10. Imagine that you are a judge in a short story competition. Mark the story out of ten and explain briefly why you marked it as you did. (See page 18 for guidelines on how to do this.)

WP **Word Power**

Find the words in the story which have similar meanings to each of the words and phrases below. The number in brackets after each one indicates the number of letters in the *answer*. The words appear in the story in the same order as the meanings given below.

1. decided (8)

2. take up (6)

3. a substance which kills germs (12)

4. amusing actions (6)

5. pulled roughly (6)

6. on time as planned (8)

7. thrown with force (6)

8. purposely (12)

9. shocked (9)

10. a group of people watching a play or a film (8)

11. stopped while doing something (11)

12. signalled to come (8)

13. cosy (4)

14. empty of people (8)

15. comrade (9)

16. follow (6)

17. work together as a team (9)

18. came out (7)

 **Points to Note**

When giving your verdict on any story you should note that we generally enjoy stories which:

- make us laugh

- have exciting or dramatic episodes

- keep us guessing as to what will happen next

- have interesting and entertaining characters

- feature a character we admire, who wins out in the end

- feature a character we dislike, who loses out in the end

- show us something about life in a new and unexpected way

- take place in a fantasy world where things happen which could never happen in real life

These points should help you to give a verdict on the story. Only a very brief answer is required

Stray Dog

Mutt was one of those dogs you could see spelt trouble. He had 'trouble' written all over him. He was a big, bounding, awkward dog. His legs were too long. His ears were too big and his bark was too loud.

No one knew how Mutt came to the village. He was one of those dogs that no one wanted. He was one of those dogs that strays from place to place. He just didn't belong to anyone and he spelt trouble. Old Mr. Dennis caught Mutt in his garden. He threw a brick at him.

Mrs. Jones caught Mutt in her kitchen just about to steal the meat. She threw a jug at him. Fang, the farm dog at Croft farm, caught Mutt in the barn. Fang sent Mutt packing with more of a limp than ever! Norman, the milkman, found Mutt asleep in the cab of his milkfloat. Norman wears big boots on his milk round. He kicked Mutt out of his cab.

Pat's father did not like dogs. When he saw Pat stroking Mutt he was cross with her. Pat's Mother had died a year ago. It was hard for Pat and her Father. Lately Pat's Father had been moody and bad-tempered. 'Leave that scruffy dog alone, Pat. He's just an old stray, and he's nothing but trouble.' Pat felt sorry for Mutt. There was something about the old dog with his big floppy ears and long awkward legs. 'Can't we look after him, Dad?' said Pat. 'He would be a good watch-dog.' Pat knew she had said the wrong thing. Her father looked really angry.

Pat's father had lost his wallet not long ago. All his money was inside it. He kept his wife's wedding ring in the wallet, too. He was sure it had been stolen from his pocket. He always put the wallet in his coat. One day he hung his coat on the kitchen door. He went down the garden to see to his bee hives. Later he found the wallet had gone. 'Someone stole that wallet,' he said. 'They took it from my coat when I was down with my bees.' Since then Pat's father had been moody and bad-tempered. Pat knew he was upset about the wedding ring.

Pat wished she had not said anything about wanting a watch-dog. Her Father was very angry. 'We don't need a watch-dog. We don't need any kind of dog. Just leave that scruffy mutt alone.'

Pat looked down at the big dog. He wagged his big, floppy tail and looked at her with his silly face. 'Go away, Mutt,' she said. 'My father doesn't like dogs and he doesn't like you. I like you, even if you are just a scruffy old dog.' Slowly, Mutt got to his feet and ran off. 'The trouble with you, Pat, is that you're soft,' said her Father. Pat knew she was soft. Mutt knew it, too.

The next day, Mutt was round at Pat's before her Father came in from

work. Pat gave Mutt some food and a dish of water. Every day from then on Mutt came round to Pat's and she would feed him. Pat was afraid, in case her Father caught Mutt there. But Mutt always went away when he heard him coming. One day Mutt came to the door with blood all over him. He could not use his back legs. Pat did the only thing she could think of. She helped Mutt down to the old shed at the end of the garden. 'Poor old Mutt,' said Pat. 'I'll soon make you better, as long as you don't make a sound.' Mutt wagged his tail and gave a silly bark.

Each day Mutt's legs got a bit better. He seemed to understand Pat and did not make a sound. Pat went to see him whenever she could. Mutt would wag his tail and eat the scraps she took him.

Then it happened! Pat's Father went down the garden to see his bees. He had six bee hives. Some of the bees were swarming. He put on his big white coat and his bee hat, with its strange black net. He put on his long rubber boots but he could not find his gloves. 'I know,' he said. 'I left them in the old shed.'

He went into the old shed. He looked so odd in his bee outfit that Mutt barked and jumped up. He shot out of the shed barking. He darted away towards the bee hives. He did not even see the swarm of bees. There's a funny thing about bees. They don't like the smell of a dog. Sometimes they will attack dogs. Some of the bees went for Mutt. They began to sting him. Mutt went mad! He ran in and out of the hives. Crash! One of the hives went over. The bees began to swarm. They swarmed all over Mutt. They swarmed everywhere. Pat's Father ran to get his gloves but he could not help Mutt.

Pat ran down the garden. 'Get back inside,' her Father yelled. 'The bees are angry. I must get the queen-bee back in the hive. Then the swarm will follow.'

It took Pat's father all evening. At last the bees were back in the hive. When he came into the house, he spoke gently to Pat. 'I'm sorry, Pat,' he said. 'That old dog is dead. He just went mad and the bees stung him. But look, where the hive fell over, see what I found.' Pat looked up with tears in her eyes. Her father had the wallet in his hand. 'It was under the hive,' he said. 'I must have dropped it. It was not stolen after all. That old dog did me a good turn. Mutt found the wallet for me, in a way.' Pat was sorry for poor old Mutt. She sobbed herself to sleep. Her father could not be cross with Pat for keeping Mutt in the shed. He was sorry he had been bad-tempered and cross with Pat.

The next day, Pat's Father was home before Pat came in. 'I don't like dogs much, Pat,' he said, 'but look in the kitchen.' Pat opened the kitchen door. There was a little puppy for her. It had a white patch over its eye. 'Look after it carefully, Pat. I'm sorry I have been so cross and bad-tempered.' 'Oh Dad!' said Pat. 'I will look after him but I don't know what to call him.' 'That's easy,' said her Father. 'Call him Patches.'

| ? | **Questions and Assignments** |

1. Describe **four** of the misfortunes which Mutt encountered when he came to the village.

2. Pat's family also suffered misfortunes. What were these?

3. Why was Mutt in the old shed at the end of the garden?

4. What did you learn about bees and bee-keeping from the story?

5. Did Pat's father change in any way in the story? Explain your answer.

6. Write about how you got your first pet *or* write about a pet you would like to have.

7. Imagine that you are a judge in a short story competition. Mark the story out of ten and explain briefly why you marked it as you did. (See page 18 for guidelines on how to do this.)

 **Word Power**

Find the words in the story which have similar meanings to each of the words and phrases below. The number in brackets after each one indicates the number of letters in the *answer*. The words appear in the story in the same order as the meanings given below.

1. clumsy (7)

2. rubbing gently (8)

3. a lost or abandoned animal (5)

4. ran quickly (6)

5. a large number of insects flying together (5)

FERRET BOY

A new boy came to our school one day. He had long, dark hair and very small, black eyes. He did not like the rest of us. He had a dirty anorak and his trousers were patched up. He had muddy boots tied up with string. He stood by himself in a corner of the playground, his hands in his trouser pockets.

We didn't notice him at first. Then Ginger saw the boy standing there. He was leaning on the fence. He was making circles in the mud with his foot. 'Hey, look,' yelled Ginger, 'look over there! There's a new kid.'

We all ran up to the new boy. We stood in a circle round him. 'What's your name, kid?' asked Ginger. 'Tell us your name.' The new boy did not speak. He did not even look up. He just went on drawing circles with his foot.

'I know who he is,' shouted Biff. 'He's that kid from the caravan at Hatch End. His dad's a rag and bone man. He comes round with a cart after rags and things.' 'He's dressed in old rags himself,' laughed Ginger. Biff began to laugh too. We all began to laugh. 'We don't want you in our school, Scruff Pot,' he called. The new boy did not move, but we did. We began to dance round him and yell out.

'Scruff Pot! Scruff Pot! Scruff Pot!' 'We don't want you in our school, Puff Scrot,' shouted Nick.

'We don't want a rag and bone kid.' Suddenly the new boy looked up. 'I won't be staying long,' he said. I wouldn't stay here long, even if you paid me.'

Ginger, Biff and Nick went up close to the new boy. Ginger held his fist up against the new boy's face. 'Go on Ginger,' we yelled, 'bash him on the nose.' Suddenly the boy pulled his hand out of his pocket. Ginger, Biff and Nick stepped back.

The boy was holding something. What was it? It was something small and furry. It was something that was alive. It was like a small, grey, furry snake, with beady black eyes and a sharp, pointed nose. I knew what it was. It was a ferret. My Grandfather had one once. 'It's a ferret,' I said.

The new boy looked at Ginger with his sharp, black eyes. 'You think you're tough?' he said. 'You're not tough. You hold the ferret.'

Ginger didn't know what to do. He didn't want to hold the ferret. Nor did Biff or Nick. 'See,' said the boy, 'you're not tough. I knew you wouldn't take him.' Nobody wanted to hold the ferret, but I did. I was not tough like Ginger or Biff. I was not tough like them but I knew how to hold a ferret. My Grandfather showed me how to hold one. I could look really tough if I held it. 'I'll hold it.' I said and I held out my hands. The new boy looked at me with his sharp, beady eyes. He looked like a ferret himself. 'He won't bite you,' he said.

I took the ferret. It felt warm and smooth. I held it like my Grandfather showed me, not too tightly. It jumped up and down in my hand, but I did not squeeze it or hold it tight. Then it was quite still. I could feel its bones through its skin.

The boy looked at Ginger again. 'You take it. Or are you scared?' Ginger went red. He did not want to look scared. 'I dare you take it,' the boy said. 'I dare you to keep it in your pocket all morning. He won't bite you.' Everyone looked at Ginger. No one said a word. The new boy looked at Ginger with his small, black eyes. There was a sly grin on his face.

The boy took the ferret from me and held it out to Ginger. 'Put him in your pocket,' he said. Slowly Ginger held out his hands and took the ferret. He jumped as the ferret jerked about in his hand. 'Don't squeeze him,' said the new boy. 'Don't hold him tight. Put him in your pocket. He likes a warm place.' Ginger put the ferret near his trouser pocket. I saw the ferret slide inside. Ginger still looked scared but he didn't say anything.

Just then the whistle went. It was time to go in. The ferret was still in Ginger's pocket as we sat in our seats. The new boy was put in our class. The teacher took his name and sat him next to me. I did not want him next to me. He smelled of horses and wood-smoke. I did not like his scruffy clothes and small, black eyes. I slid my seat as far away from him as I could.

Ferret Boy

We have to be quiet in our class. Our teacher is very strict. She gives us number work every day. The new boy did not do any work at all. He just sat there and drew circles on a piece of paper. Then he looked up at me with his sly, black eyes. 'Well, I'm off now,' he said. 'I'm off for good. You won't keep me in school for long.' Suddenly he made a funny sound through his teeth. It was like the sound of a very sharp whistle. I knew what that whistle was for. It was to call his ferret! Ginger let out a great yell. He jumped up out of his seat. His chair went over and his table went flying. 'Ouch!' he yelled. 'It bit me!'

The ferret had jumped out of his pocket and run down his leg. It ran over the classroom floor. It went all over the place, like a dart. It ran between the tables. It ran under our feet. All the girls began to yell and jump up on their seats. Everyone began to shout.

The teacher shouted at us to be quiet. Then she saw the ferret too. It made her scream and she jumped up on to her seat. 'Get it out of here! Get it out of here!' she screamed.

The new boy whistled again and the ferret darted up to him. He picked it up and put it in the pocket of his scruffy anorak. We could see the teacher was cross. She looked really mad. We were all back in our seats. The room was so quiet you could hear a pin drop. 'Now!' said the teacher. 'Who came in with that animal?' 'Please, Missus,' said the new boy. 'It was him.' He pointed at Ginger. 'He came in with it in his pocket.' We all knew Ginger was for it. Our teacher does a funny thing when she is really cross. She talks very quietly through her teeth. 'Ginger, did you bring this in?' Ginger's face was bright red. He knew he was for it.

'Yes, Miss,' he said, 'but it's not my ferret.' 'I don't care whose it is,' she said. 'How dare you bring it into my classroom!' 'Please Missus,' said the new boy. 'Shall I take the ferret outside?' 'Yes,' said the teacher, through her teeth. 'Go out and get rid of it at once.' The new boy stood up. He looked at me and winked with his sly, black eyes. 'So long,' he said to me quietly. Then he got up and went.

? Questions and Assignments

1. (a) How did the other children treat the new boy on his first day in school?
   (b) Why do you think they treated him that way?

2. (a) Explain how the new boy made Ginger look foolish.
   (b) Were you pleased that he did so? Explain why.

25

3. (a) What did the new boy dare Ginger to do?
   (b) Why do you think that Ginger accepted the dare?

4. What detail in the story suggests that the new boy had never been to school before?

5. The author compared the ferret to a dart. Explain why.

6. What evidence is there in the story that the ferret was well-trained?

7. Did you find the ending of the story pleasing? Why?

8. Describe an unexpected disturbance which took place in your class.

9. Describe a bullying incident you witnessed in primary school. (You may wish to change the names of the characters.)

10. Imagine that somebody asked you - 'who was the ferret boy?'
    Write out your reply.

11. Imagine that you are a judge in a short story competition. Mark the story out of ten and explain briefly why you marked it as you did. (See page 18 for guidelines on how to do this.)

Silver Linings

Every cloud is supposed to have one, or so I learned at my granny's knee. Isn't that where you're supposed to learn such things? My granny is full of sayings, most of them rubbish, according to my mother, who has her own sayings. Like most mothers. My granny isn't one of those grandmothers who sits and knits in the chimney corner, shrouded in shawls, if such grannies exist at all. She tints her hair auburn and is employed as manageress at a local supermarket. It's not all that 'super', I must add, as it's only got two aisles, one up and one down, but still, a job's a job these days. And money doesn't grow…

Money's a problem in our family and my granny helps keep us afloat with 'care' parcels. She dumps them down on the kitchen table muttering about the improvidence of my parents and the wasted education of my mother who had all the chances in life that she didn't have herself. Etcetera. My father is not a lot of use when it comes to providing. He does odd jobs and he comes and goes. Like driftwood, says my granny, who doesn't understand what her daughter saw in him.

I think it was probably his name. He's called Torquil. My mother's got a thing about names. Her own given name was Isobel. A good plain no-nonsense Scottish Christian name. The only person who uses it now is my granny. My mother is known to everyone else as Isabella or Bella.

My name is Samantha, which my mother uses in full, but my friends called me Sam and my brother's called Seb, short for Sebastian. My granny approves of neither the short nor the long versions. 'Sam and Seb - sounds like two cartoon characters!' She hates having to introduce us, it gives her a 'red face'. She had wanted us to be called Jean and Colin. So she calls me 'hen' and Seb, 'son'.

Anyway, to get back to silver linings. I don't know about clouds having them but for a short time we had in our possession a fur coat which had one. But, first, I'd better explain about my mother's shop.

She keeps a second-hand clothes shop in a street that's full of shops selling second-hand things, from books to old fenders and clocks to medals and feather boas (though they're scarce) and silk petticoats (usually full of snaps and runs) and woollens (usually washed in). There are also two or three bars in the street, and some cafés. We like it, Seb and I. There's always something going on. The shop's in a basement (a damp one) across the road from our flat. You can doubtless imagine what my granny thinks of it. She says the smell of the old clothes turns her stomach and folk that buy stuff like that need their heads examined.

But people do come in and buy, not that it's ever like the shops in Princes Street on a Saturday. And they tend to sit on boxes and blether to my mother for hours before they get round to buying some ghastly looking dress with a V neck and a drooping hemline that was fashionable during the war. And then they find they haven't got quite enough money to pay for it so my mother says she'll get it from them the next time they're in. You can see why we need the care parcels.

When my mother goes out on the rummage for new stock - new old stock, that is - she just shuts up the shop and leaves a note on the door saying 'Back in ten minutes' or, if I'm home from school, she leaves me in charge with my friend Morag. (Nice name, Morag, says my granny.) Morag and I amuse ourselves by trying on the clothes and parading up and down like models. We usually have a good laugh too. I like long traily dresses in black crêpe de chine and big floppy hats and Morag likes silks and satins. We don't bother with the washed-in woollies.

One day my mother came back in a taxi filled to bursting with old clothes. She was bursting with excitement too, even gave the taxi driver a pound tip. You'd have thought we were about to make our fortune!

Morag and I helped to haul in the catch. We sat on the floor in the middle of it and unpacked the bags. There were dresses of every colour of the rainbow, made of silk and of satin, of brocade and of very fine wool.

'They belonged to an old lady,' said my mother.

The dresses smelt really old when you pressed them to your face.

'She died last month.'

We shivered a little and let the dresses fall into our laps.

'She was *very* old though.'

We cheered up and turned our attention to the blouses and scarves and the satin shoes. The old lady must never have thrown anything away.

And then out of a bag I took a fur coat. Now my mother doesn't like fur coats, usually won't handle them. By that, I mean sell them. She's for Beauty Without Cruelty. As I am myself. But this coat felt kind of smooth and silky, even though it was a bit bald looking here and there, and so I slipped it on.

'I'll have to get rid of that quickly,' said my mother.

I stroked the fur.

'Poor animal,' said my mother.

I slipped my hands into the pockets. I was beginning to think there was something funny about the coat. The lining felt odd, sort of lumpy, and I thought I could hear a faint rustling noise coming from inside it. I took the coat off.

The lining had been mended in a number of places by someone who could

sew very fine stitches. I lifted the scissors and quickly began to snip the thread.

'What are you doing that for?' asked my mother irritably.

'Wait!'

I eased my hand up between the lining and the inside of the coat and brought out a five pound note. Morag gasped. And then I brought out another and another and then a ten pound one and then another five and a ten -

'I don't believe it!' said my mother, who looked as pale as the off-white blouse she was crumpling between her hands.

We extracted from the lining of the coat one thousand and ten pounds in old bank notes. They were creased and aged, but they were real enough. We sat in silence and stared at them. My mother picked up a ten pound note and peered at it in the waning afternoon light.

'She can't have trusted the bank. Old people are sometimes funny that way. Keep their money in mattresses and places.' Like old coats.

'We could go for a holiday,' I said.

'A Greek island,' murmured my mother. 'Paros. Or Naxos.'

Once upon a time she used to wander around islands, with my father, before Seb and I were born. I could see us, the three of us, lying on the warm sand listening to the soft swish of the blue blue sea.

'Are you going to keep it?' asked Morag, breaking into our trance. She's a bit like that, Morag, down-to-earth, a state of being that my granny is fully in favour of.

My mother bit the side of her lip, the way she does when she's a bit confused. She quite often bites her lip.

'Finder's keepers,' I said hopefully. Hadn't my granny taught me that?

'I did *pay* for the coat.'

Not a thousand pounds of course, we knew that.

'Who did you buy it from?' asked Morag.

'A relative of the old lady's. He was clearing out the house. He looked well enough heeled.'

'In that case -' I said.

'I'll need to think about it,' said my mother. 'In the meantime - '. She glanced about her and I got up to put on the light and draw the curtains.

What were we to do with the money?

'We could sew it back into the coat,' I suggested.

That seemed as good an idea as any other so Morag and I pushed the notes back into the lining, all but one ten pound one which my mother said we might as well keep out to buy something for supper with that evening.

'Morag,' she said, sounding a bit awkward, 'don't be saying anything about this to anyone else eh?'

'I wouldn't dream of it, Isabella.' (My mother likes my friends to call her by her Christian name. She likes Seb and me to do it too but when I'm talking about her I always refer to her as 'my mother'.)

When I chummed Morag along the street on her way home I told her I'd kill her if she did tell and we almost quarrelled as she said I'd no business to doubt her word. But it was such a big secret to keep! I felt choked with the excitement of it.

We took the fur coat across the road with us when we went home and over an Indian carry-out and a bottle of rosé wine my mother and Seb and I discussed the problem of whether we were entitled to keep the money or not. Seb and I thought there was no problem at all.

'You bought the coat, Bella,' said Seb. 'Everything in it's yours.'

'Well, I don't know. Maybe legally, but morally … I mean, I suppose I should give it back.'

'But you want to go to Greece don't you?' I said.

Her lip trembled.

Outside, it was raining. Big heavy drops were striking the window pane and the wind was making the glass rattle in its frame.

'You could both be doing with new shoes,' said our mother. 'Mind you, with money like that…' She sighed.

The next day was Saturday. We took the coat back over to the shop with us in the morning, afraid to let it out of our sight. My mother put it in a cupboard in the back room where she keeps garments that are waiting to be mended. Some are beyond redemption but they wait nevertheless.

In the afternoon, we had to go to a family wedding, on my father's side. My father was supposed to be there. My mother and I kitted ourselves out with clothes from the shop.

'Well, honestly!' declared my granny, on her arrival. She was to mind the shop while we were gone. 'I could have lent you a nice wee suit, Isobel.' She turned to look me over. 'Do you think black crêpe de chine's the right thing to be wearing at a wedding? And at your age too!' She didn't even call me hen. She couldn't have thought I looked endearing. The dress had come out of the old lady's wardrobe.

In the bus, Seb, said to our mother, 'Now don't tell Father about the money if he *is* there.'

He did turn up. He was his usual 'charming' self, never stuck for words. I was pleased enough to see him to begin with but after a bit when I saw him sweet-talking our mother and her cheeks beginning to turn pink and her eyes lighting up, I felt myself going off him. Seb and I sat side by side and drank as much fizzy wine as we could get hold of and listened to her laugh floating down the room.

'She'll tell him,' said Seb gloomily.

She did of course. And he decided to come home with us. They walked in front of us holding hands.

'When will she ever learn?' said Seb, sounding strangely like our granny.

'Good evening, Torquil,' said that lady very stiffly, when we came into the shop where she was sitting playing Clock Patience on the counter top. 'Stranger,' she couldn't resist adding.

'Hi, Ma!' He gave her a smacking kiss on the cheek. 'It's good to see you. You're not looking a day older.'

She did not return the compliment.

'Been busy?' asked my mother.

'Not exactly rushed off my feet. I sold two or three dresses and one of those tatty Victorian nightgowns - oh, and yon moth-eaten fur coat in the cupboard through the back.'

She might just as well have struck us all down with a sledge-hammer. We were in a state of total collapse for at least five minutes until my mother managed to get back the use of her tongue.

'You sold *that coat*?'

'Well, why not? You hate having fur lying around.'

'Who did you sell it to?' My mother was doing her best to stay calm.

'How should I know? Some woman. She came in asking if we'd any furs. She gave me twenty pounds for it. I didn't think you could ask a penny more. Lucky to get that.'

My mother told my granny about the money in the lining and then it was her turn to collapse. I thought we were going to have to call a doctor to revive her. My father managed it with some brandy that he had in his coat pocket.

'Oh no,' she moaned, 'oh *no*. But what did you leave it in the shop for, Isobel?'

'It was in the back shop! In the cupboard.'

They started to argue, to blame one another. Seb and I went out and roamed the streets till dark and long after looking for the woman in our fur coat. We never did see it again.

Our father left the next morning.

'Shows him up for what he is, doesn't it?' said our granny. 'He only came back for the money. He'd have taken you to the cleaners, Isobel. Maybe it was just as well. As I always say -' She stopped.

Not even she had the nerve to look my mother in the eye and say that every cloud has its silver lining.

— *Joan Lingard*

1. 'Every cloud has a silver lining.' This is the proverb from which the title is taken. Explain the proverb.

2. What do we learn about the narrator and her family in the first four paragraphs of the story?

3. Describe the street where the narrator's shop was situated.

4. Was the narrator's mother a good person to run a business? Give a reason for your answer.

5. Why did the narrator's mother not like fur coats?

6. Why was the money sewn back into the lining of the fur coat?

7. What eventually happened to the coat?

8. Write about the best or the worst bit of luck you ever had.

9. Imagine that you are a judge in a short story competition. Mark the story out of ten and explain briefly why you marked it as you did. (See page 18 for guidelines on how to do this.)

WP Word Power

Find the words in the story which have similar meanings to each of the words and phrases below. The number in brackets after each one indicates the number of letters in the *answer*. The words appear in the story in the same order as the meanings given below.

1. covered (8)

2. colours faintly (5)

3. passages (6)

4. not planning for future needs (12)

5. is in favour of (8)

6. ownership (10)

7. underground section of a building (8)

8. unpleasant; distasteful (7)

9. barely noticeable (5)

10. bad-temperedly (9)

11. breathed in sharply (6)

12. crushing; folding unevenly (9)

13. drew out (9)

14. fading (6)

15. dream (6)

16. had a right (8)

17. shook (8)

18. saving from ruin (10)

19. unhappily (8)

20. politely but coldly (7)

21. word of praise (10)

22. bring strength back (6)

THE GIANT WITH THE THREE GOLDEN HAIRS

Once upon a time a poor woman whose son was born with a mole on his cheek, and so it was foretold of him that in his fourteenth year he should marry the King's daughter. As it happened the King soon after came into the village, quite unknown to any one, and when he asked the people what news there was, they answered, "A few days since a child with a mole on his cheek was born, which is a sure sign that he will be very lucky; and, indeed, it has been foretold of him that in his fourteenth year he will marry the King's daughter."

The King had a wicked heart, and was disturbed by this prophecy, so he went to the parents, and said to them in a most friendly manner, "Give me up your child and I will care for him." At first they refused, but the stranger begged for it with much gold, and so at last they consented and gave him the child, thinking, "It is a luck-child, and, therefore, everything must go on well with it."

The King laid the child in a box and rode away till he came to a deep water, into which he threw the box, saying to himself, "This fellow now has no chance of marrying my daughter."

The box, however, did not sink, but floated along like a boat, and not one drop of water penetrated it. It floated at last down to a mill two miles from the King's palace, and in the mill-dam it stuck fast. The miller's boy, who was fortunately standing there, observed it, and drew it ashore with a hook, expecting to find a great treasure. When, however, he opened the box, he saw a beautiful child alive and merry. He took it to the people at the mill, who, having no children, adopted it for their own saying, "God has sent it to us." They took good care of the child, and it grew up a steady, good lad.

It happened one day that the King went into the mill for shelter during a thunderstorm, and asked the people whether the boy was their child. "No," they answered; "he is a foundling, who, fourteen years ago, floated into our dam in a box, which the miller's boy drew out of the water." The King observed at once, that it was no other than the luck-child whom he had thrown into the water, and so said to them, "Good people, could not the youth carry a letter to my wife the Queen? If so I will give him two pieces of gold for a reward."

"As my lord the King commands," they replied, and ordered the youth get ready.

Then the King wrote a letter to the Queen, in which he said, "So soon as this boy arrives with this letter, let him be killed and buried, and let all be done before I return."

The youth set out on his journey with the letter, but he lost himself, and at evening came into a great forest. In the gloom he saw a little light, and going up to it he found a cottage, into which he went, and saw an old woman sitting by the fire. As soon as she saw the lad she was terrified, and exclaimed, "Why do you come here; and what would you do?"

"I am come from the mill," he answered, "and am going to my lady the Queen to carry a letter; but because I have lost my way in this forest, I wish to pass the night here."

"Poor boy!" said the woman, "you have come to a den of robbers, who, when they return, will murder you."

"Let who will come," he replied, "I am not afraid: I am so weary that I can go no further;" and, stretching himself upon a bench, he went to sleep. Presently the robbers returned, and asked in a rage what strange lad was lying there. "Ah," said the old woman, "it is an innocent youth, who has lost himself in the forest, and whom I have taken in out of compassion. He carries with him a letter to the Queen."

The robbers seized the letter and read it, and understood that as soon as the youth arrived he was to be put to death. Then the robbers also took compassion on him, and the captain tore up the letter and wrote another, in which he declared that the youth upon his arrival was to be married to the Princess. They let him sleep quietly on his bench till the morning, and as soon as he awoke they gave him the letter and showed him the right road.

When the Queen received the letter she did as it commanded, and ordered a splendid marriage feast to be prepared, and the Princess was given in marriage to the luck-child, who, since he was both young and handsome, pleased her well, and they were all very happy. Some little time afterwards the King returned to his palace and found the prophecy fulfilled, and his daughter married to the luck-child. "How did this happen?" he asked. "In my letter I gave quite another command."

Then the Queen handed him the letter, that he might read for himself what it stated. The King saw at once that it had been forged by another person, and he asked the youth what he had done with the original letter that had been entrusted to him. "I know nothing about it," he replied; "it must have been changed in the forest where I passed the night."

Full of rage the King answered, "Thou shalt not escape so easily; he who would marry my daughter must fetch for me three golden hairs from the head of the Giant: bring these to me and, then you can stay on here as my son-in-law."

The King hoped by this means to get rid of him, but he answered, "The three Golden hairs I will fetch, for I fear not the Giant," and so he took leave and began his wanderings.

The road led him by a large town, where the watchman met him at the gate asked him what trade he had and what he knew. "I know everything," replied the youth.

"Then you can do us a kindness," said the watchman, "if you tell us the reason why the fountain in our market-place, out of which wine used to flow, now, all at once, does not even give water."

"That you shall know," was the answer; "but you must wait till I return."

Then he went on further and came to a rather large city, where the watchman asked him, as before, what trade he had, and what he knew. "I know everything," he replied.

"Then you can do us a kindness, if you tell us the reason why a tree growing in our town, which used to bear golden apples, does not now even have any leaves."

"That you shall know," replied the youth, "if you wait till I return," and so saying he went on further till he came to a great lake, over which it was necessary that he should pass. The ferryman asked him what trade he had, and what he knew. "I know everything," he replied.

"Then," said the ferryman, "you can do me a kindness, if you tell me why, for ever and ever, I am obliged to row backwards and forwards, and am never to be released." "You shall learn the reason why," replied the youth; "but wait till I return."

As soon as he got over the water he found the entrance into the Giant's kingdom. It was black and gloomy, and the Giant was not at home; but his old grandmother was sitting there in an immense armchair. "What do you want?" said she, looking at him fixedly. "I want three Golden hairs from the head of the Giant who lives in these regions," replied the youth, or "else I cannot obtain my bride." "That is a bold request," said the woman; "for if he comes home and finds you here it will be a bad thing for you; but still you can remain, and I will see if I can help you."

The old woman, who had magic powers, then changed him into an ant, and told him to creep within the fold of her gown, where he would be quite safe.

"Yes," he said, "that is all very well; but there are three things I am desirous of knowing: - Why a fountain, which used to spout wine, is now dry, and does not even give water. - Why a tree, which used to bear golden apples, does not now have leaves. - And why a ferryman is always rowing backwards and forwards and never gets released."

"Those are difficult questions," replied the old woman; "but do you keep quiet, and pay attention to what the Giant says when I pluck each of the three golden hairs."

As soon as evening came the Giant returned, and scarcely had he entered, when he remarked that the air was not quite pure. "I smell! I smell the flesh of man!" he exclaimed; "all is not right." Then he peeped into every corner and looked about, but could find nothing. Presently his old grandmother began to scold, screaming, "There now, just as I have dusted and put everything in order, you are pulling them all about again! Sit down and eat your supper."

When he had finished he felt tired, and the old woman took his head in her lap, and said she would comb his hair a bit. Presently he yawned, then winked, and at last snored. Then she plucked out a golden hair and laid it down beside her.

"Bah!" cried the Giant, "what are you doing?"

"I have had a bad dream," answered the old woman, "and so I plucked one of your hairs."

"What did you dream, then?" asked he.

"I dreamt that a market-fountain, which used to spout wine, is dried up, and does not even give water: what is the matter with it, pray?"

"Why, if you must know," answered he, "there sits a toad under a stone in the spring, which, if any one kills, the wine will gush out as before."

Then the old woman went on combing till he went to sleep again, and snored so that the windows shook. Presently she pulled out a second hair.

"Confound it! what are you doing?" exclaimed the Giant in a passion.

"Don't be angry," said she; "I did it in a dream."

"What did you dream about this time?" he asked.

"I dreamt that in a certain royal city there grew a fruit-tree, which formerly bore golden apples, but now has not a leaf upon it: what is the cause of it?"

"Why," replied the Giant, "at the root of the tree a mouse is gnawing. But if they kill it golden apples will grow again; if not, the mouse will gnaw till the tree dies altogether. However, let me go to sleep in peace now; for if you disturb me again you will catch a box on the ears."

Nevertheless the old woman, when she had rocked him again to sleep, plucked out a third golden hair. Up jumped the Giant in a fury and would have ill-treated her, but she pacified him and said, "Who can help bad dreams?"

"What did you dream this time?" he asked, still curious to know.

"I dreamt of a ferryman, who is forever compelled to row backwards and forwards, and will never be released. What is the reason?"

"Oh, you simpleton!" answered the Giant. "When someone comes who wants to cross over, the ferryman must give the oar into his hand; then will the other person be obliged to go to and fro, and the ferryman will be free."

Now, since the old woman had plucked the three golden hairs, and had received answers to the three questions, she let the Giant lie in peace, and he slept on till daybreak.

As soon as he went out in the morning the old woman took the ant out of the fold of her gown, and restored him again to his human form.

"There you have the three golden hairs from the King's head, and what he replied to the three questions you have just heard."

"Yes, I have heard, and will well remember," said the luck-child; and, thanking the old woman for her assistance in his trouble, he left those regions, well pleased that he had been so lucky in everything. When he came to the ferryman he had to give him the promised answer. But he said, "First row me over, and then I will tell you how you may be freed;" and as soon as they reached the opposite side he gave him the advice, "When another comes this way, and wants to pass over, give him the oar in his hand."

Then he went on to the first city, where stood the barren tree, and where the watchman waited for the answer. So he said to him, "Kill the mouse which gnaws at the root of the tree, and then it will again bear golden apples." The watchman thanked him, and gave him for a reward two asses laden with gold, which followed him. Next he came to the other city, where the dry fountain was, and he told the watchman as the Giant had said, - "Under a stone in the spring there sits a toad, which you must uncover and kill, and then wine will flow again as before."

The watchman thanked him, and gave to him, as the other had done, two asses laden with gold.

Now the lucky youth soon reached home, and his dear bride was very glad when she saw him return, and heard how capitally everything had gone with him. He brought the King what he had desired - the three golden hairs from the head of the Giant - and when his Majesty saw the four asses laden with gold he was quite pleased, and said, "Now the conditions are fulfilled, and you may have my daughter: but tell me, dear son-in-law, from whence comes all this gold? This is, indeed, bountiful treasure."

"I was ferried over a river," he replied, "and there I picked it up, for it lies upon the shore like sand."

"Can I not fetch some as well?" asked the King, feeling quite covetous.

"As much as you like; there is a ferryman who will row you across and then you can fill your sacks on the other side."

The covetous King set out in great haste upon his journey, and as soon as he came to the river beckoned to the ferryman to take him over. The man came and asked him to step into his boat, and as soon as they reached the opposite shore, the ferryman asked the King to hold the oars for a moment while he tied up the boat. The King took the oar into his hand and the ferryman sprang on shore, a free man at last.

So the King was obliged to take his place, and there he is obliged to row to and fro forever for his sins.

And there he still rows, for no-one has yet come to take the oar from him.

— The Brothers Grimm
(adapted)

? Questions and Assignments

1. What details in the title and first paragraph suggest that the story to follow is a 'fairy story'?

2. Why did the King want to adopt the child?

3. Explain why the King's first attempt at killing the child failed.

4. Describe the second meeting between the King and the boy. Explain how the boy managed to escape death a second time.

5. Outline the King's next plan to get rid of the boy - who was now his son-in-law.

6. The boy met three people on his journey to the Giant's kingdom. Who were these people and what did they each want to know?

7. Describe briefly how the boy managed to get the Giant's hairs.

8. Imagine that the boy kept a diary of his return journey. Make up a number of entries that you think he might have written into that diary.

9. Explain clearly how the boy tricked the King.

10. Suggest a number of ways in which this story is like the stories of some modern science-fiction films such as *Batman*, *Superman* or *Star-Trek*.

11. List a number of events in the story which could not happen in the real world.

12. Make up a short 'fairy story' suitable for a young child.

13. Imagine that you are a judge in a short story competition. Mark the story out of ten and explain briefly why you marked it as you did. (See page 18 for guidelines on how to do this.)

 **Word Power**

Find the words in the story which have similar meanings to each of the words and phrases below. The number in brackets after each one indicates the number of letters in the *answer*. The words appear in the story in the same order as the meanings given below.

1. forecast (8)
2. signal (4)
3. worried; annoyed (9)
4. agreed (9)
5. entered; got into (10)
6. luckily (11)
7. noticed (8)
8. orders (8)
9. darkness (almost) (5)
10. tired (5)
11. grabbed; took (6)
12. impressive; wonderful (8)
13. ornamental jet of water (8)
14. came back (8)
15. quietened; calmed (8)
16. interested (7)
17. help (10)
18. districts (7)
19. unable to produce fruit (6)
20. a gift (in return for a service) (6)
21. jealous (8)
22. jumped quickly (6)

☞ **Points to Note**

In Germany, at the beginning of the nineteenth century, two brothers, Jacob and Wilhelm Grimm, set about collecting folk tales. They travelled the countryside, persuading the people to tell them old stories which they then wrote down. In those days there was, of course, no radio or television. Even books were not very plentiful and, in any case, few people could read well. During the long winter nights people sat around the fireside and told stories, stories which had been handed down from generation to generation. The result of the brothers' efforts was the world-famous book - *'Grimms' Fairy Tales'*.

Many of the stories in the collection, such as *Cinderella, Hansel and Gretel, Sleeping Beauty, Snow White* and *Little Red Riding Hood*, have delighted children all over the world. Some of the stories are dark and frightening however and not suitable for young children.

Many of the stories feature witches, giants, goblins, sacks of gold, kings, palaces, brave handsome princes, as well as poor tailors and woodcutters whose sons often end up marrying beautiful princesses!

During their work the Grimm brothers discovered many different versions of the same stories. For example, there were over three hundred different versions of *Cinderella* in Germany alone. Of course many of the tales collected by the brothers were common to other countries, spread by sailors and travellers. Quite a number of the tales were probably inspired by living conditions of the time. For example *Little Red Riding Hood* was probably first told when wolves roamed freely throughout Europe threatening the lives of ordinary people.

The Giant with the Three Golden Hairs is one of Grimms' lesser-known fairy tales.

Conán was one of the Fenian warriors. They called him Conán Maol because he was bald. Fionn sent Conán to watch the Kerry coast for invaders.

Conán was roasting mussels over a small fire on the shore when he noticed a speck on the sea. The speck grew quickly to become a raft paddled by a huge and fierce-looking man. With one bound the stranger leaped ashore and towered over Conán.

"Little fellow," roared the giant stranger, "can you direct me to the house of Conán the Bald?"

"What do you want with him?" asked Conán, nervously.

"I want his head!" shouted the big man. "I have a nice set of heads at home in my castle in Norway. Every head is a hero's head, and now I want to add a bald head to my collection. Can you tell me where he lives?"

Conán was glad that his sheepskin cap covered his baldness."

"Conán mightn't let his head go with you as easily as you think," said Conán.

"As warriors go I'm the greatest," boasted the big Northman, beating his chest. "I've never lost a fight yet. You haven't answered my question!"

"A league forward, a league backwards, a league to the right, a league to the left, and so on. You'll come to his house sooner or later." said Conán.

The Northman stamped off, muttering "A league to the right, a league to the left . . . " Conán ran home by a short-cut to his house.

"Where are you going in all that hurry?" asked his wife. "Hide me, for heaven's sake, woman," pleaded Conán. "There's a great giant of a Northman looking for my head."

The earth began to tremble.

"He's coming this way," wailed Conán. "What am I to do?"

"Fight him," said Orla, his wife. "You're supposed to be a hero."

"I'm a hero when the odds are even," said Conán. "But I'm no match for this fellow. He's four times my size, and he's determined to have my head for his collection."

"Leave him to me, then," said his wife. "Take off that cap, put on this smock, hop into the cot there and pretend you're a baby."

Conán did what his wife told him, because he knew she was a clever woman.

The great Northman strode up to the door.

"Lady," said the Northman, "I am looking for the house of Conán the Bald. Can you tell me where he is to be found? A fool of a mussel-fisher had me walking around in circles."

? Questions and Assignments

1. What job did Fionn, leader of the Fianna, give to Conán Maol?

2. Which words in paragraph two tell us that the Northman was very big and very frightening?

3. Was the Northman a native of Ireland? Give a reason for your answer.

4. Would you agree that the Northman was a modest man? Give a reason for your answer.

5. *'The earth began to tremble'*. Explain why.

6. *'A fool of a mussel-fisher had me walking around in circles'*.
   (a) Who was the mussel-fisher?
   (b) Why did he have the Northman walking around in circles?

7. Select (a) the most clever and (b) the most stupid character in the story and, in each case, give a reason for your choice.

8. The Northman was protected by a magic spell.
   (a) Where in the story do we learn this?
   (b) What did Conán do when he heard this?

9. Give an account of each of the tricks which Conán and his wife played on the Northman.

10. Imagine that you are a judge in a short story competition. Mark the story out of ten and explain briefly why you marked it as you did. (See page 18 for guidelines on how to do this.)

WP	**Word Power**

Find the words in the story which have similar meanings to each of the words and phrases below. The number in brackets after each one indicates the number of letters in the *answer*. The words appear in the story in the same order as the meanings given below.

1. very large (4)

2. someone admired for his brave deeds (4)

3. spoke with pride about himself (7)

4. speaking quickly but not clearly (9)

5. walked with long steps (6)

6. fell apart (9)

7. spiteful; violent (7)

8. dizzy as a result of a blow (5)

9. confessed (8)

10. roared loudly (8)

11. hit with a sweeping blow (5)

12. made fun of (6)

13. very hot (8)

14. amazing; unusual (10)

15. edge (5)

16. quickly (7)

17. speaking angrily while making spitting noises (10)

18. beaten (8)

19. very big; very powerful (7)

20. floating (8)

WILLIAM'S VERSION

When William's grandmother tries to tell him a well-known fairy tale he is not too happy with her version . . . It is recommended that this story, in particular, be read aloud initially. A dramatic reading for three voices - Narrator, William and Granny - may be worth considering.

William and Granny were left to entertain each other for an hour while William's mother went to the clinic.

'Sing to me,' said William.

'Granny's too old to sing,' said Granny.

'I'll sing to you, then,' said William.

William only knew one song. He had forgotten the words and the tune, but he sang it several times anyway.

'Shall we do something else now?' said Granny.

'Tell me a story,' said William. 'Tell me about the wolf.'

'Red Riding Hood?'

'No, not *that* wolf, the other wolf.'

'Peter and the wolf?' said Granny.

'Mummy's going to have a baby,' said William.

'I know,' said Granny.

William looked suspicious.

'How do you know?'

'Well ... she told me. And it shows, doesn't it?'

'The lady down the road had a baby. It looks like a pig,' said William. He counted on his fingers. 'Three babies looks like three pigs.'

'Ah,' said Granny. 'Once upon a time there were three little pigs. Their names were —'

'They didn't have names,' said William.

'Yes they did. The first pig was called—'

'Pigs don't have names.'

'Some do. These pigs had names.'

'No they didn't.' William slid off Granny's lap and went to open the corner cupboard by the fireplace. Old magazines cascaded out as old magazines do when they have been flung into a cupboard and the door slammed shut. He rooted among them until he found a little book covered with brown paper, climbed into the cupboard, opened the book, closed it and climbed out again.

51

'They didn't have names,' he said.

'I didn't know you could read,' said Granny, properly impressed.

'C-A-T, wheelbarrow,' said William.

'Is that the book Mummy reads to you?'

'It's my book,' said William.

'But it's the one Mummy reads?'

'If she says please,' said William.

'Well, that's Mummy's story, then. My pigs have names.'

'They're the wrong pigs.' William was not open to negotiation. 'I don't want them in this story.'

'Can't we have different pigs this time?'

'No. They won't know what to do.'

'Once upon a time,' said Granny, 'there were three little pigs who lived with their mother.'

'Their mother was dead,' said William.

'Oh, I'm sure she wasn't,' said Granny.

'She was dead. You make bacon out of dead pigs. She got eaten for breakfast and they threw the rind out for the birds.'

'So the three little pigs had to find homes for themselves.'

'No.' William consulted his book.

'They had to build little houses.'

'I'm just coming to that.'

'You said they had to *find* homes. They didn't *find* them.'

'The first little pig walked along for a bit until he met a man with a load of hay.'

'It was a lady.'

'A lady with a load of hay?'

'NO! It was a lady-pig. You said *he*.'

'I thought all the pigs were little boy-pigs,' said Granny.

'It says lady-pig here,' said William.

'It says the lady-pig went for a walk and met a man with a load of hay.'

'So the lady-pig,' said Granny, 'said to the man. "May I have some of that hay to build a house?" And the man said, "Yes."— Is that right?'

'Yes,' said William. 'You know that baby?'

'What baby?'

'The one Mummy's going to have. Will that baby have shoes on when it comes out?'

'I don't think so,' said Granny.

'It will have cold feet,' said William.

'Oh no,' said Granny. 'Mummy will wrap it up in a soft shawl, all snug.'

'I don't *mind* if it has cold feet,' William explained. 'Go on about the lady-pig.'

'So the little lady-pig took the hay and built a little house. Soon the wolf came along and the wolf said—'

'You didn't tell where the wolf lived.'

'I don't know where the wolf lived.'

'15 Tennyson Avenue, next to the bomb-site,' said William.

'I bet it doesn't say that in the book,' said Granny with spirit.

'Yes, it does.'

'Let me see then.'

William folded himself up with his back to Granny, and pushed the book up under his pullover.

'I don't think it says that in the book,' said Granny.

'It's in ever so small words,' said William.

'So the wolf said, "Little pig, little pig, let me come in." And the little pig answered, "No". So the wolf said, "Then I'll huff and I'll puff and I'll blow your house down," and he huffed and he puffed and he blew the house down, and the little pig ran

'He ate the little

'No, no,' said Granny. 'The little pig ran away.'

'He ate the little pig. He ate her in a sandwich.'

'All right, he ate the little pig in a sandwich. So the second little pig—'

'You didn't tell about the tricycle.'

'What about the tricycle?'

'The wolf got on his tricycle and went to the bread shop to buy some bread. To make the sandwich,' William explained, patiently.

'Oh, well, the wolf got on his tricycle and went to the bread shop to buy some bread. And he went to the grocer's to buy some butter.' This innovation did not go down well.

'He already had some butter in the cupboard,' said William.

'So then the second little pig went for a walk and met a man with a load of wood, and the little pig said to the man, "May I have some of that wood to build a house?" and the man said, "Yes."'

'You didn't say please.'

'"Please may I have some of that wood to build a house?"'

'It was sticks.'

'Sticks *are* wood.'

William took out his book and turned the pages. 'That's right,' he said.

'Why don't you tell the story?' said Granny.

'I can't remember it,' said William.

'You could read it out of your book.'

'I've lost it,' said William, clutching his pullover. 'Look, do you know who this is?'

He pulled a green angora scarf from under the sofa.

'No. Who is it?' said Granny, glad of the diversion.

'This is Doctor Snake.' He made the scarf wriggle across the carpet.

'Why is he a doctor?'

'Because he is all furry,' said William.

He wrapped the doctor round his neck and sat sucking the loose end. 'Go on about the wolf.'

'So the little pig built a house of sticks and along came the wolf—on his tricycle?'

'He came by bus. He didn't have any money for a ticket so he ate up the conductor.'

'That wasn't very nice of him,' said Granny.

'No,' said William. 'It wasn't *very* nice.'

'And the wolf said, "Little pig, little pig, let me come in." And the ...' said, "No," and the wolf said, "Then I'll huff and I'll puff and I'll ' house down." So he huffed and he puffed and he blew the house d...... ..... then what did he do?' Granny asked, cautiously.

William was silent.

'Did he eat the second little pig?'

'Yes.'

'How did he eat this little pig?' said Granny, prepared for more pig sandwiches or possibly pig on toast.

'With his mouth,' said William.

'Now the third little pig went for a walk and met a man with a load of bricks. And the little pig said, "Please may I have some of those bricks to build a house?" and the man said, "Yes." So the little pig took the bricks and built a house.'

'He built it on the bomb-site.'

'Next door to the wolf?' said Granny.

'That was very silly of him.'

'There wasn't anywhere else,' said William. 'All the roads were full up.'

'The wolf didn't have to come by bus or tricycle this time, then, did he?' said Granny, grown cunning.

'Yes.' William took out the book and peered in, secretively. 'He was playing in the cemetery. He had to get another bus.'

'And did he eat the conductor this time?'

'No. A nice man gave him some money, so he bought a ticket.'

'I'm glad to hear it,' said Granny.

'He ate the nice man,' said William.

'So the wolf got off the bus and went up to the little pig's house and he said, "Little pig, little pig, let me come in," and the little pig said, "No." And then the wolf said, "I'll huff and I'll puff and I'll blow your house down," and he huffed and he puffed and he huffed and he puffed but he couldn't blow the house down because it was made of bricks.'

'He couldn't blow it down,' said William, 'because it was stuck to the ground.'

'Well, anyway, the wolf got very cross then, and he climbed on to the roof and shouted down the chimney, "I'm coming to get you!" but the little pig just laughed and put a big saucepan of water on the fire.'

'He put it on the gas stove.'

'He put it on the fire,' said Granny, speaking very rapidly, 'and the wolf fell down the chimney and into the pan of water and was boiled and the little pig ate him for supper.'

William threw himself full length on the carpet and screamed.

'He didn't! He didn't! *He didn't!* He didn't eat the wolf.'

Granny picked him up, all stiff and kicking, and sat him on her lap.

'Did I get it wrong again, love? Don't cry. Tell me what really happened.'

William wept, and wiped his nose on Doctor Snake.

'The little pig put the saucepan on the gas stove and the wolf got down the chimney and put the little pig in the saucepan and boiled him. He had him for tea, with chips,' said William.

'Oh,' said Granny, 'I've got it all wrong, haven't I? Can I see the book, then I shall know, next time.'

William took the book from under his pullover. Granny opened it and read, *First Aid for Beginners: A Practical Handbook.*

'I see,' said Granny. 'I don't think I can read this. I left my glasses at home. You tell Gran how it ends.'

William turned to the last page which showed a prostrate man with his leg in a splint: *compound fracture of the femur.*

'Then the wolf washed up and got on his tricycle and went to see his Granny, and his Granny opened the door and said, "Hello, William."'

'I thought it was the wolf?'

'It was. It was the wolf. His name was William Wolf,' said William.

'What a nice story,' said Granny.

'You tell it much better than I do.'

'I can see up your nose,' said William. 'It's all whiskery.'

— Jan Mark

? Questions and Assignments

1. Explain why William's singing would not be pleasing to hear.

2. *'No, not* that *wolf, the other wolf'*. Explain what William means by this remark.

3. What did William say that made Granny realise which story he wanted to hear?

4. What evidence in the story shows that William cannot read?

5. What use does William make of his book while Granny tells the story?

6. List the things William said which are likely to have shocked Granny.

7. Which of the following words best describes the character of William: cheeky, stubborn, innocent, honest? Explain your choice.

8. Which of the following words best describes the character of Granny: strict, patient, good-tempered? Explain your choice.

9. Explain why the story is called *'William's Version'*.

10. Write out the version of *The Three Little Pigs* which would have pleased William. Base your answer on the details given in the story which you have just read.

11. Imagine that Granny tells William another well-known fairy story and that again he insists on hearing his own version. Write about her efforts to tell him the story and his interruptions. You should model your answer on the story *'William's Version'*.

12. Imagine that you are a judge in a short story competition. Mark the story out of ten and explain briefly why you marked it as you did. (See page 18 for guidelines on how to do this.)

WP Word Power

Find the words in the story which have similar meanings to each of the words and phrases below. The number in brackets after each one indicates the number of letters in the *answer*. The words appear in the story in the same order as the meanings given below.

1. amuse (9)

2. sensing that someone is trying to deceive (10)

3. fell (like a waterfall) (8)

4. bargaining; discussion (11)

5. looked for information from (9)

6. new approach (10)

7. slowly and with care (10)

8. looked (6)

I had a new car. It was an exciting ＿＿＿＿＿＿i, which means
3.3 litre, long wheelbase, fuel inj＿＿＿＿＿＿＿ 129mph and
terrific acceleration. The body ＿＿＿＿＿＿＿＿＿ darker blue
and they were made of le＿＿＿＿＿＿＿＿＿uality. The
windows were electri＿＿＿＿＿＿＿＿＿＿lio aerial
popped up when I ＿＿＿＿＿＿＿＿＿＿ched it
off. The powerful en＿＿＿＿＿＿＿＿＿s, but
at sixty miles an hour ＿＿＿＿＿＿＿＿＿ith
pleasure.

I was driving up to Lo＿＿＿＿＿＿＿＿＿＿＿
haymaking in the fields and ＿＿＿＿＿＿＿＿＿d.
I was whispering along at sev＿＿＿＿＿＿＿ ＿oly in
my seat, with no more than a c＿＿＿＿＿＿ ＿e wheel to
keep her steady. Ahead of me I＿＿＿＿＿＿＿. I touched the
footbrake and brought the car to a s＿＿＿＿＿ ＿ys stopped for hitch-
hikers. I knew just how it used to fee＿＿＿＿g on the side of a country
road watching the cars go by. I hated dr＿＿＿ pretending they didn't see me,
especially the ones in big cars with three ＿mpty seats. The large expensive cars
seldom stopped. It was always the smaller ones that offered you a lift, or the
old rusty ones, or the ones that were already crammed full of children and the
driver would say, 'I think we can squeeze in one more.'

The hitch-hiker poked his head through the open window and said, 'Going
to London, guv'nor?'

'Yes,' I said. 'Jump in.'

He got in and I drove on.

He was a small ratty-faced man with grey teeth. His eyes were dark and
quick and clever, like a rat's eyes, and his ears were slightly pointed at the top.
He had a cloth cap on his head and he was wearing a greyish-coloured jacket
with enormous pockets. The grey jacket, together with the quick eyes and the
pointed ears, made him look more than anything like some sort of huge human
rat.

'What part of London are you headed for?' I asked him.

'I'm goin' right through London and out the other side,' he said. 'I'm goin'
to Epsom, for the races. It's Derby Day today.'

'So it is,' I said. 'I wish I were going with you. I love betting on horses.'

'I never bet on horses,' he said. 'I don't even watch 'em run. That's a
stupid silly business.'

'Then why do you go?' I asked.

He didn't seem to like that question. His little ratty face went absolutely blank and he sat there staring straight ahead at the road, saying nothing.

'I expect you help to work the betting machines or something like that,' I said.

'That's even sillier,' he answered. 'There's no fun working them lousy machines and selling tickets to mugs. Any fool could do that.'

There was a long silence. I decided not to question him any more. I remembered how irritated I used to get in my hitch-hiking days when drivers kept asking me questions. Where are you going? Why are you going there? What's your job? Are you married? Do you have a girl-friend? What's her name? How old are you? And so on and so forth. I used to hate it.

'I'm sorry,' I said. 'It's none of my business what you do. The trouble is, I'm a writer, and most writers are terrible nosey parkers.'

'You write books?' he asked.

'Yes.'

'Writin' books is okay,' he said. 'It's what I call a skilled trade. I'm in a skilled trade too. The folks I despise is them that spend all their lives doin' crummy old routine jobs with no skill in 'em at all. You see what I mean?'

'Yes.'

'The secret of life,' he said, 'is to become very very good at somethin' that's very very 'ard to do.'

'Like you,' I said.

'Exactly. You and me both.'

'What makes you think that I'm any good at my job?' I asked. 'There's an awful lot of bad writers around.'

'You wouldn't be drivin' about in a car like this if you weren't no good at it,' he answered. 'It must've cost a tidy packet, this little job.'

'It wasn't cheap.'

'What can she do flat out?' he asked.

'One hundred and twenty-nine miles an hour,' I told him.

'I'll bet she won't do it.'

'I'll bet she will.'

'All car makers is liars,' he said. 'You can buy any car you like and it'll never do what the makers say it will in the ads.'

'This one will.'

'Open 'er up then and prove it,' he said. 'Go on, guv'nor, open 'er right up and let's see what she'll do.'

There is a roundabout at Chalfont St Peter and immediately beyond it there's a long straight section of dual carriageway. We came out of the roundabout on to the carriageway and I pressed my foot down on the accelerator. The big car leaped forward as though she'd been stung. In ten seconds or so, we were doing ninety.

'Lovely!' he cried. 'Beautiful! Keep goin'!'

I had the accelerator jammed right down against the floor and I held it there.

'One hundred!' he shouted . . . 'A hundred and five! . . . A hundred and ten! . . . A hundred and fifteen! Go on! Don't slack off!'

I was in the outside lane and we flashed past several cars as though they were standing still - a green Mini, a big cream-coloured Citroën, a white Land-Rover, a huge truck with a container on the back, an orange-coloured Volkswagen Minibus . . .

'A hundred and twenty!' my passenger shouted, jumping up and down. 'Go on! Go on! Get 'er up to one-two-nine!'

At that moment, I heard the scream of a police siren. It was so loud it seemed to be right inside the car, and then a policeman on a motorcycle loomed up alongside us on the inside lane and went past us and raised a hand for us to stop.

'Oh, my sainted aunt!' I said. 'That's torn it!'

The policeman must have been doing about a hundred and thirty when he passed us, and he took plenty of time slowing down. Finally, he pulled into the side of the road and I pulled in behind him. 'I didn't know police motorcycles could go as fast as that,' I said rather lamely.

'That one can,' my passenger said. 'It's the same make as yours. It's a BMW R90S. Fastest bike on the road. That's what they're usin' nowadays.'

The policeman got off his motor-cycle and leaned the machine sideways on to its prop stand. Then he took off his gloves and placed them carefully on the seat. He was in no hurry now. He had us where he wanted us and he knew it.

'This is real trouble,' I said. 'I don't like it one bit.'

'Don't talk to 'im any more than is necessary, you understand,' my companion said. 'Just sit tight and keep mum.'

Like an executioner approaching his victim, the policeman came strolling slowly towards us. He was a big meaty man with a belly, and his blue breeches were skintight around his enormous thighs. His goggles were pulled up on to the helmet, showing a smouldering red face with wide cheeks.

We sat there like guilty schoolboys, waiting for him to arrive.

'Watch out for this man,' my passenger whispered. ''Ee looks mean as the devil.'

The policeman came round to my open window and placed one meaty hand on the sill. 'What's the hurry?' he said.

'No hurry, officer,' I answered.

'Perhaps there's a woman in the back having a baby and you're rushing her to hospital? Is that it?'

'No, officer.'

'Or perhaps your house is on fire and you're dashing home to rescue the family from upstairs?' His voice was dangerously soft and mocking.

'My house isn't on fire, officer.'

'In that case,' he said, 'you've got yourself into a nasty mess, haven't you? Do you know what the speed limit is in this country?'

'Seventy,' I said.

'And do you mind telling me exactly what speed you were doing just now?'

I shrugged and didn't say anything.

When he spoke next, he raised his voice so loud that I jumped. '*One hundred and twenty miles per hour*!' he barked. 'That's *fifty* miles an hour over the limit!'

He turned his head and spat out a big gob of spit. It landed on the wing of my car and started sliding down over my beautiful blue paint. Then he turned back again and stared hard at my passenger. 'And who are you?' he asked sharply.

'He's a hitch-hiker,' I said. 'I'm giving him a lift.'

'I didn't ask you,' he said. 'I asked him.'

' 'Ave I done somethin' wrong?' my passenger asked. His voice was as soft and oily as haircream.

'That's more than likely,' the policeman answered.

'Anyway, you're a witness. I'll deal with you in a minute. Driving-licence,' he snapped, holding out his hand.

I gave him my driving-licence.

He unbuttoned the left-hand breast-pocket of his tunic and brought out the dreaded books of tickets. Carefully, he copied the name and address from my licence. Then he gave it back to me. He strolled round to the front of the car and read the number from the number-plate and wrote that down as well. He filled in the date, the time and the details of my offence. Then he tore out the top copy of the ticket. But before handing it to me, he checked that all the information had come through clearly on his own carbon copy. Finally, he replaced the book in his tunic pocket and fastened the button.

'Now you,' he said to my passenger, and he walked around to the other side of the car. From the other breast-pocket he produced a small black notebook. 'Name?' he snapped.

'Michael Fish,' my passenger said.

'Address?'

'Fourteen, Windsor Lane, Luton.'

'Show me something to prove this is your real name and address,' the policeman said.

My passenger fished in his pockets and came out with a driving-licence of his own. The policeman checked the name and address and handed it back to him. 'What's your job?' he asked sharply.

'I'm an 'od carrier.'

'A *what*?'

'An 'od carrier.'

'Spell it.'

'H-O-D C-A-. . .'

'That'll do. And what's a hod carrier, may I ask?'

'An 'od carrier, officer, is a person 'oo carries the cement up the ladder to the bricklayer. And the 'od is what 'ee carries it in. It's got a long 'andle, and on the top you've got two bits of wood set at an angle. . .'

'All right, all right. Who's your employer?'

'Don't 'ave one. I'm unemployed.'

The policeman wrote all this down in the black note-book. Then he returned the book to its pocket and did up the button.

'When I get back to the station I'm going to do a little checking up on you,' he said to my passenger.

'Me? What've I done wrong?' the rat-faced man asked.

'I don't like your face, that's all,' the policeman said. 'And we just might have a picture of it somewhere in our files.' He strolled round the car and returned to my window.

'I suppose you know you're in serious trouble,' he said to me.

'Yes, officer.'

'You won't be driving this fancy car of yours again for a very long time, not after we've finished with you. You won't be driving any car again come to that for several years. And a good thing, too. I hope they lock you up for a spell into the bargain.'

'You mean prison?' I asked, alarmed.

'Absolutely,' he said, smacking his lips. 'In the clink. Behind the bars. Along with all the other criminals who break the law. And a hefty fine into the bargain. Nobody will be more pleased about that than me. I'll see you in court, both of you. You'll be getting a summons to appear.'

He turned away and walked over to his motor-cycle. He flipped the prop stand back into position with his foot and swung his leg over the saddle. Then he kicked the starter and roared off up the road out of sight.

'Phew!' I gasped. 'That's done it.'

'We was caught,' my passenger said. 'We was caught good and proper.'

'I was caught, you mean.'

'That's right,' he said. 'What you goin' to do now, guv'nor?'

'I'm going straight up to London to talk to my solicitor,' I said. I started the car and drove on.

'You mustn't believe what 'ee said to you about goin' to prison,' my passenger said. 'They don't put anybody in the clink just for speedin'.'

'Are you sure of that?'

'I'm positive,' he answered. 'They can take your licence away and they can give you a whoppin' big fine, but that'll be the end of it.'

I felt tremendously relieved.

'By the way,' I said, 'why did you lie to him?'

'Who, me?' he said. 'What makes you think I lied?'

'You told him you were an unemployed hod carrier. But you told me you were in a highly skilled trade.'

'So I am,' he said. 'But it don't pay to tell everythin' to a copper.'

'So what *do* you do?' I asked him.

'Ah,' he said slyly. 'That'd be tellin', wouldn't it?'

'Is it something you're ashamed of?'

'Ashamed?' he cried. 'Me, ashamed of my job? I'm about as proud of it as anybody could be in the entire world!'

'Then why won't you tell me?'

'You writers really is nosey parkers, aren't you?' he said. 'And you ain't goin' to be 'appy, I don't think, until you've found out exactly what the answer is?'

'I don't really care one way or the other,' I told him, lying.

He gave me a crafty little ratty look out of the sides of his eyes. 'I think you do care,' he said. 'I can see it on your face that you think I'm in some kind of a very peculiar trade and you're just achin' to know what it is.'

I didn't like the way he read my thoughts. I kept quiet and stared at the road ahead.

'You'd be right, too,' he went on. 'I *am* in a very peculiar trade. I'm in the queerest peculiar trade of 'em all.'

I waited for him to go on.

'That's why I 'as to be extra careful 'oo I'm talkin' to, you see. 'Ow am I to know, for instance, you're not another copper in plain clothes?'

'Do I look like a copper?'

'No,' he said. 'You don't. And you ain't. Any fool could tell that.'

He took from his pocket a tin of tobacco and a packet of cigarette papers and started to roll a cigarette. I was watching him out of the corner of one eye, and the speed with which he performed this rather difficult operation was incredible. The cigarette was rolled and ready in about five seconds. He ran his tongue along the edge of the paper, stuck it down and popped the cigarette between his lips. Then, as if from nowhere, a lighter appeared in his hand. The lighter flamed. The cigarette was lit. The lighter disappeared. It was altogether a remarkable performance.

'I've never seen anyone roll a cigarette as fast as that,' I said.

'Ah,' he said, taking a deep suck of smoke. 'So you noticed.'

'Of course I noticed. It was quite fantastic.'

He sat back and smiled. It pleased him very much that I had noticed how quickly he could roll a cigarette. 'You want to know what makes me able to do it?' he asked.

'Go on then.'

'It's because I've got fantastic fingers. These fingers of mine,' he said, holding up both hands high in front of him, 'are quicker and cleverer than the fingers of the best piano player in the world!'

'Are you a piano player?'

'Don't be daft,' he said. 'Do I look like a piano player?'

I glanced at his fingers. They were so beautifully shaped, so slim and long and elegant, they didn't seem to belong to the rest of him at all. They looked more like the fingers of a brain surgeon or a watchmaker.

'My job,' he went on, 'is a hundred times more difficult than playin' the piano. Any twerp can learn to do that. There's titchy little kids learnin' to play the piano in almost any 'ouse you go into these days. That's right, ain't it?'

'More or less,' I said.

'Of course it's right. But there's not one person in ten million can learn to do what I do. Not one in ten million! 'Ow about that?'

'Amazing,' I said.

'You're darn right it's amazin',' he said.

'I think I know what you do,' I said. 'You do conjuring tricks. You're a conjurer.'

'Me?' he snorted. 'A conjurer? Can you picture me goin' round crummy kids' parties makin' rabbits come out of top 'ats?'

'Then you're a card player. You get people into card games and deal yourself marvellous hands.'

'Me! A rotten card-sharper!' he cried. 'That's a miserable racket if ever there was one.'

'All right. I give up.'

I was taking the car along slowly now, at no more than forty miles an hour, to make quite sure I wasn't stopped again. We had come on to the main London-Oxford road and were running down the hill towards Denham.

Suddenly my passenger was holding up a black leather belt in his hand. 'Ever seen this before?' he asked. The belt had a brass buckle of unusual design.

'Hey!' I said. 'That's mine, isn't it? It is mine! Where did you get it?'

He grinned and waved the belt gently from side to side. 'Where d'you think I got it?' he said. 'Off the top of your trousers, of course.'

I reached down and felt for my belt. It was gone.

'You mean you took it off me while we've been driving along?' I asked, flabbergasted.

He nodded, watching me all the time with those little black ratty eyes.

'That's impossible,' I said. 'You'd have had to undo the buckle and slide the whole thing out through the loops all the way round. I'd have seen you doing it. And even if I hadn't seen you, I'd have felt it.'

'Ah, but you didn't, did you?' he said, triumphant. He dropped the belt on his lap, and now all at once there was a brown shoelace dangling from his finger. 'And what about this, then?' he exclaimed, waving the shoelace.

'What about it?' I said.

'Anyone around 'ere missin' a shoelace?' he asked, grinning.

I glanced down at my shoes. The lace of one of them was missing. 'Good grief!' I said. 'How did you do that? I never saw you bending down.'

'You never saw nothin',' he said proudly. 'You never even saw me move an inch. And you know why?'

'Yes,' I said. 'Because you've got fantastic fingers.'

'Exactly right!' he cried. 'You catch on pretty quick, don't you?' He sat back and sucked away at his home-made cigarette, blowing the smoke out in a thin stream against the windshield. He knew he had impressed me greatly with those two tricks, and this made him very happy. 'I don't want to be late,' he said. 'What time is it?'

'There's a clock in front of you,' I told him.

'I don't trust car clocks,' he said. 'What does your watch say?'

I hitched up my sleeve to look at the watch on my wrist. It wasn't there. I looked at the man. He looked back at me, grinning.

'You've taken that, too,' I said.

He held out his hand and there was my watch lying in his palm. 'Nice bit of stuff, this,' he said. 'Superior quality. Eighteen-carat gold. Easy to flog, too. It's never any trouble gettin' rid of quality goods.'

'I'd like it back, if you don't mind,' I said rather huffily.

He placed the watch carefully on the leather tray in front of him. 'I wouldn't nick anythin' from you, guv'nor,' he said. 'You're my pal. You're giving me a lift.'

'I'm glad to hear it,' I said.

'All I'm doin' is answerin' your questions,' he went on. 'You asked me what I did for a livin' and I'm showin' you.'

'What else have you got of mine?'

He smiled again, and now he started to take from the pocket of his jacket one thing after another that belonged to me - my driving-licence, a key-ring with four keys on it, some pound notes, a few coins, a letter from my publishers, my diary, a stubby old pencil, a cigarette-lighter, and last of all, a beautiful old sapphire ring with pearls around it belonging to my wife. I was taking the ring up to the jeweller in London because one of the pearls was missing.

'Now *there's* another lovely piece of goods,' he said, turning the ring over in his fingers. 'That's eighteenth century, if I'm not mistaken, from the reign of King George the Third.'

'You're right,' I said, impressed. 'You're absolutely right.'

He put the ring on the leather tray with the other items.

'So you're a pickpocket,' I said.

'I don't like that word,' he answered. 'It's a coarse and vulgar word. Pickpockets is coarse and vulgar people who only do easy little amateur jobs. They lift money from blind old ladies.'

'What do you call yourself, then?'

'Me? I'm a fingersmith. I'm a professional fingersmith.' He spoke the words solemnly and proudly, as though he were telling me he was the President of the Royal College of Surgeons or the Archbishop of Canterbury.

'I've never heard that word before,' I said. 'Did you invent it?'

'Of course I didn't invent it,' he replied. 'It's the name given to them who's risen to the very top of the profession. You've 'eard of a goldsmith and a silversmith, for instance. They're experts with gold and silver. I'm an expert with my fingers, so I'm a fingersmith.'

'It must be an interesting job.'

'It's a marvellous job,' he answered. 'It's lovely.'

'And that's why you go to the races?'

'Race meetings is easy meat,' he said. 'You just stand around after the race, watchin' for the lucky ones to queue up and draw their money. And when you see someone collectin' a big bundle of notes, you simply follows after 'im and 'elps yourself. But don't get me wrong guv'nor. I never takes nothin' from a loser. Nor from poor people either. I only go after them as can afford it, the winners and the rich.'

'That's very thoughtful of you,' I said. 'How often do you get caught?'

'Caught?' he cried, disgusted. '*Me* get caught! It's only pickpockets get caught. Fingersmiths never. Listen, I could take the false teeth out of your mouth if I wanted to and you wouldn't even catch me!'

'I don't have false teeth,' I said.

'I know you don't,' he answered. 'Otherwise I'd 'ave 'ad 'em out long ago!'

I believed him. Those long slim fingers of his seemed able to do anything.

We drove on for a while without talking.

'That policeman's going to check up on you pretty thoroughly,' I said. 'Doesn't that worry you a bit?'

'Nobody's checkin' up on me,' he said.

'Of course they are. He's got your name and address written down most carefully in his black book.'

The man gave me another of his sly, ratty little smiles. 'Ah,' he said. 'So 'ee 'as. But I'll bet 'ee ain't got it all written down in 'is memory as well. I've never known a copper yet with a decent memory. Some of 'em can't even remember their own names.'

'What's memory got to do with it?' I asked. 'It's written down in his book, isn't it?'

'Yes, guv'nor, it is. But the trouble is, 'ee's lost the book. 'Ee's lost both books, the one with my name in it and the one with yours.'

In the long delicate fingers of his right hand, the man was holding up in triumph the two books he had taken from the policeman's pockets. 'Easiest job I ever done,' he announced proudly.

I nearly swerved the car into a milk-truck, I was so excited.

'That copper's got nothin' on either of us now,' he said.

'You're a genius!' I cried.

''Ee's got no names, no addresses, no car number, no nothin',' he said.

'You're brilliant!'

'I think you'd better pull in off this main road as soon as possible,' he said. 'Then we'd better build a little bonfire and burn these books.'

'You're a fantastic fellow,' I exclaimed.

'Thank you guv'nor,' he said. 'It's always nice to be appreciated.'

— *Roald Dahl*

? Questions and Assignments

1. What luxury features could be found in the narrator's car?

2. Why did the author use the phrase *'whispering along at seventy miles an hour'*?

3. Why did the narrator always stop for hitch-hikers?

4. In what ways did the hitch-hiker remind the narrator of a rat?

5. What puzzled you about the hitch-hiker as you read the story for the first time?

6. What was the hitch-hiker's view on betting on horses?

7. What made the hitch-hiker decide that the narrator was a successful writer?

8. *'The big car leaped forward as though she'd been stung'*. What point is being made in this sentence?

9. Would you agree that the policeman spoke sarcastically to the narrator? Explain.

10. What details are given about the policeman which are likely to make the readers dislike him?

11. Describe clearly what the policeman did with his book of tickets.

12. The hitch-hiker claimed that he was a hod-carrier. Did you believe him? Explain why.

13. (a) Why did the author describe the way in which the hitch-hiker rolled and lit his cigarette as a *'remarkable performance'*?

    (b) Did you suspect anything when you read this description for the first time? Explain.

14. At what point in the story do we learn exactly how the hitch-hiker made his living?

15. Describe how you felt about the way the story ended.

16. Imagine that you are a judge in a short story competition. Mark the story out of ten and explain briefly why you marked it as you did. (See page 18 for guidelines on how to do this.)

WP Word Power

Find the words in the story which have similar meanings to each of the words and phrases below. The number in brackets after each one indicates the number of letters in the *answer*. The words appear in the story in the same order as the meanings given below.

1. not fake (7)
2. driven; powered (8)
3. strong (8)
4. dear; costly (9)
5. tightly crowded (7)
6. very big (8)
7. empty; expressionless (5)
8. annoyed (9)
9. eye protectors (7)
10. moved shoulders (8)
11. looked without blinking (6)
12. walked slowly in a relaxed way (8)
13. pieces of information (7)
14. crime (7)
15. examined; looked to make sure (7)
16. put back (8)
17. shocked; very worried (7)
18. law breakers (9)
19. written request to appear in court (7)
20. extremely (12)
21. out of work (10)
22. secretly; cunningly (5)
23. carried out; did (9)
24. vanished (11)
25. amazing (10)
26. graceful; tasteful (7)
27. hanging loosely (8)
28. looked quickly (7)
29. changed direction suddenly (7)

SPIT NOLAN

SPIT NOLAN was a pal of mine. He was a thin lad with a bony face that was always pale, except for two rosy spots on his cheekbones. He had quick brown eyes, short, wiry hair, rather stooped shoulders, and we all knew that he had only one lung. He had had a disease which in those days couldn't be cured, unless you went away to Switzerland, which Spit certainly couldn't afford. He wasn't sorry for himself in any way, and in fact we envied him, because he never had to go to school.

Spit was the champion trolley-rider of Cotton Pocket; that was the district in which we lived. He had a very good balance, and sharp wits, and he was very brave, so that these qualities, when added to his skill as a rider, meant that no other boy could ever beat Spit on a trolley - and every lad had one.

Our trolleys were simple vehicles for getting a good ride downhill at a fast speed. To make one you had to get a stout piece of wood about five feet in length and eighteen inches wide. Then you needed four wheels, preferably two pairs, large ones for the back and smaller ones for the front. However, since we bought our wheels from the scrapyard, most trolleys had four odd wheels. Now you had to get a poker and put it in the fire until it was red hot, and then burn a hole through the wood at the front. Usually it would take three or four attempts to get the hole bored through. Through this hole you fitted the giant nut-and-bolt, which acted as a swivel for the steering. Fastened to the nut was a strip of wood, on to which the front axle was secured by bent nails. A piece of rope tied to each end of the axle served for steering. Then a knob of margarine had to be slanced out of the kitchen to grease the wheels and bearings. Next you had to paint a name on it: *Invincible* or *Dreadnought*, though it might be a motto: *Death before Dishonour* or *Labour and Wait*. That done, you then stuck your chest out, opened the back gate, and wheeled your trolley out to face the critical eyes of the world.

Spit spent most mornings trying out new speed gadgets on his trolley, or searching Enty's scrapyard for good wheels. Afterwards he would go off and have a spin down Cemetery Brew. This was a very steep road that led to the cemetery, and it was very popular with trolley-drivers as it was the only macadamised hill for miles around, all the others being cobblestones for horse traffic. Spit used to lie in wait for a coal-cart or other horse-drawn vehicle, then he would hitch *Egdam* to the back to take it up the brew. *Egdam* was a name in memory of a girl called Madge, whom he had once met at Southport Sanatorium, where he had spent three happy weeks. Only I knew the meaning of it, for he had reversed the letters of her name to keep his love a secret.

It was the custom for lads to gather at the street corner on summer evenings and, trolleys parked at hand, discuss trolleying, road surfaces, and also show off any new gadgets. Then, when Spit gave the sign, we used to set off for Cemetery Brew. There was scarcely any evening traffic on the roads in those days, so that we could have a good practice before our evening race. Spit, the unbeaten champion, would inspect every trolley and rider, and allow a start which was reckoned on the size of the wheels and the weight of the rider. He was always the last in the line of starters, though no matter how long a start he gave it seemed impossible to beat him. He knew that road like the palm of his hand, every tiny lump or pothole, and he never came a cropper.

Among us he took things easy, but when occasion asked for it he would go all out. Once he had to meet a challenge from Ducker Smith, the champion of the Engine Row gang. On that occasion Spit borrowed a wheel from the baby's pram, removing one nearest the wall, so it wouldn't be missed, and confident he could replace it before his mother took baby out. And after fixing it to his trolley he made that ride on what was called the 'belly-down' style - that is, he lay full stretch on his stomach, so as to avoid wind resistance. Although Ducker got away with a flying start he had not that sensitive touch of Spit, and his frequent bumps and swerves lost him valuable inches, so that he lost the race with a good three lengths. Spit arrived home just in time to catch his mother as she was wheeling young Georgie off the doorstep, and if he had not made a dash for it the child would have fallen out as the pram overturned.

It happened that we were gathered at the street corner with our trolleys one evening when Ernie Haddock let out a hiccup of wonder: 'Hey, chaps, wot's Leslie got?'

We all turned our eyes on Leslie Duckett, the plump son of the local publican. He approached us on a brand-new trolley, propelled by flicks of his foot on the pavement. From a distance the thing had looked impressive, but now, when it came up among us, we were too dumbfounded to speak. Such a magnificent trolley had never been seen! The riding board was of solid oak, almost two inches thick; four new wheels with pneumatic tyres; a brake, a bell, a lamp, and a spotless steering-cord. In front was a plate on which was the name in bold lettering: *The British Queen*.

'It's called after the pub,' remarked Leslie. He tried to edge it away from Spit's trolley, for it made *Egdam* appear horribly insignificant. Voices had been stilled for a minute, but now they broke out:

'Where'd it come from?'

'How much was it?'

'Who made it?'

Leslie tried to look modest. 'My dad had it specially made to measure,' he said, 'by the gaffer of the Holt Engineering Works.'

He was a nice lad, and now he wasn't sure whether to feel proud or ashamed. The fact was, nobody had ever had a trolley made by somebody else. Trolleys were swopped and so on, but no lad had ever owned one that had been made by other hands. We went quiet now, for Spit had calmly turned his attention to it, and was examining *The British Queen* with his expert eye. First he tilted it, so that one of the rear wheels was off the ground, and after giving it a flick of the finger he listened intently with his ear close to the hub.

'A beautiful ball-bearing race,' he remarked, 'it runs like silk.' Next he turned his attention to the body. 'Grand piece of timber, Leslie - though a trifle on the heavy side. It'll take plenty of pulling up a brew.'

'I can pull it,' said Leslie, stiffening.

'You might find it a shade *front-heavy*,' went on Spit, 'which means it'll be hard on the steering unless you keep it well oiled.'

'It's well made,' said Leslie. 'Eh, Spit?'

Spit nodded. 'Aye, all the bolts are counter-sunk,' he said, 'everything chamfered and fluted off to perfection. But -'

'But what?' asked Leslie.

'Do you want me to tell you?' asked Spit.

'Yes, I do,' answered Leslie.

'Well, it's got none of *you* in it,' said Spit.

'How do you mean?' says Leslie.

'Well, you haven't so much as given it a single tap with a hammer,' said Spit. 'That trolley will be a stranger to you to your dying day.'

'How come,' said Leslie, 'since I *own* it?'

Spit shook his head. 'You don't own it,' he said, in a quiet, solemn tone. 'You own nothing in this world except those things you have taken a hand in the making of, or else you've earned the money to buy them.'

Leslie sat down on *The British Queen* to think this one out. We all sat round, scratching our heads.

'You've forgotten to mention one thing,' said Ernie Haddock to Spit, 'what about the *speed*?'

'Going down a steep hill,' said Spit, 'she should hold the road well - an' with wheels like that she should certainly be able to shift some.'

'Think she could beat *Egdam*?' ventured Ernie.

'That,' said Spit, 'remains to be seen.'

Ernie gave a shout: 'A challenge race! *The British Queen* versus *Egdam*!'

'Not tonight,' said Leslie. 'I haven't got the proper feel of her yet.'

'What about Sunday morning?' I said.

Spit nodded. 'As good a time as any.'

Leslie agreed. 'By then,' he said in a challenging tone, 'I'll be able to handle her.'

Chattering like monkeys, eating bread, carrots, fruit, and bits of toffee, the entire gang of us made our way along the silent Sunday-morning streets for the big race at Cemetery Brew. We were split into two fairly equal sides.

Leslie, in his serge Sunday suit, walked ahead, with Ernie Haddock pulling *The British Queen*, and a bunch of supporters around. They were optimistic, for Leslie had easily outpaced every other trolley during the week, though as yet he had not run against Spit.

Spit was in the middle of the group behind, and I was pulling *Egdam* and keeping the pace easy, for I wanted Spit to keep fresh. He walked in and out among us with an air of imperturbability that, considering the occasion, seemed almost godlike. It inspired a fanatical confidence in us. It was such that Chick Dale, a curly-headed kid with a soft skin like a girl's, and a nervous lisp, climbed up on to the spiked railings of the cemetery, and, reaching out with his thin fingers, snatched a yellow rose. He ran in front of Spit and thrust it into a small hole in his jersey.

'I pwesent you with the wose of the winner!' he exclaimed.

'And I've a good mind to present you with a clout on the lug,' replied Spit, 'for pinching a flower from a cemetery. An' what's more, it's bad luck.' Seeing Chick's face, he relented. 'On second thoughts, Chick, I'll wear it. Ee, wot a 'eavenly smell!'

Happily we went along, and Spit turned to a couple of lads at the back. 'Hy, stop that whistling. Don't forget what day it is - folk want their sleep out.'

A faint sweated glow had come over Spit's face when we reached the top of the hill, but he was as majestically calm as ever. Taking the bottle of cold water from his trolley seat, he put it to his lips and rinsed out his mouth in the manner of a boxer.

The two contestants were called together by Ernie.

'No bumpin' or borin',' he said.

They nodded.

'The winner,' he said, 'is the first who puts the nose of his trolley past the cemetery gates.'

They nodded.

'Now, who,' he asked, 'is to be judge?'

Leslie looked at me. 'I've no objection to Bill,' he said. 'I know he's straight.'

I hadn't realized I was, I thought, but by heck I will be!

'Ernie here,' said Spit, 'can be starter.'

With that Leslie and Spit shook hands.

'Fly down to them gates,' said Ernie to me. He had his father's pigeon-timing watch in his hand. 'I'll be setting 'em off dead on the stroke of ten o'clock.'

I hurried down to the gates. I looked back and saw the supporters lining themselves on either side of the road. Leslie was sitting upright on *The British Queen*. Spit was settling himself to ride belly-down. Ernie Haddock, handkerchief raised in the right hand, eye gazing down on the watch in the left, was counting them off - just like when he tossed one of his father's pigeons.

'Five - four - three - two - one - *Off*!'

Spit was away like a shot. That vigorous toe push sent him clean ahead of Leslie. A volley of shouts went up from his supporters, and groans from Leslie's. I saw Spit move straight to the middle of the road camber. Then I ran ahead to take up my position at the winning-post.

When I turned again I was surprised to see that Spit had not increased the lead. In fact, it seemed that Leslie had begun to gain on him. He had settled himself into a crouched position, and those perfect wheels combined with his extra weight were bringing him up with Spit. Not that it seemed possible he could ever catch him. For Spit, lying flat on his trolley, moving with a fine balance, gliding, as it were, over the rough patches, looked to me as though he were a bird that might suddenly open out its wings and fly clean into the air.

The runners along the side could no longer keep up with the trolleys. And now, as they skimmed past the half-way mark, and came to the very steepest part, there was no doubt that Leslie was gaining. Spit had never ridden better; he coaxed *Egdam* over the tricky parts, swayed with her, gave her her head, and guided her. Yet Leslie, clinging grimly to the steering-rope of *The British Queen*, and riding the rougher part of the road, was actually drawing level. Those beautiful ball-bearing wheels, engineer-made, encased in oil, were holding the road, and bringing Leslie along faster than spirit and skill could carry Spit.

Dead level they sped into the final stretch. Spit's slight figure was poised fearlessly on his trolley, drawing the extremes of speed from her. Thundering beside him, anxious but determined, came Leslie. He was actually drawing ahead - and forcing his way to the top of the camber. On they came like two charioteers - Spit delicately edging to the side, to gain inches by the extra downward momentum. I kept my eyes fastened clean across the road as they came belting past the winning-post.

First past was the plate *The British Queen*. I saw that first. Then I saw the heavy rear wheel jog over a pothole and strike Spit's front wheel - sending him in a swerve across the road. Suddenly then, from nowhere, a charabanc came speeding round the wide bend.

Spit was straight in its path. Nothing could avoid the collision. I gave a cry of fear as I saw the heavy solid tyre of the front wheel hit the trolley. Spit was flung up and his back hit the radiator. Then the driver stopped dead.

I got there first. Spit was lying on the macadam road on his side. His face was white and dusty, and coming out between his lips and trickling down his chin was a rivulet of fresh red blood. Scattered all about him were yellow rose petals.

'Not my fault,' I heard the driver shouting. 'I didn't have a chance. He came straight at me.'

The next thing we were surrounded by women who had got out of the charabanc. And then Leslie and all the lads came up.

'Somebody send for an ambulance!' called a woman.

'I'll run an' tell the gatekeeper to telephone,' said Ernie Haddock.

'I hadn't a chance,' the driver explained to the women.

'A piece of his jersey on the starting-handle there . . .' said someone.

'Don't move him,' said the driver to a stout woman who had bent over Spit. 'Wait for the ambulance.'

'Hush up,' she said. She knelt and put a silk scarf under Spit's head. Then she wiped his mouth with her little handkerchief.

He opened his eyes. Glazed they were, as though he couldn't see. A short cough came out of him, then he looked at me and his lips moved.

'Who won?'

'Thee!' blurted out Leslie. 'Tha just licked me. Eh Bill?'

'Aye,' I said, 'old *Egdam* just pipped *The British Queen.*'

Spit's eyes closed again. The women looked at each other. They nearly all had tears in their eyes. Then Spit looked up again, and his wise, knowing look came over his face. After a minute he spoke in a sharp whisper:

'Liars. I can remember seeing Leslie's back wheel hit my front 'un. I didn't win - I lost.' He stared upward for a few seconds, then his eyes twitched and shut.

The driver kept repeating how it wasn't his fault, and next thing the ambulance came. Nearly all the women were crying now, and I saw the look that went between the two men who put Spit on a stretcher - but I couldn't believe he was dead. I had to go into the ambulance with the attendant to give him particulars. I went up the step and sat down inside and looked out the little window as the driver slammed the doors. I saw the driver holding Leslie as a witness. Chick Dale was lifting the smashed-up *Egdam* on to the body of *The British Queen*. People with bunches of flowers in their hands stared after us as we drove off. Then I heard the ambulance man asking me Spit's name. Then he touched me on the elbow with his pencil and said:

'Where *did* he live?'

I knew then. That word 'did' struck right into me. But for a minute I couldn't answer. I had to think hard, for the way he said it made it suddenly seem as though Spit Nolan had been dead and gone for ages.

— Bill Naughton

? Questions and Assignments

1. What evidence in the first paragraph suggests that Spit Nolan did not belong to a rich family?

2. According to the narrator what were the qualities of a good trolley rider?

3. List the items needed to make a trolley.

4. Why was Cemetery Brew different from other roads in the district?

5. How do we know that Spit Nolan and the narrator were very close friends?

6. On two occasions the narrator tells us that Spit Nolan was impossible to beat in a trolley race. Find the sentences in the story where we are told this and write them out.

7. Describe the reaction of the other lads when they first saw *The British Queen.*

8. Why do you think that Leslie *'wasn't sure whether to feel proud or ashamed'*?

9. During your first reading of this story
   (i)   Who did you want to win the race? Why?
   (ii)   Who did you think would win? Why?

10. (i)   Explain why Spit had a good start in the race?
    (ii)   What helped Leslie catch up with him?
    (iii) What detail in the story gives us a good idea of the speed at which the riders travelled?

11. Explain how the accident happened.

12. Close to the ending of the story our fears grow that Spit will not survive. What details does the narrator include to cause us to fear that Spit was to die? At what stage do we know for certain?

13. Describe an occasion when you or a friend of yours was involved in an accident.

14. Imagine that you are a judge in a short story competition. Mark the story out of ten and explain briefly why you marked it as you did. (See page 18 for guidelines on how to do this.)

WP Word Power

Find the words in the story which have similar meanings to each of the words and phrases below. The number in brackets after each one indicates the number of letters in the *answer*. The words appear in the story in the same order as the meanings given below.

1. were jealous of (6)
2. attached; tied (8)
3. fault-finding (8)
4. put back to front (8)
5. talk about (7)
6. examine closely (7)
7. very sure (9)
8. came towards (10)
9. silent from a surprise or a shock (11)
10. filled with air (9)
11. unimportant; not standing out (13)
12. skillful (6)
13. carefully (8)
14. expecting things to go well (10)
15. grabbed suddenly or quickly (8)
16. barely noticeable (5)
17. people involved in a contest (11)
18. strong; energetic (8)
19. a slight bulge along the middle of a road (6)
20. without warning (8)
21. holding tightly (8)
22. force created by a moving body (8)
23. a crash between two objects (9)
24. spoke quickly and with little thought (7)
25. saying (something) over and over again (9)

Sim Dalt had two long, loose arms, spindly legs, a bony face with gleaming brown eyes, and, from the age of twelve, was reckoned to be a bit touched in the head.

Goalkeeping was the main interest in Sim's life. In his nursery days the one indoor pastime that satisfied him was when his mother kicked a rubber ball from the living-room into the kitchen, while Sim stood goal at the middle door. It was rare even then that he let one pass.

He later attended Scuttle Street elementary school, where he was always gnawed with the ferocious wish for four o'clock, when he could dash to the cinder park to play goalie for some team or other. Even in the hot summer days, Sim would cajole a few non-players into a game of football. "Shoot 'em in, chaps," he would yell, after lovingly arranging the heaps of jackets for the goalposts, "the harder the better."

At twelve he was picked as goalkeeper for his school team. "If you let any easy 'uns through," the captain, Bob Thropper, threatened him, "I'll bust your shins in!"

But he had no need to warn Sim, for it was rare indeed that anyone could get a ball past him.

It was near the end of the season, and Scuttle Street were at the top of the league and in the final for the Mayor's Shield, when a new and very thorough inspector visited the school. He found Sim's scholastic ability to be of such a low order that he directed him at once to Clinic Street special school.

"I suppose you could continue to play for us until the end of the season," said Mr. Speckle, at a meeting of the team, "and then, at least, you'll be sure of a medal."

"What, sir!" interposed Bob Thropper. "*A cracky school* lad play for us? Ee, sir, that *would* be out of order!"

"But what shall we do about a goalkeeper?" asked the teacher.

"Goalkeepers!" snorted Bob. "I could buy 'em and sell 'em."

"What," asked Sim, staring at Bob, "what do you mean, 'buy 'em an' sell 'em'?"

"I mean that they're ten a penny," grunted Bob, "especially daft 'uns." And having made his point he snapped: "Off with them togs, mate — we want 'em for our next man." And Sim sadly removed his boots, stockings, and shorts, but when it came to the jersey, he hesitated, but Bob grabbed at it: "Buy 'em an' sell 'em," he growled, "that's me."

There was a tear close to Sim's eye. "I'll never buy you," he hissed, "but I might *sell* you one day."

In adapting himself to his new life he was quick enough to grasp any advantage it might offer. He organised games in the schoolyard, and for two years enjoyed some hectic, if not polished, goalkeeping. And at the age of fifteen, when his mother took him round to different factories for work, he simulated idiocy so as not to be taken on.

"Now stop this shinanikin," his mother scolded him, "you're no more barmy than I am. And you know it."

"You shoulda told the school-inspector that," remarked Sim.

Every morning, with the 'normal intelligence' boys gaping enviously at him through the factory windows, Sim would set out for the cinder park, bouncing and heading a football along the street.

At the age of nineteen he accepted his first job, since it did not interfere with his way of life; also, it had possibilities. It was at Brunt's Amusement Arcade, where the chief attraction was a "Beat the Goalie" game. There were goal-posts that appeared to be full size, and a real football, and all comers were invited to try to score. It cost threepence for a try, and anyone who scored received sixpence in return. Sim, of course, got the job of goalkeeper.

Maggie Brunt, the owner, was a wizened, red-eyed woman. "How's it goin', lad?" she would say, giving sly slaps of apparent goodwill on various parts of the goalkeeper's person. By this cunning form of greeting she had caught out a stream of employees who had been fiddling — having one pocket for Maggie and one for themselves.

She tried it out on Sim, time after time, and never once was there the faintest jingle of metal, until finally she decided that the lad must be simple, if not honest. The fact was that Sim — who did things with singular efficiency when he had to — had constructed a special pocket, copiously insulated with cottonwool, and provided with various sections for different coins. Had Maggie turned him upside-down and shaken him like a pepper-pot she would not have heard the faintest jingle, so expertly was it contrived.

There came a day, after some six thrifty years, when Maggie decided to sell the Arcade — and Sim was able to buy it from her. "Bless you, lad," sighed Maggie, "they say you're gone in the head, but I wish there were more like you."

"It wouldn't do," remarked Sim, and not without a touch of regret he removed the cottonwool from his pocket.

Bob Thropper's visit to the Arcade was the start of a remarkably prosperous boom for Sim. Bob was a thickset, dark-jowled footballer by this time, and the idol of the Hummerton crowd. His tremendous kicking power

had broken many goal-nets, winded or knocked senseless a number of goalkeepers, and on one occasion, it was said, had actually smashed a crossbar.

One night, just after a cup-tie victory, Bob and his team-mates, merry though not drunk, were passing the Arcade, when one suggested having some sport with Sim.

"Skipper," whispered Stan Mead, "you smash one in!"

Stan Mead dived into his pocket for threepence, when Sim called out: "Like to make it pounds instead of pence?"

The challenge was taken up at once, and in a moment eleven pound notes were flung down, and Sim covered these with as many out of his pocket. Then Bob Thropper drew back, took his short, confident run, and let go one of his famous drives. Sim was up like a flash, and brought it down with a stylish assurance.

Then with a casual air he threw the ball back. "Are you covering the twenty-two quid?" he asked.

The money was covered in two minutes. "What about waiting till somebody nips off for your football boots?" asked Stan Mead.

Bob shook his head. "I could lick this loon," he snorted, "in my bare feet" — and with that he took a second shot. It was good — but not good enough. Sim leapt and caught it on his chest. Bob's face went darker than ever. "Fetch my boots," he hissed at Stan Mead, "an' I'll smash him to bits."

A huge crowd swayed the Arcade when Bob Thropper prepared to make the third attempt. The forty-four pounds had been covered, so that there was a pile of pound notes on an orange box, with a brick on top of them. After having his boots tied up, Bob Thropper removed his jacket, took off his collar and tie, and nodded to Stan Mead to place the ball. The crowd went silent as he took the short run, and then kicked.

The ball flashed forward — it went like lightning, a knee-high shot. "*Goal!*" yelled a voice from behind. But a long thin figure whizzed through the air. There was a thud, the figure dropped to the ground. Nobody could be sure what had happened — until Sim stood up. His face was white. But he had the ball clutched against his heart. Slowly he went towards the orange box and picked up the money. "Closing time!" he whispered in a low, clear voice. The crowd set up a sudden cheer — volley after volley.

From that night on Sim Dalt became famous as "The goalie Bob Thropper could never beat!" The Arcade flourished. Sim got offers from many teams, including one from Hummerton club itself.

"When I join your club," he told them, "it'll not be as a goalie."

And it was not many years before Sim's words came true, for there came a chance for him to buy a considerable portion of club shares, and he was voted a director.

One September morning early in the season he was taken round and introduced to all the players.

"Meet Bob Thropper," said the co-director, "our most famous centre-forward."

Sim looked at the man before him. "Centre-forwards," he remarked significantly, "I can buy 'em an' sell 'em — or," he added, "I can at least sell 'em."

Some vague and long-forgotten moment of memory was evoked in Bob Thropper at these words.

He stood there frowning. Then, as Stan Mead nudged him and spoke, it all came back to him clearly.

"Bob, you'd better be looking for a nice pub to retire to," Stan whispered feelingly, "because this chap means it."

— *Bill Naughton*

? Questions and Assignments

1. What is your first impression of
   (i) Sim Dalt?
   (ii) Bob Thropper?

2. Explain fully why Sim was dropped from the Scuttle Street school team.

3. Why was Sim not offered a factory job?

4. Describe his first *'job'*.

5. How did Maggie Brunt check if her employees were *'fiddling'*?

6. How did Sim manage to buy the arcade?

7. Would you agree that Sim Dalt got double revenge on Bob Thropper? Explain.

8. Did you consider the ending satisfying? Why?

9. Write about an occasion when you got revenge on somebody or when somebody got revenge on you.

10. Imagine that you are a judge in a short story competition. Mark the story out of ten and explain briefly why you marked it as you did. (See page 18 for guidelines on how to do this.)

WP **Word Power**

Find the words in the story which have similar meanings to each of the words and phrases below. The number in brackets after each one indicates the number of letters in the *answer*. The words appear in the story in the same order as the meanings given below.

1. very thin (7)
2. hobby (7)
3. persuade (6)
4. warned of punishment (10)
5. unusual (4)
6. interrupted (10)
7. snapped (7)
8. paused for a moment (9)
9. making a change to suit new conditions (8)
10. exciting and energetic (6)
11. pretended (9)
12. jealously (9)
13. took up an offer (8)
14. shrivelled (7)
15. protected (9)
16. thought out (9)
17. sorrow (6)
18. an offer of a contest (9)
19. appearing relaxed and unconcerned (6)
20. dull sound (4)
21. held tightly (8)
22. grew successful (10)
23. part (7)
24. hazy; unclear (5)
25. called to mind (6)

THE LION

Tim stood patiently at the edge of the small crowd and waited for the appearance of the man he called Putrid in his mind.

He was a young boy. His thin hands were clasped behind his back. This was the third day he had come to watch the feeding of the animals of the circus. Tim hadn't been inside to see the circus. He could never raise the price of it, even the matinee, but the feeding of the animals was for free. Anybody could come and watch. It was a small menagerie. Just a lioness and a tiger and a few monkeys and Samson.

Samson was the lion. It was near his cage Tim always stood. It wasn't a big cage. It barely fitted the body of the lion. Tim felt his own limbs cramped when he looked at the cage. Samson wasn't like a lion you would see in books or a picture. His mane was not bushy. It was nearly worn away. There was only a bit of it left around his head, up near his ears. He didn't roar either. Even when he was provoked he would only loose off a sort of half-hearted growl. You know the sort of small bush that a lion has near the end of his tail. Samson didn't have that either. It was worn away. His tail was mottled, sort of mean-looking. You could see his ribs too. He wasn't a fat lion. Tim was very fond of Samson. He preferred him to the others; to the pacing tiger with the fearful eyes and to the yawning lioness. He even preferred him to the monkeys, although the monkeys were good fun.

The Lion

The other children had run up to the far side of the field. There was Putrid coming out with the bucket. It was a bucket of meat. Raw meat. The sides of the bucket were stained with old blood and fresh blood. Tim felt a wave of dislike coming over him again at the sight of the man with the bucket.

He was a small man, very black-haired, always seeming to want a shave. He was carrying a pole in his hand with a steel prod on the end of it. Tim felt the muscles of his stomach tightening at the sight of him. Always the same. Opening the slot in the cage of the tiger and the lioness and poking in the meat to them. He talked to those nicely enough always. They grabbed the meat and held it between their claws and squatted at the eating of it. Then he turned his face towards the cage of Samson and went into his act.

Before he could start the act, Tim turned to Samson, and he said to him: 'Don't mind him, Samson. Don't mind him. He is very ignorant.' Samson may have heard him. He turned his head towards him and blinked his great eyes, and then went back to his dreaming. Almost against his will Tim turned his eyes to watch Putrid.

There he was several yards away, crouching like an ape, the bucket in one hand, the pole in the other. The kids were around him laughing at his antics.

'Here's the fiercest one of them all, mind,' he was saying, pointing to Samson with his nose, like a dog. 'Fresh outa the jungles of Africa. Looka the red in his eyes. Watch the stretch of the claws. Only to be approached with great caution. Careful with him now. He can stretch a limb five foot through the bars to get at ye.'

He circled around as if he was stalking. Tim watched him in disgust. He knew that the best parts would be gone from the bucket. Samson never got anything from him but the bare leavings of the others. The kids were delighted with Putrid. They started to imitate him, crouching and stalking and laughing. Suddenly Putrid darted towards the cage, inserted the prod and stuck it in Samson's side. The lion moved, almost grunting. He couldn't move far. He didn't growl. He didn't roar. Tim would have given anything to hear him roaring with anger. He didn't.

'See that,' says Putrid. 'Hear the roaring of him. Waken the dead he would. Oh, a fierce animal, kids. But, you don't have to be afraid of him. Watch this.' He left down the bucket and the pole and he ran crouching behind the cage and caught hold of Samson's tail. He pulled it as hard as he could, so that the body of the lion was pulled back to the end bars.

'See that,' he was shouting. 'The only fierce animal in captivity to be held by the tail. He'll go mad, so he will. Watch him tear the cage to pieces.'

Tim's finger-nails were biting into his palms. Samson rose almost wearily, straightening himself, crouching because he could not stand upright in the cage, pulling against the pull on his tail, almost staggering on his pads as Putrid suddenly released him. The lion's head hit the bars on the other side. He didn't object.

Because he's old, I suppose, Tim thought. He wouldn't have done that to him when he was young. He conjured up a picture of Samson meeting Putrid in a jungle clearing. Putrid wouldn't be unkind then, Tim bet. Samson would just tear Putrid to pieces. Tim savoured that.

Putrid was rubbing his hands.

'Nothin' to it, mind,' he was saying. 'I've pulled lions by the tail in every continent in the world. But this one is real fierce when he's feedin'. Oh, real fierce when he's feedin'.'

He didn't open the slot. He pulled the bar and opened the whole door of the cage. Tim wished that Samson would spring out on top of him. He didn't. Putrid hit him on the head with the prod. You could hear the sound of it. Samson just blinked his eyes and pulled back.

'No play in him at all today,' said Putrid. 'Here, Fanny, have your chips.' He up-ended the bucket and flung the contents of it straight into the lion's face. The lion must have looked funny with the things on his face, the bystanders were dying laughing. The scraps fell off his face then onto the floor of the cage.

Putrid banged the door and locked it.

'Bah,' he said, 'No play for him at all today. What a lion. Come on, we'll get to the monkeys.'

They followed him. One of them, before going, tentatively took a pull at the lion's tail which was still hanging through the bars. He let it go quickly and ran after them shouting, 'Hey, fellas, I did it, I pulled his tail.'

Putrid patted him on the head.

'Man,' he said, 'you'll be a lion-tamer yet, so you will.'

They laughed.

Tim was looking at Samson.

'Maybe he doesn't mean it,' he was saying to him. 'But don't mind him. He has to die sometime and then he won't be after you.'

He felt tears in his eyes. Because I'm young, he thought. Like you would cry about a drowning kitten.

Samson started to clean his face. It took him some time. Then he sniffed at the food between his paws. It didn't interest him. He lifted his head and looked away at the sky.

At this moment Tim got the thought that maybe Samson was sick. He knew they didn't use him in the circus. Just the lioness and the tiger. They just carted him around to be a father, they said. And suddenly in his mind's eyes he saw the wood outside the town. You came down a hill to it and climbed another hill out of it, and in the hollow there was a clear stream that babbled over stones and the wood was wide and dappled with sunlight. A place like that Samson would be at home, with the birds and the trees and the bracken, and he would get well and growl and roar and nobody would disturb him, and Putrid couldn't torture him.

On this thought, Tim reached up (he had to stretch a lot) and he pulled back the steel bolt and he opened the door of the cage.

'Come on, Samson,' he said, 'I will take you to a place that you will like. It won't be like the jungle. But it'll be nearly as good. Come on! Please come on before anybody comes.'

Samson didn't want to come.

Tim pulled himself up onto the floor of the cage until he was hanging on his chest. He stretched an arm until his hand could take hold of the remaining mane and he tugged it gently.

'Come on, Samson,' he said. 'Come on.'

Samson resisted, but then he started to go with the pull of the small hand on his mane and walked beside him, past the caravans, out the gate and into the street of the town.

They walked calmly down the middle of it.

If you can ripple a pond with a pebble you can entirely upset it by throwing a large boulder into it. The pond will explode. It was like that now with the town as the first person looked at the boy and the lion.

This was a fat woman with a shopping basket. She looked and she looked again, and then she dropped her basket and opened her mouth very widely and screamed and turned and ran screaming.

Everybody claimed afterwards that it was this woman who led to the unnatural panic with her screaming. Only for her, they said, nobody would have paid the least attention to the boy and the loose lion. Perhaps, but if you are walking up a street and you see a lion walking towards you, I doubt if you will stop to ask any questions. Your skin will crawl, you mouth will dry, the hair will rise on the back of your neck and you will seek safety in flight. Everybody did now. The street, thronged with people, cleared as if a plague had swept through it. People ran into the first open shop door, fighting to get in and to bang the doors behind them, and peer out through the glass. Screaming women and shouting men, all panic-stricken. They ran into cars and closed the doors of them and shot up the windows of them and peered palely through them.

The Lion

Tim walked solemnly on, talking to Samson, almost unconscious of the confusion he was leaving behind him. He turned from the busy shopping and market street into the wide Square. This was roomier and people had more time to find safety and to reflect.

Tim paused at the top of the Square and became aware of all the disturbance he was causing and also became aware of the line of police gradually and very cautiously closing in on him. His hand tightened on Samson, and he stopped, and Samson stopped and looked at the circle of men approaching him. He raised a lip and snarled, and the advancing line came to a dead stop, all except the Inspector, a tall man with blue eyes, who came close to the boy and the lion with nothing under his arm except a light cane. He had sense. He had called the circus people. Out of one corner of his eye he saw them approaching now, out of the street into the Square, loaded with ropes and bars and hauling a cage on wheels which they lifted down from a van.

'Take it easy, boy,' said the Inspector. 'Don't get excited. Nothing will happen. Don't excite him.'

Tim's mouth was dry. He suddenly realised that his hopes were at an end. He hadn't thought of the town and the police.

If he could have gone a back way, nobody might have noticed. Now, he thought sadly, Samson would never see the wood.

The Inspector was surprised as he closed on him. The boy had no fear, and as he looked closely at the lion, he saw there was no need for anybody to fear. All the same, who knew? The lion looked old and thin and helpless, but one slash at the boy was all that was needed.

The men were closing from behind, cautiously, the ropes held in loops.

'Leave the lion and come here to me.' said the Inspector.

Tim shook his head.

'No, no,' he said, his small hand tightening on the lion.

'You'll have to leave him go,' said the Inspector. 'The men are behind you. They are going to throw ropes over him. You'll have to come to me.'

'Don't let Putrid touch him,' said Tim.

The Inspector didn't know what he was talking about.

'All right,' he said.

'Good-bye, Samson,' said Tim then, pressing his hand deeply into the lion's neck. He didn't look at him any more. He bent his head and walked to the Inspector. The Inspector heaved a sigh and caught his hand. He watched for a short time as the ropes landed, and the lion was secured. Like a pent-up breath relieved, there was laughter and calling and shouting. He noticed the small, black, dirty little fellow cavorting around the lion as they put him into the

91

cage. He went docilely, peacefully. But this chap was putting on an act for the surrounding people. And they were laughing at his antics.

'All right,' said the Inspector 'let's go down and get off the streets and see what this is all about.'

Tim found himself alone in a small room with just a desk and a bright fire, and the Inspector who didn't seem so tall when he was sitting down.

'Now Tim,' he said, 'tell me. Did you open the cage?'

'Yes sir,' said Tim.

'Why?' he asked.

'I wanted to bring him out to the woods,' Tim said. 'So that he would get well and Putrid wouldn't torture him.'

Tim told him about Putrid.

'I see,' said the Inspector.

'Samson is not well,' said Tim. 'You should have seen him. He wouldn't roar nor nothing. And he should have. He should have eaten Putrid. But he didn't do nothing. Just sat when he stuck things into him and pulled his tail and everything. You see, Samson should be in the woods to get well.'

'I see,' said the Inspector. He took up the telephone and called a number into it. He tapped with a pencil on the desk as he waited. His eyes were hard. Tim was frightened again.

'That you, Joe?' he asked. 'Yes, it's me. I want you down here in about ten minutes. Bring your bag of tricks with you. Yes, I'll explain to you then. It's urgent.'

He put down the phone. He pressed a button and started to write lines on a sheet of paper. Another policeman came in.

'Here,' he said. 'Go down to the J.P. down the road and get him to sign that.' The policeman went.

'All right, Tim,' said the Inspector, 'come on and we'll go out and wait for Joe'.

'What are you going to do with me?' Tim asked. 'Will I have to go to jail?' The Inspector looked at him for a moment, then put his hand on his head.

'No Tim,' he said. 'No jail. On the other hand, no medal either. They don't give out medals for the kind of good deed you do. Come on.'

They went out. The Inspector opened the door of a car and put Tim in before him. There was a bulky red-faced man behind the wheel.

'Hello, Joe' said the Inspector. 'This is Tim, a friend of mine.'

'Hello, Tim,' said Joe. 'Glad the Inspector has decent friends for a change.'

The policeman came breathless, then shoved in the paper through the window.

'He made no trouble about it?' the Inspector asked.

'Not a bit,' said the policeman, laughing. 'Said he'd sign an order to burn the circus as well.'

The Inspector laughed.

'Fine. All right, Joe.'

The car moved away.

'What's all this about a lion?' Joe asked. 'Everybody is talking about it.'

'That's the lion you are going to see,' said the Inspector. He explained to Tim. 'Joe is a doctor of animals, Tim. He cares for animals, like a doctor cares for people.

Tim was interested.

'Oh,' he said. 'Will you make Samson well?'

'He will, Tim, don't worry,' said the Inspector.

Joe was a bit bewildered, but kept silent under the appeal of the Inspector's wink.

The car stopped outside the circus entrance. The town had returned to normal.

'You stay here, Tim,' said the Inspector. 'We won't be long.'

They left him. Tim opened a window. He could smell the circus. He didn't want to go in there again.

Joe was looking at Samson.

'What do you think?' the Inspector asked.

'I'm afraid so,' said Joe.

'You wait here', said the Inspector.

He found the owner. He presented him with the signed order.

'You can't do that,' he protested. 'It's illegal. There's nothing wrong with him. Just because some crazy kid let him out. That's no reason. Here, Alphonsus. Come here. He knows. He keeps them fed. You know that Samson is all right, isn't he? Isn't Samson all right?'

'Strong as a lion,' said Alphonsus, chuckling.

'You are Putrid,' said the Inspector suddenly to Aphonsus. He thought how vivid had been the boy's description of him. 'You're a dirty sadistic little man,' he said, 'and if a lion doesn't tear you to pieces some day, some honest man will kick your puddens out.'

Putrid's mouth was open in astonishment.

The owner protested.

'Here,' he said. 'You can't say things like that.'

'You keep that fella away from your animals,' said the Inspector and walked away from them.

Joe was at the cage. He was putting away a syringe. Samson was lying on the floor of the cage, his legs stiffened straight out from him. His chest was not rising.

They looked at the body of the lion.

'He should have been destroyed years ago,' Joe said.

'Poor devil,' said the Inspector. He put his hand through the bars of the cage and rested it on the body of Samson.

'That's from Tim, Samson,' he said, and then walked back to the car. They got in.

They could sense the silence of the boy.

'What happened?' he asked.

Joe started the car.

The Inspector put his arm round Tim's shoulders.

'Samson is gone back to the woods, Tim,' he said. You watch. One time maybe when you are playing in that wood, you might see Samson standing in the sunlight.'

'Resting on the soft leaves?' said Tim eagerly.

'That's right,' said the Inspector.

— *Walter Macken*

? Questions and Assignments

1. What does the author tell us about Samson in order to make us feel sorry for him?

2. How did Putrid treat Samson? What was his reason for doing so?

3. How did the people behave when Tim led Samson through the town?

4. *'His eyes were hard'*. Explain clearly why the author wrote this sentence.

5. What sentence in the story tells us that Samson was dead?

6. Do you think that the person who wrote this story liked circuses? Explain why.

7. Give your own views on (i) circuses (ii) zoos.

8. Imagine that somebody asked you - 'Who was Samson?' Write out your reply.

9. Imagine that you are a judge in a short story competition. Mark the story out of ten and explain briefly why you marked it as you did. (See page 18 for guidelines on how to do this.)

WP Word Power

Find the words in the story which have similar meanings to each of the words and phrases below. The number in brackets after each one indicates the number of letters in the *answer*. The words appear in the story in the same order as the meanings given below.

1. joined together (7)
2. afternoon performance with low admission prices (7)
3. collection of animals (9)
4. annoyed; made angry (8)
5. stooping with knees bent (8)
6. care (7)
7. creeping up on an animal to catch it (8)
8. copy (7)
9. tiredly (7)
10. walking unsteadily (10)
11. enjoyed; relished (8)
12. people who stop to watch something (10)
13. hesitantly (11)
14. smelled (7)
15. marked with splashes of colour (7)

16. to cause suffering on purpose (7)
17. a large stone (7)
18. crowded (8)
19. a disease which spreads quickly (6)
20. struck with sudden fear (5-8)
21. stopped briefly (6)
22. confusion; disorder (11)
23. pulling (7)
24. tied safely (7)
25. dancing; leaping around (9)
26. a very short time (6)
27. puzzled (10)
28. not legal (7)
29. objected strongly (9)

I looked again at the slip of paper where I had written down my visits. "Mr. Dean, 3 Thompson's Yard. Old dog ill". There were quite a lot of these yards in Darrowby. They were, in fact, like pictures from an old book. Some of them opened off the market-place and many more were scattered behind the main streets, hidden away from the world. You would pass through an archway and then suddenly you were in a little courtyard where all the cottages faced each other across the rough cobblestone street.

In front of the houses, small gardens had been cut out and planted with marigolds or roses. But at the far end of the square, the houses were in a tumbledown condition and some were abandoned with their windows boarded up.

Number Three was the last house on that side of the square and it looked as if it wasn't going to last any longer. The paint was flaked off the doors and the old wood on the porch was rotting away. When I knocked on the door, a small white-haired man answered. His face was pinched with age but his eyes were bright and cheerful. He wore a shabby woollen cardigan, patched trousers and slippers.

"I've come to see your dog." I said, and the old man smiled.

"Oh, I'm glad you've come, sir," he said. "I'm getting a bit worried about the old chap. Come inside, please." He led me into the small sitting room. "I'm alone now," he went on. "I lost my wife over a year ago. She used to think the world of that old dog."

As I looked around, I could see the sad traces of poverty everywhere. The worn-out lino, the wallpaper peeling from the wall, the cold and empty fireplace, and on the table the old man's sparse dinner was laid out. All he had to eat that night was a bit of bacon, a few fried potatoes and a cup of tea. This was life on the old age pension.

In a corner, lying on a folded blanket lay my patient, a cross-bred labrador. He must have been a powerful dog in his day, but the signs of age showed in the white hairs around his muzzle and the jelly-look in his eyes.

"Getting on a bit, isn't he, Mr. Dean?"

"Aye, he is that. Nearly fourteen, but he's been like a pup, galloping about until these last few weeks. Wonderful dog, is old Bob. Never offered to bite anyone in his life. Children can do anything with him. He's my only friend now. I hope you'll be able to put him right."

"Is he off his food, Mr. Dean?"

"Yes, clean off. And that's a strange thing because, by heaven he could eat.

Up to now, he always sat by me at meal times and put his head on my knee, but he hasn't been doing it lately."

I looked at the dog with growing uneasiness. The stomach was very swollen and I could see the tell-tale signs of pain: the catch in his breathing, the slack lips and the frightened look in the eyes. When his master spoke, the tail thumped on the blankets twice and a quick look of interest came into the eyes, but just as quickly, the old animal slumped on the blankets again. I passed my hand over the dog's stomach and felt the accumulated fluid beneath the skin. He must have been feeling great pain. "Come on, old boy." I said. "Let's see if we can turn you over." The dog made no resistance and I gently rolled him over on his side. And then, without a doubt, I noticed the cause of the illness. Under the skin, I could see the slightly raised lump and when I felt it, my fears for the dog became even greater. For beneath the thin muscle of the flank, I felt the hard knotted mass and I knew immediately that this was a cancer and because of the size, it would not be able to be removed. I stroked the old dog's head. This was not going to be easy.

"Is he going to be ill for long?" asked the man, and again came the thump, thump of the dog's tail on the floor. "You know, it's miserable when I don't have Bob following me around as I do my little jobs."

"I'm sorry, Mr. Dean, but I'm afraid this is something very serious. You see this large swelling? It is caused by an internal growth."

"You mean... cancer?" the old man said faintly.

"Yes, I'm sorry. I'm so sorry. The disease has progressed too far for anything to be done. I wish there was something I could do to help him, but there isn't."

The old man looked bewildered and his lips trembled. "Then he's going to die?"

I swallowed hard. "Well, we really can't leave him to die, can we? He's in great pain now, and it will soon be an awful lot worse. Don't you think it would be kindest to put him to sleep? He's had a good long life." I tried to be brisk and business-like, but it didn't work. My heart went out to the poor old man. He looked so lonely already.

The old man was silent, then he said, "Just a minute." Slowly and painfully, he knelt down beside the dog. He did not speak, but ran his hand over the grey muzzle and ears again and again, and all the while the dog's tail thumped on the floor with joy. Mr. Dean knelt there a long time and I looked around the room at the faded pictures and broken armchair.

At last the old man struggled to his feet and with his eyes turned downward asked, "All right, will you do it now?"

I filled the syringe and said the things I always said, "You needn't worry. This is absolutely painless. Just put him to sleep, it's the easiest way for the poor old fellow." The dog did not move as the needle was inserted, and as the drug went through his veins, he began to relax and the anxious expression left his face. By the time the injection was finished, he was not breathing anymore.

"Is that it?" the old man whispered.

"Yes, that's it," I said. "He's out of pain now."

Mr. Dean stood completely still, his eyes turned gently to the old dog, and his hands shaking. Then he looked at me and I could see the strength coming into his face again. "Yes, that's right. We couldn't leave him to suffer, could we? I'm grateful to you for what you have done. And now, what do I owe you for your services, sir?'

"Oh, that's all right, Mr. Dean. I was passing by here anyway on my rounds. It was no trouble."

The old man was astonished. "But you can't do that for nothing."

"Now, please, say no more about it, Mr. Dean. It's all right." I said good-bye and went out of the house. As I passed through the bustle of the crowds on the street, I could see only the bare little room, the old man and his dead dog.

As I walked towards my car, I heard a shout behind me. The old man was half-running towards me in his slippers. His cheeks were streaked and wet, but he was smiling. In his hand he held a small brown object.

"You've been very kind, sir. I've got something for you." He held out the object and I looked at it. It was a tattered brown ribbon, and at the end of it was a tarnished medal, awarded to Mr. Dean for bravery during the war. "Go on, it's for you," he said, and I could see the pride in his eyes. This medal was worth something, and so had his dog been worth something, and Mr. Dean wanted to give. The passing of his beloved dog had to be marked with a precious gift, for it was an important occasion.

I took the medal respectfully and thanked him. Then I walked on. When I looked back he was still standing there, watching me go.

— *James Herriot*

? Questions and Assignments

1. How do we know from the opening paragraph of the story that a vet is telling the story?

2. What details in the story tell us that Mr. Dean was poor?

3. What details in the story tell us that there was much affection between Mr. Dean and his dog?

4. *"This was not going to be easy"* says the vet to himself in the story. What was not going to be easy? Why?

5. How did the vet know that the old dog had cancer?

6. What part of the story did you find particularly sad?

7. Why did the vet take the medal?

8. Write about an old person with whom you are friendly.

9. Imagine that you are a judge in a short story competition. Mark the story out of ten and explain briefly why you marked it as you did. (See page 18 for guidelines on how to do this.)

WP Word Power

Find the words in the story which have similar meanings to each of the words and phrases below. The number in brackets after each one indicates the number of letters in the *answer*. The words appear in the story in the same order as the meanings given below.

1. spread out (9)
2. left; given up (9)
3. covered entrance to a house (5)
4. old and worn (6)
5. signs (6)
6. not enough; inadequate (6)
7. running on four legs (9)
8. increased in size (7)
9. fell weakly (7)
10. collected; gathered (11)
11. liquid (5)

12. lump (4)
13. taken away (7)
14. very unhappy (9)
15. advanced (10)
16. lively and cheerful (5)
17. uneasy; worried (7)
18. spoke quietly (9)
19. amazed (10)
20. torn; ragged (8)
21. dull; not shining (9)
22. event (8)

ST. BRENDANS COMMUNITY SCHOOL
BIRR, CO. OFFALY

STEEPLEJACKS

The brickworks at the edge of the town had been closed down for many years and wind and rain had made wrecks of the old kilns and drying sheds. Nearby in the deep pit lay a pond of greenish water and across it on sunny days there stretched a shadow of the tall brick chimney with its lightning-conductor, a chimney that was a landmark for miles around.

One day it was rumoured that the brickworks was to be reopened and the rumour became a fact when Tim Rooney, a famous steeplejack, arrived one morning with three assistants to repoint and renovate the tall chimney. After much manoeuvering and hammering the ladder was placed upright against the face of the chimney, and from the top of it Tim gazed down at his three workmates who were shading their eyes against the sun and staring up at him. From the broad lip of the chimney he hauled out abandoned jackdaws' nests and flung the bundles of sticks into the air, and after putting his hammers in a

straw basket that was suspended from a pulley-block he plucked at the ropes and signalled to his men to lower away. He watched the basket move to the ground in short, irregular jerks, and before climbing down the ladder himself he looked across the fields to the houses at the edge of the town where smoke rose untroubled from the chimney pots and freshly washed shirts hung limp from the lines in the backyards. The sight of the clothes made him thirsty and he licked his dry lips and resting his hands on the topmost rung of the ladder, now warm under the sun, he began to descend with slow and definite rhythm.

"Well," he said on reaching the ground and clapping the red dust from his hands, "there's a grand view from the top. Three counties lie below you," he exaggerated, "and you can gaze down the throats of all the chimney pots in the streets beyond." "Well, John," he addressed the youngest of the group, a lad of 18, "what about that jaunt you're to make to the top? When you're married you'll be able to boast to your children how you climbed to the top of the tallest chimney in the town."

John's gaze travelled slowly to the top of the chimney but he didn't move or speak.

"He boasted all week he'd climb it," said George, the eldest of the group.

"Nobody's forcing him if he doesn't want to go," Tim declared, unwilling to encourage him. "We'll take our lunch first."

"I'm not afraid," John answered and spat on his hands. "It'd be better if I'd climb on a fasting stomach. I'll go before we take our lunch."

"It would be better for us all if you would," George mocked. "You'll be seasick before you're halfway up."

"I was never seasick in my life."

"Hard for you! The biggest boat you were ever in was a swing-boat in the children's playground."

"Here goes!" John answered, fastened his belt and cartwheeled towards the base of the chimney. He gripped the side of the ladder with one hand, bowed gracefully, and said, "You're now about to witness an exhibition of how a chimney should be climbed. There's nothing in it, gentlemen, as long as you keep your head. Nothing in it."

"Hear! Hear!" George applauded and eyed him humorously. Tim said nothing.

The lad climbed some rungs rapidly and then with slow caution ascended another four. His toe dislodged a piece of mortar and he heard it clink against the ladder on its way to the ground. He paused, frightened. Above him he saw the ladder converge at the top like railway lines. He had a long way to go yet, and on looking down to measure his distance from the ground he saw, in one

swaying moment, the old drying sheds buckle and stretch like an accordion.

He held grimly to the ladder and allowed his head to clear. Sweat oozed in blobs on his forehead and his hands became clammy. In front of him he saw tiny hairs of moss growing like moles between the bricks and he noticed with rising terror that some the the bricks were cracked. He closed his eyes, swallowed with difficulty, and made an attempt to descend. His foot missed the lower rung and his trouser-leg caught on it and rolled back, and for a moment he felt the free air on his bare leg. He drew his two feet together, twined his arms round a rung of the ladder and remained still.

A tizzling sound trembled through the sides of the ladder. They were hammering on it, signalling to him to come down. He was afraid to move or to look up or look down. He heard Tim call up to him, but what advice was given he couldn't make out. The grey rope at the side of the ladder tautened and presently the basket halted beside him, but when he put a hand on it, it swung away from him and in an instant he gripped the rung above his head and closed his eyes to shut out the drunken tilting of the chimney.

"Hold tightly, John, like a good lad," Tim shouted, his voice near at hand. "Hold tightly and don't look down."

Tim was now directly below him: "Don't be afeared," he was saying, "give me your right foot. Let it loose and I'll guide it. That's the stuff. Now give me your left foot. Hold tight with your hands and leave the feet to me . . . Here we go again. Put the right foot down and now the left beside it. That's the way it's done. That's the ticket! We'll make a steeplejack out of you yet, never fear. Off we go again. First the right and now the left."

"Are we nearly there?" John asked without turning his head.

"We haven't far to go. Keep looking up and you'll be safe in port before you know where you are."

Tim hurried down the last few rungs: John followed him and on reaching the ground his workmates clapped loudly.

"It's not as easy as it looks," he breathed, his face a green colour and his eyes large with fright. "Was I up far?"

"You were near the top."

"I was like hell."

"I warned you you'd be seasick but you wouldn't heed me."

"Give over," Tim said. "We all have to learn. For a first attempt he didn't do badly."

"Never again," John said and sat on the ground which swayed like the deck of a ship.

Tim patted him on the shoulder: "Breathe in the air deeply and you'll be as right as rain in no time."

They helped him to his feet and gave him a drink of water from a can that lay in the long grass out of the sun. They spread newspapers in the cool shade of the hedge, opened their lunchboxes, and took out their thermos flasks. In front of them across the sunny field the windows of the houses were all open and the smoke from the chimneys lay in a smother above the roofs.

"It's so still here," Tim said, "it'd be a nice place for a cemetery. But you'll not be going there for a while yet, John."

John smiled like a convalescent and his hand trembled as he took the cup of tea that Tim poured out for him. He drank it slowly, and when he had finished he lay back on the grass and felt his nausea slip away from him. For awhile he listened to the men talking, and then closing his eyes he tried to relax. He dozed over, but the smell from the men's pipes made him feel sickish and he sat up and rubbed his forehead. Above the hedge towered the chimney and as he stared at it he saw a young boy halfway up the ladder.

"Tim, look!" and he turned pale and felt his head grow light. Tim peered through the leaves in the hedge and saw the boy nearing the top of the chimney.

"For the love of God, men, don't budge, don't breathe," he ordered. "There's a young lad at the top of the ladder. Keep still and don't frighten him."

The two men turned and watched the boy lever himself on to the lip of the chimney and sit dangling his legs as if he were seated on a roadside wall.

"We mustn't show ourselves," Tom urged, "mustn't let him know we see him. If he has the head to climb up, he'll have the head to get down."

Suddenly the boy ceased dangling his legs and crawled on his knees round the lip of the chimney. He did the complete circle and on reaching the top of the ladder he turned his back to descend. He twined his arms round the topmost rung and clung to it without moving. The men watched and waited, bending the branches of the hedge to see better.

"He's staying there because he can't get down," John said. "I know what it's like - he's afraid to move. We must do something. Tim. Go up after him; help him the way you helped me."

"Take it cool; that boy will get down all right. I know what I'm talking about."

"He's stuck. He's afraid to move - anyone can see that! I'm going for the fire brigade; they'll get him down," John said, springing to his feet.

"Don't make a fool of yourself. Stay where you are. That boy has a head for heights, I tell you. He'll manage by himself if we leave him alone and not startle him."

The boy still clung to the top rung, but made no attempt to descend.

"I can't bear to look at him any longer," John said, and before his workmates could stop him he was running along the hedge to the town.

At that moment, slowly and steadily, the boy began to descend, sometimes halting to look around him.

"That's the way, my boy," Tim breathed to himself, "that's the way to do it. But for the love of God, don't look down. Come on, another rung. You're just half way. Come on, what are you hesitating for!"

From their look-out behind the hedge they watched intently every movement that he made. They saw him halt, rub each hand in turn on his jersey, look up, and once more begin to ascend.

"Did you ever see the like of that for cheek since God made you? There's the makings of a great steeplejack in that boy," George said.

"He has the head all right, but I wish I had my hands on him before John fetches the fire brigade," Tim said. "I should have left someone on watch when we were at our lunch."

The boy had now reached the top of the ladder and after struggling on to the lip of the chimney he stood up on it, walked round to the lightning-conductor and gripped it like a Roman soldier with his spear. At that moment a woman came out of the end house across the fields and taking damp clothes from her washing basket she hung them on the line. Then, shading her eyes, she called to left and right: "Jackie, Jackie, Jackie." She didn't see him crouched at the top of the chimney, and when she had gone back to the house he descended the ladder rapidly and raced across the fields.

"Thanks be to God he's safe anyway," Tim said and rose to his feet. "Never again will I leave the ladder without a watchman."

He walked across the field to the end house and on reaching the open door he called to the woman as she moved about the dark kitchen and asked if he could have a word with her son.

"I hope he hasn't been up to any mischief, Mister," she said, coming to the door.

"Nothing much. I was wondering if you'd like him to be a steeplejack."

"A steeplejack! What on earth's that?"

"My job - pointing and renovating mill chimneys."

The woman smiled: "It is our Jackie! He hasn't the heart of a rabbit, Mister, and that's the truth."

"I can tell you he climbed to the top of the brickyard chimney when we'd our backs turned."

"He wouldn't do the like of that, Mister!" she said and stared at him.

"He did, indeed. Ask him yourself."

She beckoned Jackie beside her and looked closely at the red dust on his jersey and trousers.

"Where were you?" she shouted and gripped his shoulder.

"Over in the brickfields, Mother."

"What were you doing?"

"Looking around and playing."

"Playing at what?"

Jackie lowered his head but didn't answer.

"You climbed the ladder to the top of the chimney," Tim challenged him.

"Speak up to the man, Jackie, where's your manners!"

Jackie plucked at a loose thread on his jersey.

"You walked round the lip of the chimney and put your hand on the lightning conductor," Tim pressed.

"Merciful God!" the mother exclaimed and sat down on a chair. "Wait till I get my breath back. My boyo, but you're a heartscald. You'd some poor body's blessing about you when you weren't killed stone dead."

"He has a head for heights. You should let him follow his gift. He's a born climber, a born steeplejack."

"He'll not be able to climb into bed when I'm done with him . . . And wait till his father hears about it... It's the last chimney he'll climb in this life . . . Oh, you'll be in your good safe school tomorrow if you're fit to go . . . I'm thankful to you, Mister, for if I'd seen him at the top of the chimney the sight'd never left my eyes."

The bell of the fire brigade could be heard approaching the edge of the town.

"I'll have to go," Tim said. "But when the lad's the age keep my job in mind for him. There's good money in it."

He hurriedly took his leave and headed across the field to the hedge where his two workmates awaited him.

— Michael McLaverty

? Questions and Assignments

1. Explain the phrase - *'a chimney that was a landmark for miles around'*.

2. Why did Tim Rooney arrive at the brickworks?

3. Explain why John climbed the ladder.

4. List all the things which caused John to stop and panic during his climb.

5. What kind of character was Tim Rooney? Did you admire him or not? Explain why.

6. In the story we are told that John *'turned pale and felt his head go light'*. Explain why.

7. After reaching the top of the chimney did Jackie come straight down again? Explain exactly what he did.

8. Explain the phrase - *'He has a head for heights'*.

9. Do you thing that John would ever make a good steeplejack? Explain.

10. What did you think of the ending of the story?

11. Write about an occasion when you panicked with fright.

12. Imagine that you are a judge in a short story competition. Mark the story out of ten and explain briefly why you marked it as you did. (See page 18 for guidelines on how to do this.)

WP   Word Power

Find the words in the story which have similar meanings to each of the words and phrases below. The number in brackets after each one indicates the number of letters in the *answer*. The words appear in the story in the same order as the meanings given below.

1. greatly damaged objects (6)

2. something well-known on the landscape (8)

3. (a story) passed from person to person which might not be true (8)

4. helpers (10)

5. restore(8)

6. deserted (9)

7. hung (9)

8. go downwards (7)

9. described something as being greater than it actually is (11)

10. look for a long period (4)

11. urge (9)

12. tied (8)

13. demonstration (10)

14. went upwards (8)

15. moved from position (9)

16. words to help someone make a decision (6)

17. tightened (8)

18. held tightly (7)

19. sick feeling (6)

20. move slightly (5)

21. stopped (6)

22. quickly (7)

REQUIEM FOR JOHNNY MURTAGH

I was not speeding. I was cruising along and almost home. Three and a half hours out of Dublin, and I was within five miles of my destination.

One moment I had an open stretch of country road in the long beam of my headlight, the next his grotesque face and wildly waving arms filled the windscreen. I drove the brake-pedal into the floor and stiffened behind the wheel. The tyres gripped and gave an almightly drag against the car. There was no frost on the road, no water. Nevertheless, I didn't stand a chance.

There was a thud as I rammed him below the belt, and a louder thud as his head smashed downwards on the bonnet.

There he rested until the car skidded to a halt.

I jumped out and turned him over on the bonnet. He was moaning. So he was still alive.

I screamed at him, 'How did you get in front of me? How did you get there?'

He just kept moaning, and the only coherent word I could make out were, 'Can't sleep.'

I looked up the road, and down the road. There wasn't a wisp of car-light coming from either direction. What would I do? I was in a frenzy. There was no house for half-a-mile on either side. What should I do?

The rules of thumb were easily recalled. Telephone the police. Call an ambulance, a doctor, a priest to administer the last rites for fear he should die. Never leave the scene of an accident.

There wasn't a police station for fifteen miles, nor a telephone that I knew of for at least a mile. Anyway, how could I leave him there to go for help?

He was still sprawled across the bonnet, muttering, 'Can't sleep. Can't sleep.'

I had recognised him, of course - Johnny Murtagh - the second his face flashed in the headlight, even though I hadn't laid eyes on him for several years. He was noted for his eccentric habits. Ever since he left the primary school he had withdrawn from the company of his peers, and continued to live with his mother in their little three-roomed cottage. And what a cottage! It was one of the most forlorn sights on the landscape. While other families built bright new homes, the Murtagh cottage got more and more bedraggled. It was reputed to be filthy inside, and Johnny had all the appearance of such a lifestyle. His face was black with dirt, and his old clothes were similarly caked with grime. I couldn't make out whether he was bleeding or not.

I decided to do the only thing that seemed sensible. I rolled up my overcoat and made a pillow on the back seat. As gently as I could, I lifted him off the bonnet and edged him into the car.

'Johnny, I'm going to take you to the hospital. Are you in much pain?'

'Can't sleep.'

What if his back was broken? Or his neck? What if his skull were fractured? I was terrified. What if he died in my car on the way to Sligo? I caught his chin and shook his head gently. 'Johnny, Johnny, open your eyes. Do you recognise me?'

To my relief he did open his eyes. There was a wild and vacant stare, but he gradually focussed on my face.

'Peter Sullivan,' he mumbled slowly.

'I knocked you down, Johnny. But it wasn't my fault. You came right out in front of me. You came at me from nowhere.'

He nodded, as if agreeing.

'Don't worry. I'll get you to the hospital. You'll be all right.'

I jumped into the driving seat, and turned the car quickly, back in the direction of Sligo town. Again I heard him muttering. 'Can't sleep.' Better to keep him awake, I thought, better not let him lose consciousness.

'What were you doing on the road, Johnny?'

'Can't sleep.'

Scarcely half-a-mile down the road I hit the brow of the little hill above Farranaharpy. The sudden bounce made Johnny cry out and I slowed down. He was certainly in pain. It is perhaps twenty miles from Templeboy to the town of Sligo and there are many humps and hollows on the road. Not Hell's flags would have been more painful to traverse than the road to Sligo that night, with Johnny groaning in agony every time the car lunged.

I tried to keep him talking, even though I had remembered it was a person with a drug-overdose you were supposed to keep conscious. While there were sounds out of him, he was at least still alive.

'We're in Skreen now, Johnny, just passing the creamery. Do you send milk to the creamery?'

'Can't sleep.'

'Is it beef then, Johnny? Have you got a few cattle on the land?' I thought of the pitiable cluster of little fields that were his farm, growing more ragwort and thistles than grass.

'Can't sleep.'

'What do you want to sleep for Johnny? No one pays you for sleeping. It's a waste of time.'

'Australia.'

I almost turned my head and caused another accident, I was so surprised by the suddenness of this new word.

'Australia. It's a fine country, Johnny. I've never been there. I wouldn't mind going some time. On holidays. I wouldn't emigrate or anything. Would you like to go to Australia, Johnny?'

'When I sleep.'

'What do you mean by that, Johnny?'

'Australia. When I sleep.'

'Ah, yes. You dream of Australia when you're asleep.'

'No dream. Wife, child, house, Australia, sleep.'

'I don't understand, Johnny. You have a wife, a child, a house, in Australia when you're asleep?'

'Yes.'

'And that's why you want to go to sleep so badly?'

'Yes.'

His wits were certainly forsaking him, but I was relieved to have him talking.

'Tell me about Australia, Johnny. What is your wife's name?'

'Annie.'

'Is she pretty?'

'Yes. Blonde.' And I could detect a warmth in his tone despite the painful gasps that he gave with every syllable.

'And your child. Is it a boy or a girl?'

'Lisa.'

'We're well on the way, Johnny. Those are the street lamps in Ballisodare you can see now. And, tell me, do you have a job in Australia?'

'Builder's Yard.'

'That must be hard work, carrying bags of cement and the like. But I suppose you are well paid. Did you say you have a house?'

'Bungalow. Nice.'

'Australia is a big country, I believe. What part of Australia do you have your house in?'

'Geraldton. North of Perth.'

By then I had reached the grounds of the hospital. I drove straight up to the casualty door, halted in front of it, and ran inside to get help.

I explained to the orderlies how the accident had happened as they deftly lowered him onto a stretcher. I followed them inside and took a seat in the cubicle until the doctor came.

After a rapid examination, while I again recounted the details of the accident, the doctor declared: 'We'll have to get him to the theatre right away.'

Alone again, I stood over Johnny, looking down into his face.

'They're taking you to Emergency,' I said. 'They will look after you. And I'll wait around to see how you get on, so that I can tell your mother.'

He didn't respond for a moment. Then he looked up at me with a pleading glance.

'Ring her for me.'

'Who, Johnny?'

'Annie, in Australia.'

'Sure, Johnny, sure I will. What's her number?'

'726514. Geraldton.'

I took out my cigar box and wrote the number on it.

'What message will I give her, Johnny?'

He paused and thought.

'Tell her I'll be back.'

'Fine, Johnny. I'll ring this number, speak to Annie, and give her your message.'

'Promise.'

'I promise.'

The orderlies had come to wheel him away at this stage. As he was moving out of the cubicle he cast me a slight sheepish grin through the distortions pain had wreaked on his swarthy features.

'Peter,' he said.

'Yes, Johnny.'

'They call me John in Australia.'

Whatever they might do for his poor broken body, I thought the medical profession would have an even greater problem putting to rights his poor deranged mind.

I went outside to be in the open air, to be alone, possibly to be in the direct line of vision of the Almighty. For, if ever I was close to praying, I was close to it that night.

The car I had abandoned was obtrusively close to the door, so I sat in and drove it around to the visitors' parking area. Craving a little comfort, I lit a cigar and smoked it slowly. Through the windows of the wards on the ground floor I could see the nurses tending their patients. It seemed an intimate little world, self-contained, but totally remote from where I sat isolated in the car park.

Having sucked whatever consolation I could from the cigar, I returned to the Casualty Ward, and waited.

It was perhaps an hour later that the doctor came looking for me.

'I have bad news,' he said solemnly. 'He died before we could do anything. He had severe internal injuries. I'm sorry. Will you inform the next-of-kin? And of course you will have to report it to the authorities.'

I was in a daze as I left the hospital. I was in a daze as I gave a detailed account of the accident to the police sergeant. I was in a daze as I drove back the long lonely road to Templeboy, wondering how I would tell Mrs Murtagh that I had killed her only son.

Approaching the door of the cottage I caught a glimpse of her through the window. She was sitting beside the fire watching television. She opened the door to my knock and then went back to lower the volume on the television set.

'I have bad news for you, Mrs Murtagh,' I said.

She lifted her hand to her mouth. 'It's Johnny,' she gasped. 'Isn't it?'

'It is, Mrs Murtagh. He's been in an accident.'

'Oh, God. He's not dead, is he?'

I paused for a moment to let the suspicion of my awful tidings take root in her mind.

'He's dead, Mrs Murtagh.'

She knotted her fist and stuck it so far into her mouth, I thought she would swallow it. She curled into the armchair and buried her head in the crook of her arm.

'I'm sorry, Mrs Murtagh,' I said, desperate to say or do something, and I sat in another armchair on the opposite side of the fire.

The house deserved its reputation for squalor. Every detail, from the pock-marked blistering paintwork to the tattered vinyl covering on the floor, contributed to the overall effect. There were dirty saucepans and broken mugs arrayed on the dresser. And the kitchen table was loaded indiscriminately with items of food and used dishes.

'How did it happen?' she asked eventually, between sobs.

I explained exactly how the accident had occurred.

She didn't blame me. 'Sure God knows it wasn't your fault. Whatever way his wits were rambling, poor Johnny mustn't have known where he was.'

'He kept repeating that he couldn't sleep, as if he were demented.'

'He turned strange lately, sure enough,' she nodded.

'But what was his problem with sleep?'

'He was a great sleeper until a couple of weeks ago. Sometimes he worried me, he would sleep so long. He might go to bed at eight or nine o'clock, and still he wouldn't rise till twelve or one the next day. It was unnatural. And I declare to God it was impossible to rouse him when he was asleep. I often roared at him and pulled at him, but to no avail. Not an eye would he open. So I left him to his ways, sleeping longer and longer. Then, some time recently, I noticed he was having trouble getting to sleep at night. I used to hear him in his room, pacing around the floor, and coming out here sometimes to make a cup of tea. Tea was his great weakness, but wasn't it a small failing in one who neither smoked nor drank?'

'He mentioned Australia.'

'Australia,' she repeated slowly. 'Yes, he had some notion about Australia. I often wondered if he was thinking of emigrating. He used to tear out any little piece from the newspaper where there was a mention of Australia. And the odd time he went into Sligo or Ballina he came back with an armful of magazines and brochures from the travel agents' offices, all about Australia. Come on and I'll show you where he had a box full beside his bed.'

She led the way through the door into the bedroom and switched on a light. The smell of stale sweat was over-powering. She walked over the articles of clothing that were littered on the floor. His bed was an army-style bunk with a few grey and brown blankets thrown on top. She lifted the lid of a large timber box that stood by the head of the bed. I sat down to look inside.

It was, as the old woman had indicated, filled to the brim with pages from newspapers, magazines, travel brochures. And, sure enough, they were all about Australia. I examined some of them. It was the usual - photographs of beaches, kangaroos, Aborigines and Ayers Rock.

'Poor Johnny,' she said. 'Isn't it terrible to think that he's gone, and how he wasted his life either sleeping or lying here reading those old magazines.'

I felt that I had at last reached an understanding of the unfortunate man I had killed, and I felt a great sorrow for a stunted life and the stunted lives of so many more like Johnny.

The old woman would accept none of my offers of help. Nor did she want the company of any friends or neighbours for the night. So I left the house, having arranged to return in the morning to take her to the hospital.

My state of mind had improved somewhat as I finally began to drive the last few miles to Dromore West. I was not guilty. The old woman did not hold me responsible. I had done everything that a person could do or should do in such circumstances. But then the man's dying wish flashed across my mind. The telephone call. Of course, it was only part of his strange elaborate fantasy. Wouldn't I be as big a lunatic as he if I were to go ringing a telephone in Australia? Still there was something solemn and binding about a promise made to a dying man, and I knew I would have no peace until I had kept my word. I was approaching Quinn's pub and noticed it was still open despite the late hour. Knowing they had a public telephone, I wheeled in off the street.

I was also drawn by the drink, and felt it would bring me some relief. Tom Quinn looked at me with curiosity when he had placed the double whiskey and a pint of beer on the counter in front of me.

'Are you all right?' he enquired.

I told him of the accident.

'The Lord have mercy on the dead,' he said slowly, and, turning to the three men who were drinking at the other end of the bar, he informed them: 'Peter here has been in an accident down the road. Poor old Johnny Murtagh is dead.' The three of them gathered around me and, once more, I had to repeat the details of the accident.

'He kept saying that he couldn't sleep, as if that were the problem,' I said, by way of reflection.

'If Johnny Murtagh couldn't sleep, it was a severe handicap to him.'

There was a brief silence and then one of them burst into compulsive giggling. Another spluttered. Finally the three of them and Tom Quinn were all caught in a swell of uncontrollable laughter.

'He couldn't sleep. Sure the man had exhausted the quota he had been given for a lifetime.'

The incongruity of their laughter quickly helped to suppress it.

'We didn't mean any disrespect to the dead,' explained Tom Quinn when they had finally re-assumed an appropriate solemnity.

'No disrespect at all to poor Johnny, probably the most inoffensive poor devil that ever wore shoe leather.'

I knew these three men by sight, but I couldn't name them.

'Do you know if he had any friends in Australia?' I asked. 'Or anyone he might have known that emigrated there?'

Each of the four men thought deeply, but agreed with one another that there was no one from the locality who had gone to Australia, and Johnny was never known to have had any friends or acquaintances outside the locality.

'It's just that he asked me to call a number in Australia.'

'That's strange, all right,' said Tom. 'But the only way you'll find out is to give it a ring.'

I had swallowed the whiskey and was halfway through the pint of beer. The soothing effect of the alcohol was restoring me to my business-like self. I got Tom to give me the change of a ten pound note in silver coins, and went out to the telephone box.

The operator was remarkably quick, considering she was making contact with the other side of the earth. I heard her asking, 'Is that Geraldton 726514?' Then, returning to me, she asked me to insert the coins and press the button.

'Could I speak to Annie, please?' I asked confidently.

'Yes, this is Annie speaking,' came the reply in a lovely feminine Australian drawl. My confidence was demolished. I almost dropped the telephone. Why my blood didn't stop flowing at that moment I will never understand.

'Hello, hello,' she called out when I didn't respond.

'I'm a friend of John Murtagh,' I eventually managed to articulate.

'You're a friend of John's,' her voice lifted with enthusiasm, 'and you're from Ireland too, I can tell by the accent. John isn't here. In fact I'm very worried about him because I haven't seen him for the past two weeks. It's so unlike him to disappear like this.'

I was in a state of utter confusion. What was I to say? What was his message? - That he would be back. What sort of a message from a dead man was that to give to a woman? He didn't know he was going to die when he gave me the message. Did he? What kind of vortex was I getting pulled into?

'Your daughter,' I queried tentatively.

'Little Lisa. Oh, she's fine, but she's missing her daddy so much.'

I could take no more.

'Listen, Annie,' I said, 'I'll phone back in a few days.'

'Yes, do that. I'm sure he'll be back by then. And he will certainly enjoy hearing from an Irish friend.'

'Thank you, Annie. Goodbye.'

I hung up the receiver and had to lean against the back of the box for a few minutes to try and regain my composure and my faltering hold on reality.

After a while I ventured back to the bar and swallowed the remains of my beer, immediately ordering another pint and double whiskey.

'Well, did you get through?' asked Tom Quinn as he placed the drink in front of me. He refused payment. 'It's on the house.'

'Yes, I got the number all right. Someone answered, but they never heard of Johnny Murtagh.'

'I'm not surprised that they never heard of Johnny in Australia,' ruminated one of the men.

'Sure if Johnny hadn't been famous for sleeping, we wouldn't have heard of him even here.'

I could sense the laughter welling up again, and felt that this time I might join in.

— Jack Harte

? Questions and Assignments

1. What details in the opening paragraph tell us that the accident took place at night in a remote part of Ireland?

2. What does the narrator remember about Johnny Murtagh?

3. Why did the narrator continue talking to Johnny as they drove to the hospital?

4. *'His wits were certainly forsaking him'*. Why did the narrator say this about Johnny?

5. What did the narrator promise Johnny before he was brought into the emergency theatre?

6. What do we learn of Johnny's sleeping habits from his mother? What was unusual about them?

7. What evidence in the story shows that Johnny was never in Australia?

8. Why did the narrator decide to ring the number in Australia?

9. Why were the men in the pub laughing?

10. Explain why the narrator was shocked when he phoned the number which Johnny had given him?

11. Would you agree that this is a strange and mysterious story? Explain why. What is your view on how the story ended?

12. Write about a strange or mysterious event in which you were involved or heard about.

13. Imagine that you are a judge in a short story competition. Mark the story out of ten and explain briefly why you marked it as you did. (See page 18 for guidelines on how to do this.)

WP Word Power

Find the words in the story which have similar meanings to each of the words and phrases below. The number in brackets after each one indicates the number of letters in the *answer*. The words appear in the story in the same order as the meanings given below.

1. end of a journey (11)
2. distorted and ugly (9)
3. making a low noise to indicate pain (7)
4. clear; understandable (8)
5. place; location (5)
6. lying flat and spread out (8)
7. odd; strange (9)
8. sad; forsaken (7)
9. empty (6)
10. travel over (8)
11. collection; group (7)
12. go to live in a different country (8)
13. abandoning; leaving (9)
14. single storey house (8)
15. medical attendants (9)
16. carefully and skillfully (6)
17. caring for; looking after (7)
18. cut off; alone (8)
19. dirt; neglect (7)

II - Poetry

• People write poetry as a way of showing their feelings about all the things that affect us in life - from the most serious to the most trivial. Poetry gives us insight into the thoughts and feelings of others and, in doing so, often helps us to look at things in a new and different way.

Over the course of this section, we will learn to identify some of the devices used by poets to express their feelings and influence their readers, and we will examine how they work in different poems. However, understanding and enjoying poetry does not depend on being able to spot poetic devices. When you read a certain poem and think to yourself "I felt like that too, about . . ." then that poem has worked its magic on you.

Of course, some poems do not reveal their full meaning on a first reading. Like listening to a new song, a new poem may require a number of readings before it begins to 'grow' on you. Even after this, you may still not understand each line. Don't worry! The secret is to try to enjoy it and not to be put off because you're puzzled about the meaning of a few lines. As often as not, it can be the poet's fault - he or she may have been unable to find the right words to get the message across to you.

A RECIPE FOR HAPPINESS

An ounce of tv
A slice of disco dancing
Mix up well
With a squeeze of summer sunbaking
Half a cup of raging on Saturday night
And a large tablespoon of tickling the dog
Add a freshly picked ticket to the Grand Final
Stir in a splash of lazing around the pool
Add the mess of records and clothes on my bedroom floor
Bake slowly with a really good late night video
Add a pinch of messing round on lazy afternoons
Sprinkle with a couple of beaut barbecues
Pour in my oldest and most favourite jeans
Serve with a real good helping of family fun.
And there you are — the recipe's done.

— *Hugh Clement*

? Questions and Assignments

1. The term *'recipe'* means a set of cooking instructions. What words and phrases, used in this poem, could be found in a recipe?

2. Make a list of the 'ingredients' given above e.g. T.V., disco dancing etc.

3. What does the poet mean by *'raging on Saturday night'*?

SONG OF THE RAIN

Night,
And the yellow pleasure of candle-light . . .
Old brown books and the kind fine face of the clock
Fogged in the veils of the fire — its cuddling tock,

The cat,
Greening her eyes on the flame-litten mat;
Wickedly wakeful she yawns at the rain
Bending the roses over the pane,
And a bird in my heart begins to sing
Over and over the same sweet thing —

Safe in the house with my boyhood's love,
And our children asleep in the attic above.

— *Hugh McCrae*

? Questions and Assignments

1. In the first stanza, what *things* cause the poet to feel happy? In the case
   of each, which words or phrases suggest that the poet is happy?

2. Explain the phrases *'Greening her eyes'* and *'flame-litten mat'*.

3. *'Bending the roses over the pane'*. What impression of the weather do
   we get from this line?

4. Why is the poet happy?

SHELTER

The wind and the rain
    Are beating the windows
Lashing the tree-tops
    Beyond the dark fields

The ships and the sailors
    Are tossed on the ocean,
The fish are all hiding
    Their fins in the deep.

The small birds are clinging
    To sway of the branches,
The fox from his hunting
    Slinks back to his den

The sheep on the mountain
    Are huddled together,
The rabbits are burrowed
    Deep down in the earth.

A dog far away
    Complains in the darkness,
The brown flood is swirling
    Against the stone bridge

I hope there is no one
    Lost without shelter,
Out on the wet roads
    Or up in the hills.

I'm warm under blankets
    Safe from the weather,
Feeling my eyelids
    Surrender to sleep

The great world is turning
    Under the heavens,
This is a moment
    I wish I could keep.

           — *Michael Coady*

? Questions and Assignments

1. What words and phrases are used by the poet to capture the power of the storm?

2. The poet imagines what some creatures are doing during the storm. Explain in your own words what they are doing.

3. Say why you think the poet chose each of the following words: *slinks, huddled, complains, swirling.*

4. What are the poet's thoughts on the storm?

5. *'This is a moment/I wish I could keep'.* Why do you think the poet wants to keep that moment?

6. Explain how this poem is similar to *Song of the Rain*.

The night was creeping on the ground;
She crept and did not make a sound
Until she reached the tree, and then
She covered it, and stole again
Along the grass beside the wall.

I heard the rustle of her shawl
As she threw blackness everywhere
Upon the sky and ground and air,
And in the room where I was hid:
But no matter what she did
To everything that was without,
She could not put my candle out.

So I stared at the night, and she
Stared back solemnly at me.

— *James Stephens*

? Questions and Assignments

1. What is the poet describing in this poem?

2. (a) To what does the poet compare *'The night'*?
   (b) What words and phrases help to make the comparison clear?

3. What was *'The night'* unable to do?

4. Make a list of the words that rhyme.

5. Is this poem similar in any way to *Song of the Rain* and *Shelter*? Explain.

STOPPING BY WOODS ON A SNOWY EVENING

Whose woods these are I think I know,
His house is in the village though;
He will not see me stopping here
To watch his woods fill up with snow.

My little horse must think it queer
To stop without a farmhouse near
Between the woods and frozen lake
The darkest evening of the year.

He gives his harness bells a shake
To ask if there is some mistake.
The only other sound's the sweep
Of easy wind and downy flake.

The woods are lovely, dark and deep.
But I have promises to keep,
And miles to go before I sleep,
And miles to go before I sleep.

— Robert Frost

? **Questions and Assignments**

1. The poet seems relieved that the owner of the woods will not see him looking at the snow falling on the woods. Why do you think this is so?

2. How do we know that the event in the poem occurred in December? Can you give the exact date?

3. The poet stopped to gaze on a wood at the side of the road. What could he see on the other side of the road?

4. How do we know that the scene is deserted?

5. How did the horse respond when the poet decided to stop?

6. Do you think that the poet is a complete stranger or a native of the place described in the poem? Explain your answer.

7. What words suggest that the poet found the scene very peaceful and pleasant?

8. What do we learn about the poet in the final stanza?

MY SHIP

When I was a lad my bed was the ship
that voyaged me far through the star-dusted night
to lands forever beyond the world's lip
dark burning olive lands of delight
across blood-red oceans under the stars
lorded by the scarlet splendour of Mars.

It is only a bed now spread with eiderdown
and the sheets merciless chains holding me down.

— *Christy Brown*

? Questions and Assignments

1. The title of the poem is *'My ship'*. Explain exactly what kind of ship the poet is writing about.
2. What are the words *'star-dusted'* used to describe? Do you think it is a good choice of words? Give a reason for your answer.
3. What meaning do you get from the third line of the poem?
4. Are the lands to which the poet travels, pleasant lands? Give a reason for your answer.
5. Explain the phrase *'blood-red oceans'*.
6. How is Mars described?
7. Explain how the poem describes two different stages of the poet's life.
8. Give the poem a different title and explain your choice.
9. Write out the main ideas of the poem in your own words.

WHEN ALL THE OTHERS

When all the others were away at Mass
I was all hers as we peeled potatoes.
They broke the silence, let fall one by one
Like solder weeping off the soldering iron;
Cold comforts set between us, things to share
Gleaming in a bucket of clean water.
And again let fall. Little pleasant splashes
From each other's work would bring us to our
senses.

So while the parish priest at her bedside
Went hammer and tongs at the prayers for the dying
And some were responding and some crying
I remembered her head bent towards my head,
Her breath in mine, our fluent dipping knives —
Never closer the whole rest of our lives.

— *Seamus Heaney*

? Questions and Assignments

1. Explain the phrase *'I was all hers . . .'*
2. Did the poet talk to his mother as they worked? Refer to the poem to support your answer.
3. To what did the poet compare the dropping of the potatoes into the bucket of water?
4. What do you think the poet means by *'cold comforts'*?
5. Explain what you think is meant by *'Little pleasant splashes/From each other's work would bring us to our senses.'*
6. What special meaning did peeling the potatoes have for the poet?
7. The first part of the poem deals with the poet's memory of Sunday mornings. What is remembered in the second part?
8. How did people react as the prayers for the dying were said?
9. What is meant by the expression *'hammer and tongs'*?
10. Explain, in your own words, what the poem is about.

THE ENCOUNTER

Over the grass a hedgehog came
Questing the air for scents of food
And the cracked twig of danger.
He shuffled near in the gloom. Then stopped.
He was sure aware of me. I went up,
Bent low to look at him, and saw
His coat of lances pointing to my hand.
What could I do
To show I was no enemy?
I turned him over, inspected his small clenched paws,
His eyes expressionless as glass,
And did not know how I could speak,
By touch or tongue, the language of a friend.

It was a grief to be a friend
Yet to be dumb; to offer peace
And bring the soldiers out ...

— *Clifford Dyment*

? **Questions and Assignments**

1. What was the hedgehog *'questing'* (watching out for)?
2. How do we know that the meeting took place in late evening?
3. What word does the poet use to describe the movement of the hedgehog? Do you think that it is a good word? Explain.
4. What happened when the poet went to look closely at the hedgehog?
5. Explain the poet's problem in your own words.
6. Describe, in your own words, how the hedgehog behaved when the poet turned him over.
7. If you were writing to the poet about this poem, what would you say to him? Compose a short letter you might write.

BATS

A bat is born
Naked and blind and pale.
His mother makes a pocket of her tail
And catches him. He clings to her long fur
By his thumbs and toes and teeth.
And then the mother dances through the night
Doubling and looping, soaring, somersaulting -
Her baby hangs on underneath.
All night, in happiness, she hunts and flies.
Her high sharp cries
Like shining needlepoints of sound
Go out into the night and, echoing back,
Tell her what they have touched.
She hears how far it is, how big it is,
Which way it's going:
She lives by hearing.
The mother eats the moths and gnats she catches
In full flight; in full flight
The mother drinks the water of the pond
She skims across. Her baby hangs on tight.
Her baby drinks the milk she makes him
In moonlight or starlight, in mid-air.
Their single shadow, printed on the moon
Or fluttering across the stars,
Whirls on all night; at daybreak
The tired mother flaps home to her rafter.
The others all are there.
They hang themselves up by their toes,
They wrap themselves in their brown wings.
Bunched upside-down, they sleep in air.
Their sharp ears, their sharp teeth, their quick sharp faces
Are dull and slow and mild.
All the bright day, as the mother sleeps,
She folds her wings about her sleeping child.

— Randall Jarrell

? Questions and Assignments

1. What do we learn about young bats in the first five lines?

2. *'And then the mother dances through the night'*. What idea is the poet trying to get across in this line?

3. List the words used by the poet to describe the flight of the bat. Are they good descriptive words? Explain your answer in each case.

4. *'She lives by hearing.'* How does the poem help us to understand this?

5. What other unusual powers does the bat possess? In answering you should note the phrase *'In full flight'*.

6. The poet also uses the word *'flaps'* to describe the movement of the bat. Why do you think he chose this word?

7. Describe how bats spend the day.

8. Poets sometimes help us to see things in a different way or to change our attitude to something. Has this poem shown you something in a new light or changed your attitude in any way? Explain how.

THE SANDPIPER

At the edge of tide
He stops to wonder,
Races through
The lace of thunder.

On toothpick legs
Swift and brittle,
He runs and pipes
And his voice is little.

But small or not,
He has a notion
To outshout
The Atlantic Ocean.
— *Robert Frost*

? **Questions and Assignments**

1. Where does the bird stop?

2. Do you think that the second line of the poem is actually true? Explain.

3. What do you understand by the line *'lace of thunder'*?

4. (a) What words are used to describe the sandpiper's legs?
   (b) Do you think that these words are good choices? Explain why.

5. What do we learn about the nature of the sandpiper from the final verse?

SHEEP AND LAMBS

All in the April evening,
    April airs were abroad,
The sheep with their little lambs
    Passed me by on the road.

The sheep with their little lambs
    Passed me by on the road;
All in the April evening
    I thought on the Lamb of God.

The lambs were weary, and crying
    With a weak, human cry.
I thought on the Lamb of God
    Going meekly to die.

Up in the blue, blue mountains
    Dewy pastures are sweet;
Rest for the little bodies,
    Rest for the little feet,

But for the Lamb of God,
    Up on the hill-top green,
Only a cross of shame
    Two stark crosses between.

All in the April evening,
    April airs were abroad,
I saw the sheep with their lambs,
    And thought on the Lamb of God.

— Katherine Tynan

? Questions and Assignments

1. In what season is the poem set?

2. What thought came into the poet's mind when she saw the sheep and lambs?

3. Where were the sheep and lambs being brought?

4. What will the mountains provide for the lambs?

5. Say why you think the poet chose to use each of these particular phrases: *'blue, blue mountains'*; *'dewy pastures'*; *'a cross of shame'*.

CLAIMS

My father had a motor car:
It was his pride and joy.
He would have taught me how to drive
If I had been a boy.

But girls grow into women
And women are to blame,
According to my father,
For each insurance claim.

We're just not built for things like cars.
Dad says we mustn't moan:
Men are built for speed and strength,
Women for the home.

My mother used to drive a bit
Until the accident:
Parking in the multi-storey,
A wing mirror got bent.

It wasn't really Mum's fault,
There simply wasn't space.
You'd think to hear my father rant
She'd damned the human race.

My mother didn't argue,
She says she saves her breath,
Dad homes in for a blazing row
Like vultures swoop on death.

'Women drivers,' said my dad
'No one need discuss:
Women should accept their lot
And meekly take the bus.'

Which makes it such a pity,
Such wretched awful luck,
That Dad has driven his new car
Half way up a truck.

What makes it worse in Dad's eyes
(And the police's book)
Is that the truck was neatly parked
And father didn't look.

His seat belt meant that he was safe,
Though the car's beyond repair;
What hurt him was the firemen laughed
As they cut him free from there.

He sometimes takes the subject up,
Explains the crash away.
My Mum and I say nothing,
Much to Dad's dismay.

Claims

But part of what Dad taught me,
I must admit, remains:
Men are built with speed and strength
But hardly any brains.

— David Kitchen

? Questions and Assignments

1. Who is supposed to be speaking in this poem?

2. Why did Dad not teach his daughter to drive his car?

3. (a) Describe Dad's attitude to women and to women drivers?
   (b) What was his excuse for this attitude?

4. Describe Dad's accident. How was it different from Mum's car accident?

5. What did Dad find most painful about his accident?

6. What message or idea do you get from this poem?

WHY?

Why are the leaves always green, Dad?
Why are there thorns on a rose?
Why do you want my neck clean, Dad?
Why do hairs grow from your nose?

Why can dogs hear what we can't, Dad?
Why has the engine just stalled?
Why are you rude about Aunt, Dad?
Why are you going all bald?

Why is Mum taller than you, Dad?
Why can't the dog stand the cat?
Why's Grandma got a moustache, Dad?
Why are you growing more fat?

Why don't you answer my questions?
You used to: you don't anymore.
Why? Tell me why. Tell me why, Dad?
Do you think I am being a bore?

— *John Kitching*

? Questions and Assignments

1. Who do you think is speaking in this poem? Explain your choice.

2. List the questions which could be answered simply.

3. List the questions which would be difficult to answer.

4. Which of the questions do you think Dad found most annoying? Why?

5. (a) List all the pairs of words in the poem which rhyme with each other.
    (b) Write out a further three words which rhyme with each pair.

6. Count the number of syllables in each line. Do you see a pattern? Explain.

7. Make up an imaginative, yet silly, answer for each of the questions which would, nevertheless, satisfy the curiosity of a child.

AWAY FROM IT ALL

Conjure up a whole new moon,
    A landscape loud with hungry owls,
A road that clings where mountains soar
    And separate from hills.

October: and a car climbs up
    The mountain, staggers on the slope,
Gives up, oh roughly half-way there.
    The snoring engine goes to sleep.

A family clambers out: a man,
    A woman and a boy and girl;
They're lost without their zonked-out car.
    They feel the wind creep up and snarl.

They look around: there's nothing there,
    Well, nothing that they recognise;
They hear the thunder, then they feel
    The downpour falling from the skies.

They seek a shelter, trudge along the road,
    They want a light to match the beaming moon;
They march in silence for a mile,
    Though they are four each one's alone.

Another mile, and then they see
    A beacon in the distant dark;
Their footsteps quicken, they approach
    A mansion in a massive park.

Although it's lit, the place looks odd:
    The door is open; no one's there.
They enter, shout a greeting, get
    An echo from the empty air.

'Ah well,' says father, 'it'll do.
    We need a shelter for the night.'
They take two rooms, the beds are made;
    They fall asleep in seconds flat.

Under the moon the mansion lifts,
    It hovers in the gloom awhile;
Bright lights blaze out, a sound escapes,
    The whisper of a whirring wheel.

Then up the structure goes, straight up
    And launches through the atmosphere.
They'll wake up where they started out,
    A zillion millions from anywhere.

            — *Alan Bold*

? Questions and Assignments

1. What is frightening and eerie about the landscape described in the first stanza?

2. Describe the event which takes place in stanzas two and three.

3. *'They feel the wind creep up and snarl.'* What kind of animal comes to mind in this line? Explain why.

4. What do the family do next?

5. Describe the weather.

6. What is the mood of the family? Refer to the poem to support your answer.

7. What distance do they walk before they see the light?

8. Explain what is odd about the mansion.

9. *'An echo from the empty air.'* Explain this line.

10. Was the father happy to find the shelter? Explain.

11. Does the ending surprise, puzzle or amuse you? Explain why.

A year after the outbreak of World War One in 1914 Australia joined the war. Shiploads of soldiers set off on a long sea journey to Turkey; their aim was to defeat the Turks who were fighting on the German side. When the Australian army landed they were completely outnumbered. Many young Australian soldiers were killed and many more were maimed for life. Ernie Bogle, who was born in 1950, wrote THE BAND PLAYED WALTZING MATILDA, in which he imagines how one of the survivors might tell of his experiences.

THE BAND PLAYED WALTZING MATILDA

When I was a young man I carried a pack,
I lived the free life of a rover;
From the Murray's green basin to the dusty outback,
I waltzed my Matilda all over.
Then in Nineteen-fifteen, the country said, "Son,
It's time you stopped roving, there's work to be done."
So they gave me a tin hat and they gave me a gun,
And sent me away to the war.

> *And the band played Waltzing Matilda,*
> *As the ship pulled away from the quay,*
> *And midst all the cheers, flag-waving and tears,*
> *We sailed off to Gallipoli.*

How well I remember that terrible day,
How our blood stained the sand and the water.
And how in that hell that they called Suvla Bay,
We were butchered like lambs at the slaughter.
Johnny Turk he was ready, he'd primed himself well,
He showered us with bullets and he rained us with shell,
And in five minutes flat he'd blown us all to hell,
Nearly blew us right back to Australia.

> *And the band played Waltzing Matilda,*
> *When we stopped to bury the slain;*
> *We buried ours, the Turks buried theirs,*
> *Then we started all over again.*

And those that were left, we tried to survive,
In a sad world of blood, death and fire.
And for ten weary weeks I kept myself alive,
Though around me the corpses piled higher.
Then a big Turkish shell knocked me heels over head,
And when I woke up in my hospital bed,
I saw what it had done and I wished I was dead,
Never knew there were worse things than dying.

For I'll go no more Waltzing Matilda,
All round the green bush far and free.
To hump tent and pegs, a man needs both legs,
No more Waltzing Matilda for me.

So they gathered the crippled and wounded and maimed,
And they shipped us back home to Australia.
The legless, the armless, the blind and insane.
The brave wounded heroes of Suvla.
And when our ship pulled into Circular Quay,
I looked at the place where my legs used to be,
And thanked Christ there was nobody waiting for me,
To grieve, to mourn and to pity.

But the band played Waltzing Matilda,
As they carried us down the gangway,
But nobody cared, they just stood and stared,
And they turned their faces away.

So now every April I sit on my porch,
And I watch the parade pass before me.
And I see my old comrades, how proudly they march
Reviving old dreams and past glory.
The old men march slowly, old bones stiff and sore,
Tired old men from a forgotten war,
And the young people ask, "What are they marching for?"
I ask myself the same question.

But the band plays Waltzing Matilda
And the old men they answer the call.
But as year follows year, they get fewer and fewer
Someday no-one will march there at all.

— *Eric Bogle* (b. 1950)

? Questions and Assignments

1. What put a stop to the poet's rovings?
2. What details capture the horror of the battlefield?
3. *'Never knew there were worse things than dying'*. What point is being made in this line?
4. Write out the line which tells us what the shell did to the narrator.
5. What words and phrases does the poet use to give us an idea of the injuries which war inflicts on soldiers?
6. Explain how the scene of their departure was different from the scene of their return.
7. What message do you get from the final verse and chorus?
8. Do you think that this is a good anti-war song? Explain why.
9. In the words of the song a soldier looks back on his life. Retell his lifestory in your own words.

WHO KILLED DAVEY MOORE?

Who killed Davey Moore,
Why an' what's the reason for?

"Not I," says the referee,
"Don't point your finger at me.
I could've stopped it in the eighth
An' maybe kept him from his fate,
But the crowd would've booed, I'm sure,
At not gettin' their money's worth.
It's too bad he had to go,
But there was a pressure on me too, you know.
It wasn't me that made him fall.
No, you can't blame me at all."

Who killed Davey Moore,
Why an' what's the reason for?

"Not us," says the angry crowd,
Whose screams filled the arena loud.
"It's too bad he died that night
But we just like to see a fight.
We didn't mean for him t' meet his death,
We just meant to see some sweat,
There ain't nothing wrong in that.
It wasn't us that made him fall.
No, you can't blame us at all."

Who killed Davey Moore,
Why an' what's the reason for?

"Not me," says his manager,
Puffing on a big cigar.
"It's hard to say, it's hard to tell,
I always thought that he was well.
It's too bad for his wife an' kids he's dead,

But if he was sick, he should've said.
It wasn't me that made him fall.
No, you can't blame me at all."

Who killed Davey Moore,
Why an' what's the reason for?

"Not me," says the gambling man,
With his ticket stub in his hand.
"It wasn't me that knocked him down
My hands never touched him none.
I didn't commit no ugly sin,
Anyway, I put money on him to win.
It wasn't me that made him fall.
No, you can't blame me at all."

Who killed Davey Moore,
Why an' what's the reason for?

"Not me," says the boxing writer,
Pounding print on his old typewriter,
Sayin' "Boxing ain't to blame,
There's just as much danger in a football game."
Sayin', "Fist fighting is here to stay,
It's just the old American way.
It wasn't me that made him fall.
No, you can't blame me at all."

Who killed Davey Moore,
Why an' what's the reason for?

"Not me," says the man whose fist
Laid him low in a cloud of mist,
Who came here from Cuba's door
Where boxing ain't allowed no more.
"I hit him, yes, it's true,
But that's what I am paid to do.
Don't say 'murder,' don't say 'kill.'
It was destiny, it was God's will."

Who killed Davey Moore,
Why an' what's the reason for?

— *Bob Dylan*

? Questions and Assignments

1. How did the referee excuse himself?
2. Why did the people in the crowd not think they were to blame?
3. How did Davey Moore's manager explain that he was innocent?
4. Why did the gambling man not consider himself responsible for Davey Moore's death?
5. Describe the boxing writer's attitude to boxing?
6. How did Davey Moore's opponent see his position?
7. Who do you think was responsible for Davey Moore's death? Give reasons for your answer.

BACK IN THE PLAYGROUND BLUES

Dreamed I was in a school playground, I was about four feet high
Yes dreamed I was back in the playground, and standing about four feet high
The playground was three miles long and the playground was five miles wide

It was broken black tarmac with a high fence all around
Broken black dusty tarmac with a high fence running all around
And it had a special name to it, they called it the Killing Ground.

Got a mother and a father, they're a thousand miles away
The Rulers of the Killing Ground are coming out to play
Everyone thinking: who they going to play with today?

> You get it for being Jewish
> Get it for being black
> Get it for being chicken
> Get it for fighting back
> You get it for being big and fat
> Get it for being small
> O those who get it get it and get it
> For any damn thing at all

Sometimes they take a beetle, tear off its six legs one by one
Beetle on its black back rocking in the lunchtime sun
But a beetle can't beg for mercy, a beetle's not half the fun

Heard a deep voice talking, it had that iceberg sound;
"It prepares them for Life" — but I have never found
Any place in my life that's worse than the Killing Ground.

— *Adrian Mitchell* (b. 1932)

? Questions and Assignments

1. Who is the narrator in the poem?

2. Would you agree that the poet exaggerates in line three? Can you suggest why?

3. Identify another exaggeration in the poem and explain why it is there.

4. Who are the rulers of the *Killing Ground*?

5. *'Everyone thinking: who they going to play with today?'* What do you understand this line to mean?

6. (a)   What is the *'it'* mentioned in the short lines?
   (b)   What type of people get *'it'*?

7. What do we learn about the rulers of the *Killing Ground* from the second last stanza?

8. (a)   Who is the owner of the *'deep voice'*?
   (b)   Why did the poet describe it as having an *'iceberg sound'*?

9. *'It prepares them for Life.'* Who is speaking here and what is meant?

10. Do you think the poet's school days were happy days? Refer to the last line to support your answer.

11. Do you think that this is a good poem about bullies? Say why you think so.

LAMENT FOR LUCY

She dwelt among th' untrodden ways
    Beside the springs of Dove:
A maid whom there were none to praise
    And very few to love.

A violet by a mossy stone
    Half-hidden from the eye;
Fair as a star, when only one
    Is shining in the sky.

She lived unknown, and few could know
    When Lucy ceased to be;
But she is in her grave, and oh,
    The difference to me!

— William Wordsworth

?   **Questions and Assignments**

1. What do we learn about Lucy's life from the first stanza?

2. The poet uses two comparisons in the second stanza. Explain what each of these comparisons are and say why they are used.

3. (a)   What were the poet's feelings towards Lucy?
   (b)   What lines in the poem tell us about the poet's feelings?

4. In poetry a *'Lament'* is a poem which commemorates the loss of something/somebody. Is this a suitable title for this poem? Explain.

In this poem Jeff writes about how he felt when his older brother, Lee, died suddenly from meningitis while they were in Rome on holidays. The boys' father recalls - "Some days after we returned from Rome, Jeff wrote a poem. He started it one evening. worked on it steadily the next day and then took two hours to type it out on a borrowed type-writer." The poem's strength is its honesty and simplicity, as Jeff tries to come to terms with his brother's death.

A BOY THIRTEEN

He had red hair,
Was thin and tall,
One could never eat as much as he,
He hiked in the sierras,
Went back-packing and even planned
a trip for the family,
Even got me to join Boy Scouts,
Always wanted me to back-pack with him,
We went to Germany,
He and I went to German schools and learned German,
Then it came time for our trip to Rome,
By train,
He and I couldn't wait to come back to
Germany and go sledding,
We passed through the Alps on the way
to Rome,
I looked up to him,
I twelve and He 'A BOY THIRTEEN',
He was five feet and nine inches tall,
I remember very well looking up and there
He was with the train window down, his head
a little way out with the wind blowing
his red hair as he watched the Alps
passing by,
He was my brother,
My only brother,
One I could play Baseball with,
Someone I could talk to.

In Germany he had bought a camera,
A single lens reflex,
He had a lot of new things going on,
Then on Feb. 6 He died.
He my only brother the one I planned to
back-pack with, the guy I wanted to sled with,
the person I looked up to, the boy that
played baseball with me, the guy with a
new camera, my brother who I could talk to, the
one who could eat as no one else, my brother that
was five feet and nine inches tall, tall and thin with
red hair 'THE BOY THAT WAS THIRTEEN'.
He died because he happened to breathe in some bacteria
that probably can only be seen under some special microscope,
I guess all I can say is I loved him and needed him and that
I don't understand.

— Jeff

? Questions and Assignments

1. What does Jeff remember about his brother's appearance?

2. Jeff recalls in some detail one special moment shared with his brother. Describe this moment in your own words.

3. What kind of activities did Jeff's brother enjoy?

4. *'He had a lot of new things going on.'* What does this line tell us about Jeff's brother?

5. Were you surprised at any point during your first reading of this poem? If so, say where you were surprised and explain why.

6. (a) What do you think of this poem? Did you find it moving, shocking or sad?
   (b) Do you think it is well written? Explain why.

A nurse in a Scottish hospital found this poem in an old lady's bedside locker after she had died.

A CRABBIT OLD WOMAN WROTE THIS

What do you see nurses, what do you see?
Are you thinking when you are looking at me -
A crabbit old woman, not very wise,
Uncertain of habit, with far-away eyes,
Who dribbles her food and makes no reply
When you say in a loud voice - 'I do wish you'd try'.
Who seems not to notice the things that you do,
And forever is losing a stocking or shoe.
Who, unresisting or not, lets you do as you will,
With bathing and feeding, the long day to fill.
Is that what you are thinking, is that what you see?
Then open your eyes, nurse, you're not looking at me.

I'll tell you who I am as I sit here so still,
As I use at your bidding, as I eat at your will.
I'm a small child of ten with a father and mother,
Brothers and sisters, who love one another.
A young girl of sixteen with wings on her feet,
Dreaming that soon now a lover she'll meet;
A bride soon at twenty - my heart gives a leap,
Remembering the vows that I promised to keep;
At twenty-five now I have young of my own,
Who need me to build a secure, happy home;
A woman of thirty, my young now grow fast,
Bound to each other with ties that should last;
At forty, my young sons have grown and are gone.
But my man's beside me to see I don't mourn.
At fifty once more babies play round my knee,
Again we know children, my loved one and me.
Dark days are upon me, my husband is dead,
I look at the future, I shudder with dread.
For my young are all rearing young of their own,
And I think of the years and the love that I've known.

152

I'm an old woman now and nature is cruel -
Tis her jest to make old age look like a fool.
The body it crumbles, grace and vigour depart,
There is now a stone where I once had a heart;
But inside this old carcase a young girl still swells,
And now and again my battered heart swells.
I remember the joys, I remember the pain,
And I'm loving and living life over again.
I think of the years all too few - gone too fast,
And accept the stark fact that nothing can last.
So open your eyes, nurses, open and see,
Not a crabbit old woman, look closer - see ME!

— *Anonymous*

? Questions and Assignments

1. Who is speaking in this poem?
2. What does the old lady suspect the nurses think about her?
3. Give an account, in your own words, of the old lady's lifestory.
4. *'I look at the future, I shudder with dread.'* What do you understand this line to mean?
5. *'. . . and nature is cruel.'* Why do you think the old lady says this?
6. Do you think that the old lady is angry at the nurses? Give reasons for your answer.
7. What is your response to this poem? (Does it change your outlook in any way? How? Does it frighten you? Why? Will it change your view of old people? Explain.)

HE WAS . . .

He was . . .
a boy who became
a man
a husband
a father.

He was . . .
a good goalie,
a rotten batsman,
not bad at darts.

He was . . .
second cornet in the works band;
a man who brought his pay-packet straight home
without stopping at the pub;
a man who enjoyed his dinner.

He was . . .
forgetful,
rarely on time,
sometimes tongue-tied,
at a loss for what to say.

He was . . .
always honest,
never sober at Christmas,
often puzzled by the world.
He was . . .
. . . my dad.

— *John Cunliffe*

? Questions and Assignments

1. What were the father's strong points?
2. What were his weak points?

LIGHTNING

At a decent distance
From the heads of men
I happen

And am gone.
This is how
I light up heaven

And define the dark.
You think I must
Be something of an exhibitionist,

A dramatic braggart of light?
I am a mere moment
Between this and that

Yet so much that moment
I
Illumine the sky

And the small homes of men,
Flash through their fears, spotlight their joys.
My deepest nature is quiet and private
I cannot escape the noise.

— *Brendan Kennelly*

? **Questions and Assignments**

1. Who is speaking in this poem?

2. Explain in your own words what is said.

3. What do you understand by each of the following phrases?
   'At a decent distance', 'a mere moment', 'I cannot escape the noise'.

4. Boastful; Modest; Mocking; Vicious; Spiteful; Shy.
   (a) Which of these words best describes the lightning?
   (b) Which word least describes the character of the lightning? Explain your choices.

HUNGER

I COME among the peoples like a shadow.
I sit down by each man's side.
None sees me, but they look on one another,
And know that I am there.

My silence is like the silence of the tide
That buries the playground of children;
Like the deepening of frost in the slow night,
When birds are dead in the morning.

Armies trample, invade, destroy,
With guns roaring from earth and air.
I am more terrible than armies,
I am more feared than the cannon.

Kings and chancellors give commands;
I give no command to any;
But I am listened to more than kings
And more than passionate orators.

I unswear words, and undo deeds.
Naked things know me.
I am first and last to be felt of the living.
I am Hunger.

— *Laurence Binyon*

? | **Questions and Assignments**

1. Hunger speaks in this poem. In the first line he compares himself to a shadow. Do you think that this is a good comparison? Explain.
2. '*. . . but they look on one another, / And know that I am there.*' What do you understand this extract to mean?
3. In what way is Hunger (a) like and (b) unlike armies?
4. '*But I am listened to more than kings.*' Do you think this is so? Give a reason for your answer.
5. '*Naked things know me.*' What point do you think the poet is making here?
6. Explain why the poet uses the words '*first*' and '*last*' in the second last line.

THE MOON

The moon has a face like the clock in the hall;
 She shines on thieves on the garden wall,
On streets and fields and harbour quays,
 And birds asleep in the forks of the trees.

The squalling cat and the squeaking mouse,
 The howling dog by the door of the house,
The bat that lies in bed at noon,
 All love to be out by the light of the moon.

But all of the things that belong to the day
 Cuddle to sleep to be out of the way;
And flowers and children close their eyes
 Till up in the morning the sun shall rise.

— Robert Louis Stevenson

? Questions and Assignments

1. What colour is the face of the hall-clock? Explain your choice.

2. What kind of noises can be heard at night, according to this poem?

3. Explain how the final verse is different from the first two verses.

4. (a) List all the pairs of words in the poem which rhyme with each other.
   (b) Write out a further three words which rhyme with each pair.

5. Explain, in your own words, what the poem is about.

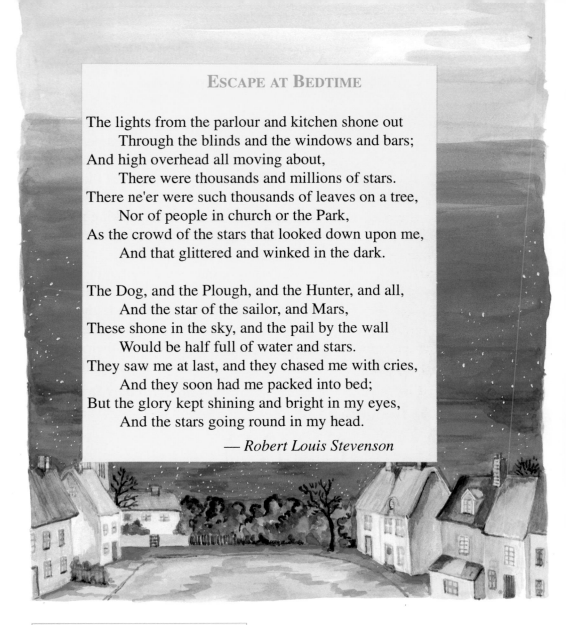

ESCAPE AT BEDTIME

The lights from the parlour and kitchen shone out
    Through the blinds and the windows and bars;
And high overhead all moving about,
    There were thousands and millions of stars.
There ne'er were such thousands of leaves on a tree,
    Nor of people in church or the Park,
As the crowd of the stars that looked down upon me,
    And that glittered and winked in the dark.

The Dog, and the Plough, and the Hunter, and all,
    And the star of the sailor, and Mars,
These shone in the sky, and the pail by the wall
    Would be half full of water and stars.
They saw me at last, and they chased me with cries,
    And they soon had me packed into bed;
But the glory kept shining and bright in my eyes,
    And the stars going round in my head.

— *Robert Louis Stevenson*

? Questions and Assignments

1. What details in the first verse tell us that it was night-time?

2. Why does the poet refer to *'leaves'* and *'people'* in the first verse?

3. (a)   What words does the poet use to describe the action of the stars?
   (b)   Which word do you prefer? Why?

4. What do you think the poet means by the *'star of the sailor'*?

5. What idea is the poet trying to get across when he tells us that the pail *'would be half full of water and stars'*?

OLD DOG

Toward the last in the morning she could not
get up, even when I rattled her pan.
I helped her into the yard, but she stumbled
and fell. I knew it was time.

The last night a mist drifted over the fields;
in the morning she would not raise her head -
the far, clear mountains we had walked
surged back to mind.

We looked a slow bargain: our days together
were the ones we already had.
I gave her something the vet had given,
and patted her still, a good last friend.

— *William Stafford*

? **Questions and Assignments**

1. What signs are there in the first stanza that the dog is very old?

2. *'I knew it was time.'* What is meant by this line?

3. *'The last night a mist drifted over the fields.'*
   Why do you think the poet included this information?

4. What does the poet remember about the dog?

5. Describe the scene of the dog's final moments.

6. What were your thoughts and feelings after reading this poem?

THE ANIMALS

The animals are herded slowly from green fields
to be eaten by gentlemen in restaurants. The fish
swim in the river for the pan of an experienced cook.
The wheat grows golden for loaves served at a fair price
in the shops. Even the birds in the trees
are aimed at by happy sportsmen. So the lovers of nature
make fatal advances towards the object of their affection.
And those living in cities who hate the country
and know where their bread-and-butter comes from don't care
as they walk in parks which are innocent of agriculture.

— *George Buchanan*

? Questions and Assignments

1. What happens to the animals?

2. Where do the fish end up?

3. For what purpose does the wheat grow?

4. What happens to the *'birds in the trees'*?

5. What does the poet mean by
   (a) *'fatal advances'*?
   (b) *'object of their affection'*?
   (c) *'innocent of agriculture'*?

6. Do the people of the city care about the creatures of nature? Refer to the poem to support your answer.

7. This poem looks at how animals live and die. What is the poet's attitude towards the animals? Do you find this attitude very extreme or unbalanced? Explain why.

LION

Poor prisoner in a cage,
I understand your rage
And why you loudly roar
Walking that stony floor.

Your forest eyes are sad
As wearily you pad
A few yards up and down,
A king without a crown.

Up and down all day,
A wild beast for display,
Or lying in the heat
With sawdust, smells and meat,

Remembering how you chased
Your jungle prey, and raced,
Leaping upon their backs
Along the grassy tracks.

But you are here instead,
Better, perhaps, be dead
Than locked in this dark den;
Forgive us, lion, then,
Who did not ever choose,
Our circuses and zoos.

— Leonard Clark

? Questions and Assignments

1. To whom is the poet speaking?

2. What words and phrases in the first stanza show us how the poet felt towards the lion?

Lion

3. How does the lion spend his day?

4. Why does the poet speak of the lion as *"A king without a crown"*?

5. (a) What words in the poem suggest that the cage is not a nice place?

   (b) What does each of the words you have chosen suggest to you about the cage?

6. For whom does the poet ask forgiveness in the last three lines?

7. What do you understand the last two lines of the poem to mean?

8. List (a) four reasons for and (b) four reasons against having circuses and zoos.

9. (a) What message do you think the poet is trying to get across in this poem?

   (b) Is there a similar message to be found in the poem *'A Caged Bird in Springtime'*? Explain

10. Do you think that birds and animals should be kept in captivity? Give reasons for your answer.

BETTER BE KIND TO THEM NOW

A squirrel is digging up the bulbs
In half the time Dad took to bury them.

A small dog is playing football
With a mob of boys. He beats them all,
Scoring goals at both ends.
A kangaroo would kick the boys as well.

Birds are so smart they can drink milk
Without removing the bottle-top.

Cats stay clean, and never have to be
Carried screaming to the bathroom.
They don't get their heads stuck in railings,
They negotiate first with their whiskers.

The gecko walks on the ceiling, and
The cheetah can outrun the Royal Scot.
The lion cures his wounds by licking them,
And the guppy has fifty babies at a go.

The cicada plays the fiddle for hours on end,
And a man-size flea could jump over St Paul's.

If ever these beasts should get together
Then we are done for, children.
I don't much fancy myself as a python's pet,
But it might come to that!

$\qquad$ — D. J. Enright

? Questions and Assignments

1. How does the squirrel show he is better than Dad?
2. How does the small dog show that he can outdo the boys?
3. In what way do (i) the birds show they are clever?
   (ii) the cats show they are smarter than children?
4. What is the warning the poet gives in the last stanza?
5. What is the importance of the word *"now"* in the title?

THE CAGED BIRD IN SPRINGTIME

What can it be,
This curious anxiety?
It is as if I wanted
To fly away from here.

But how absurd!
I have never flown in my life,
And I do not know
What flying means, though I have heard,
Of course, something about it.

Why do I peck the wires of this little cage?
It is the only nest I have ever known.
But I want to build my own,
High in the secret branches of the air.

I cannot quite remember how
It is done, but I know
That what I want to do
Cannot be done here.

I have all I need -
Seed and water, air and light,
Why, then, do I weep with anguish,
And beat my head and my wings
Against those sharp wires, while the children
Smile at each other, saying: 'Hark how he sings'?

— *James Kirkup*

? Questions and Assignments

1. Explain who is speaking in this poem.

2. In the first two lines the bird seems to be puzzled and anxious about something. What do you think it is?

3. *'But how absurd!'* Why does the bird say this?

4. *'It is the only nest I have ever known.'* What do we learn from this line?

5. The bird says that what she wants to do *'cannot be done here'*. Why not?

6. The final part of the poem begins with the line *'I have all I need'*. Do you agree that the bird has all she needs? Explain your answer.

7. Why do the children smile?

THE DEFENCE

A silent murderer,
A kestrel came today,
Canny marauder
In search of prey.

He scanned the ground for signs,
Hovered on the lifting air,
His claws poised ready to snatch
Some victim off to his lair.

But swallows gathered fast,
Closed in from all around,
Sounding a shrill alarm,
Filling the sky with furious sound.

They soared into the sky,
And peeled off to attack,
Jabbing with dagger beak and needling cry
To drive the killer back.

The kestrel wavered once,
Then, like a useless glove
Thrown down, he tumbled on the wind
And fled from the birds above.

And we who sat and watched,
We too had been afeared,
Had held our bated breath.
But now we stood up and cheered.

— *Geoffrey Summerfield*

? **Questions and Assignments**

1. Why is the kestrel described as a silent murderer?

2. Select three words from the second stanza which describe the actions of the kestrel. What do each of these words tell us about the nature of the kestrel?

3. Describe clearly what the swallows did when the kestrel appeared.

4. Why does the poet compare the kestrel to a useless glove?

5. Who else witnessed the event?

Poetry Workshop

Writing your own Poetry

The following are just some of the things which poets attempt to do when they set about writing poems. In this section we will try writing a few poems in each of these three groups:

* Making word pictures of places, people and events.
* Describing things which make them sad, happy, angry or amused.
* Touching the reader's feelings and perhaps changing the reader's outlook in some way.

A good way to get started on poetry writing is to use another poem as a model for your own efforts. For example, the first poem in the poetry section, *'Recipe for Happiness'*, will serve as a useful model for your own personal recipe for happiness.

A RECIPE FOR HAPPINESS

An ounce of tv
A slice of disco dancing
Mix up well
With a squeeze of summer sunbaking
Half a cup of raging on Saturday night
And a large tablespoon of tickling the dog
Add a freshly picked ticket to the Grand Final
Stir in a splash of lazing around the pool
Add the mess of records and clothes on my bedroom floor
Bake slowly with a really good late night video
Add a pinch of messing round on lazy afternoons
Sprinkle with a couple of beaut barbecues
Pour in my oldest and most favourite jeans
Serve with a real good helping of family fun.
And there you are — the recipe's done.
                                        — *Hugh Clement*

Assignment **1**

The following **five** steps should be followed when attempting to write any poem. Use these steps now to write a poem similar to *'Recipe for Happiness'*.

Step 1. Brainstorming

Begin with a *brainstorming* session. For this you will need a blank page and a pen or biro. Next let your imagination loose. List all the things which make you happy. As well as obvious things such as 'Last day of term' or 'Christmas morning', try to come up with less obvious things. Write down anything that comes into your head.

Many of the things on your list should be special to you; try to include things that may not apply to other people in the class. These can be little things e.g. a song, a special kind of food, someone's voice, a particular sound, a certain place and time, a precious memory. Often it is these little things that will give your poem its own novel spark and will make it more memorable.

Don't worry about sentences or spellings - use single words or phrases. Fill the page.

Step 2. Selecting

Next read over your list and cross out anything with which you are not entirely happy. Now take what remains on the list and decide on the order in which they will appear in the poem. There are many different ways of doing this. For example, you could start with those things that made you happy when you were very young and work your way towards the present time. You could also group all the indoor things that make you happy and then move on to the outdoor things, or you could decide to present them in random order etc...

Step 3. First Draft

Now make a first attempt at writing your poem. Write your effort neatly on a new page, leaving plenty of space between the lines. The purpose of this is to give you room to make changes and additions. This is called your *first draft*.

Step 4. Improving Your First Draft

Here are some devices used by poets when writing poetry. You may find these useful in your efforts to prepare your final draft.

(a) *Choose Your Words Carefully*

Choose the best words - examine each word in your first draft to see if you could replace it with another word which would help the reader imagine more clearly what you are describing.

Watch out particularly for verbs (words that describe actions). For example the word 'strolled' is more descriptive than the word 'walked' and the phrases 'the wind whispered' or 'the wind howled' are more descriptive than the phrase 'the wind blew'. Can you replace any verbs in your draft with better ones?

Adjectives are another group of words that are useful e.g. *pale* moon, *golden* sun, *tall* trees, *purple* heather, *yellow* candlelight. Adjectives tell us more about nouns. Can you add any suitable adjectives to your draft?

(b) *Comparisons*

Poets use comparisons to help us form pictures of things in our imaginations e.g. *'the wind ... crying like a lost child'*, *'as warm as toast'*, *'shines like a jewel'*, *'big as a polar bear'*. Of course we also use comparisons in our everyday speech. How many times have you heard phrases such as: *'as cold as ice'*, *'as black as coal'*, *'as old as the hills'*? These comparisons have become dull and stale from overuse. In your writing you should try to avoid these well-known comparisons or clichés and invent new, more exciting comparisons of your own.

(c) *Rhyme and Rhythm*

Some poems have words arranged in such a way that the last word in a line rhymes with a word in another line. Patterns vary from poem to poem. For example, in the poem *My Ship* (page 127): line 1 rhymes with line 3; 2 with 4; 5 with 6, and 7 with 8. Writing poems which rhyme can be difficult as it is often hard to think of a suitable word to rhyme with another.

Poems may also have a rhythm - a pattern of beats - which is repeated in the poem. For example, when you read *The Band Played Waltzing Matilda* (page 141) you will notice a certain rhythm or beat. Using rhythm in your own poetry can sometimes be difficult as it means getting a certain number of beats into each line.

Rhyme and rhythm give poems a sing-along 'musical' feel.

However poetry does not have to have rhymes and rhythms.When a poem has lines of varying length and no rhyming pattern it is called 'free verse' e.g. *A Boy Thirteen*. It might be a good idea to write your *'Recipe for Happiness'* in free verse.

Step 5. Final draft

When you have finally made up your mind about all the changes to your first draft write the new version in very neat handwriting on a new page. This is called the *final draft*. You may like to draw a few suitable illustrations to 'set it off'.

Assignment 2

Here are some extracts from a number of poems which you can use as models for some poems of your own. You should follow **Steps 1-5** given above when you attempt to write any poem of your own.

1.   ORDERS OF THE DAY

Get up!
Get washed!
Eat your breakfast!
That's my mum,
Going on and on and on and on . . .

Sit down!
Shut up!
Get on with your work!
That's my teacher,
Going on and on and on and on . . .

Come here!
Give me that!
Go away!
That's my big sister,
Going on and on and on and on . . .

Get off!
Stop it!
Carry me!
That's my little sister,
Going on and on and on and on . . .
                                        — *John Cunliffe*

Think of some of the things which people always seem to be saying to you and put them in a poem. Use this poem as a model.

2. **THINGS PEOPLE DO**

My brother's stripped his motorbike
Although it's bound to rain.
My sister's playing Elton John
Over and over again.

— *Kit Wright*

List four more members of your family - *Auntie Kathy, Uncle Paul, Cousin Jim, Grandad* - and, after each name, list something they always seem to be doing. Give two lines to each person and try to follow the rhyming pattern and rhythm of the example above.

Now try similar poems featuring some people from (i) your class and (ii) your town or neighbourhood.

3. **CHRISTMAS THANK YOUS**

Dear Auntie
Oh, what a nice jumper
I've always adored powder blue
and fancy you thinking of
orange and pink
for the stripes
how clever of you

Dear Uncle
The soap is
terrific
So
useful
and such a kind thought and
how did you guess that
I'd just used the last of
the soap that last Christmas
brought?

Dear Gran
Many thanks for the hankies
Now I really can't wait for the flu
and the daisies embroidered
in red round the 'M'
for Michael
how thoughtful of you

Dear Cousin
What socks!
and the same sort you wear
so they must be
the last word in style
and I'm certain you're right that the
luminous green
will make me stand out a mile

Dear Sister
I quite understand your concern
it's a risk sending jam in the post
But I think I've pulled out
all the bits
of glass
so it won't taste too sharp
spread on toast

Dear Grandad
Don't fret
I'm delighted
So don't think your gift will
offend
I'm not at all hurt
that you gave up this year
and just sent me
a fiver
to spend

— Mick Gowar

In this poem Mick Gowar thanks some of his relations for the christmas gifts they sent him. Read the poem and consider if he is happy with all the gifts. Would you think that his tone is a little sarcastic in places? Make up your own poem, modelled on *Christmas Thank Yous*, in which you thank some relations for the gifts they sent to you for christmas.

4.   # A CHILD'S CALENDAR

No visitors in January.
A snowman smokes a cold pipe in the yard.

The June bee
Bumps in the pane with a heavy bag of plunder.

Strangers swarm in July
With cameras, binoculars, bird books.

— G.M. Browne

The above three stanzas are from a twelve stanza poem. In each stanza the poet describes one thing which he associates with each particular month of the year.

(i) Write your own *'Calendar'* poem using the extract above as a model.
(ii) Write a second poem, *'My Week'*, again using the extract above as a model.

5.   **BEACHCOMBER**

Monday I found a boot -
Rust and salt leather.
I gave it back to the sea, to dance in.

Tuesday a spar of timber worth thirty bob.
Next winter
It will be a chair, a coffin, a bed.

Thursday I got nothing, seaweed,
A whale bone,
Wet feet and a loud cough.

— G.M. Browne

In this extract a beachcomer gives an account of his week's work. It is set in the past.

(i) Write a poem in which a modern-day beachcomber gives an account of his/her week's findings.
(ii) Select someone with another occupation and write a poem, modelled on *Beachcomber*, in which they give an account of a week in their job.

III - Writing Skills 1

SENTENCES

When somebody says *"The men walked down to the river"* we know what is meant. However, if *"The men walked down to the river to"* was said, we would wait to hear the remainder of the statement.

"The men walked down to the river" is a **sentence** because it is complete and makes sense.

"The men walked down to the river to" is not a complete statement and is therefore not a sentence. The statement can be completed by adding a phrase such as *"watch the boats go by"*.

 **Assignment 1** | **MAKING SENTENCES**

There are 14 sentences in the list below. Identify each sentence by its number. In the case of those that are not sentences, turn them into sentences by making suitable additions.

1. When the concert started.
2. The dog is playful and he snaps at people's legs.
3. At night the light shines through the windows.
4. If we get paid on Friday and we meet Peter.
5. Elephants live to be a good age.
6. It is shaped like a star.
7. If it had ever lived, the unicorn would have been a strange creature.
8. Pure gold is bright and shiny.
9. You will never see a live unicorn.
10. It is a mile long.
11. When they die.
12. If the rain stops.
13. The prisoners are carefully guarded.
14. Although some people are afraid of bats.
15. When the teacher returned and found the class making noise.
16. Children who fear dogs.
17. Tom is always late but.
18. When they came we were delighted.
19. Farther along the path.
20. When the teacher came back, she found the class was sitting quietly.
21. Electricity can kill.
22. After reaching the top of the mountain.
23. At the foot of the hill.
24. As a result of his win.
25. Every little helps.
26. Nobody cares.

Assignment **2** **PUNCTUATION AND SENTENCES**

All capital letters and full stops have been removed from each of the passages below. Rewrite each of the passsages, putting in capital letters at the start of sentences and full stops at the end of sentences. The number of sentences in each passage is given at the end of the passage. Remember that *names of people always begin with a capital letter* and that the word *'I'* is always a capital letter. After sentences that form questions you should insert a question mark (?) instead of a full stop.

1. ben awoke to a frosty, bright christmas morning already the tiny cottage was filled with appetising smells ben fetched his bulky parcels from where he had hidden them and ran downstairs to give them to his family never had he felt so keenly the pleasure of giving (**4** sentences)

2. as we were leaving the cafe with our hot-dogs we bumped into a kid pushing through the narrow doorway i recognised him straight away he was a punk, about seventeen years old he used to go to our school, until he'd been thrown out i had dropped my hot-dog and when i bent down to pick it up the punk slammed his boot down on my hand the hot-dog was squashed flat and ketchup oozed out between my fingers i cried out in pain (**7** sentences)

3. is a brown egg more nourishing than a white egg the colour of an egg's shell really has nothing to do with the amount of nutrition contained inside the contents of an egg contain substances that will be food for the developing chick the colouring of the shell is the last part in a long process when the egg forms inside the hen the colour of the shell acts as a camouflage, so that the egg will be protected from any animal that is looking for food (**5** sentences)

4. puppets are small animal or human figures worked by a person who is called a puppet-master, or puppeteer a good puppeteer can charm his audience by making even the simplest puppet move and speak in a way that seems almost human a puppet may be only a handkerchief draped over the hand, or it may be a figure strung with wires so that it can perform many different movements there are six basic types of puppet one of the most common is the glove puppet or hand puppet, which is worn on the hand the first finger is put into the neck, and the thumb and second finger into the arms two of the best-known puppets, punch and judy, are nearly always made as glove puppets (**7** sentences)

5. the two aliens approached the ship they walked all around it, feeling the battered surface and inspecting the point of impact they came to the door and struggled with it until something fell into place and the door slid open one of them went in when he came out, the two seemed to speak briefly, and then the door was closed they began scraping the last of the earth away from around the crushed landing gear the ship tilted again, sharply, and one of them had to leap to safety. (**7** sentences)

6. the morning sun now coming in through the window fell on it and, as if led by the sun, jonathan walked across and looked inside one look was enough he fell back with a wild cry dracula lay asleep on a bed of earth his face was no longer pale but deep red, and his hair, instead of its usual black, was now iron-grey blood ran from the corners of his mouth, down his neck and on to his clothes his whole body was swollen with blood he smelt of blood and on his face was the look of a wild animal that has killed and fed until it can feed no more (**8** sentences)

CROSSWORD NO. 1

Across

1 Speedy.

3 Flying emblem.

6 Catches the wind.

8 Two alike.

9 We write on this.

11 Maker of honey.

13 Holly fruit.

16 A talking examination.

17 Close securely.

18 A walking expedition.

19 An underwater scuttler.

Down

1 He clenched his _____ in anger.

2 Jump over a rope.

4 Shakespeare wrote a play called *King _____*.

5 Clothing. (_ _ _ B)

7 Shirts have washing instructions on a _____ inside the collar.

8 Looks closely (P _ _ _ _).

10 Apples £1.20 _____ dozen.

12 Each of them.

13 You may fish from one (or draw money from one).

14 It takes this time for the Earth to go around the Sun.

15 A weapon maybe, — or a group with similar interests.

CAPITAL LETTERS

There are twelve basic rules for the use of capital letters. We will begin with **Rules 1 - 7**.

Rule 1. **At the start of each sentence.**
- Our class won the school league.
- It was late when he arrived.

Rule 2. **To begin both surnames and first names.**
- Mary, Paul, Joan, Daniel, Liam, Peter, Nuala.
- Byrne, Daly, Hanley, McCarthy.

Rule 3. **For initials.**
- J.D. Smith, T. O'Neill.
- R.T.E., I.N.T.O., C.I.E., T.D., R.S.P.C.A., E.S.B.

Rule 4. **For days of the week, months of the year and holidays.**
- Friday, Saturday, February, April.
- Christmas, Easter, St. Patrick's Day.

Rule 5. **Brand Names.**
- She drinks Fanta.
- She bought a Nissan Bluebird.
- He plays a Fender guitar.
- He won a Sony cassette player and a Yamaha motor-cycle.

Rule 6. **To begin titles that are used as part of personal names.**
- Lord Longford.
- Count Dracula.
- Captain Murphy.
- Miss Dunne.

Rule 7. **To begin abbreviated (shortened) words.**
- Mr. Murray.
- Mrs. Nolan.
- Dr. Brown.
- Botanic Ave.
- Dublin Rd.
- O'Connell St.

(Note that abbreviated words always end with a full stop.)

178

| Assignment | 3 | USING CAPITALS CORRECTLY |

In each of the following paragraphs all capitals have been omitted. Refer to **Rules 1-7** above to rewrite each paragraph with capital letters correctly included. After you have rewritten each paragraph correctly, list all the words to which you gave capitals. Then write the rule number that made you decide that the word should have a capital. The first assignment is completed for you.

Example

Assignment

1. my neighbour, peter byrne, works for the esb sometimes he works on sundays last year he worked on easter sunday

Answer

My neighbour, Peter Byrne, works for the ESB. Sometimes he works on Sundays. Last year he worked on Easter Sunday.

Rules Used

My **1.**	Peter Byrne **2.**	ESB **3.**	Sometimes **1.**
Sundays **4.**	Last **1.**	Easter Sunday **4.**	

---

2. ms smith's panasonic video recorder was stolen last christmas she returned home on new year's eve and, paul mullins, her neighbour, told her that her house had been broken into on friday night he said that he had contacted sgt o brien our local garda

3. a religion teacher in our school, fr dunne, plays the piano sometimes he brings in a casio keyboard and plays it for our class and margaret sullivan sings the headmaster, mr buckley, came in one day and sang an elvis song he was awful

4. on tuesday last a lorry backed into my brother's old opel kadett the lorry belonged to dc dog foods ltd the lorry driver said that it was my brother's fault as he had parked the opel in a dangerous place my brother wrote to mr cahill who is the owner of the company

5. on mayday there was a big parade in our town it was sponsored by toyota ms carbery, who teaches us maths, won first prize in the adults fancy dress competition she was dressed up as queen elizabeth the first she was interviewed by a reporter from utv and was presented with a mitsubishi camcorder her boyfriend, peter eason, went as prince charles he came second last

CAPITAL LETTERS (RULES 8-12)

Rule 8. **For the names of specific continents, countries, provinces, cities, towns, mountains, rivers, lakes, streets, parks, buildings, etc.**
- Europe, Ireland, France, Munster, Dublin, Cardiff, Reading, Naas, Alps, Galtees, Wicklow Mountains, Aran Islands, Liffey, River Lee, Grafton Street, Patrick Street, Phoenix Park, Hyde Park, St. Stephen's Green, Navan Vocational School, Greendale College, Cumberland House, Oak Drive, Willow Gardens etc.

The examples below illustrate how capital letters are used for names of specific places only.

She lives in *D*ublin. - She lives in the *c*ity.
They travelled to *T*ralee. - They travelled to *t*own.
There is snow on the *G*altees. - There is snow on the *m*ountains.
Our class visited the *A*ran *I*slands. - The class visited islands on the *l*ake.
I go to *G*lenroe *C*ommunity *S*chool. - I go to a *c*ommunity *s*chool.

Rule 9. **To begin the key words in the titles of books, films, plays, songs, poems, magazines, newspapers, etc.**
- Hamlet.
- The Day of the Jackal.
- The Phoenix.
- The Irish Times.
- The Merchant of Venice.
- The Green Fields of France.
- Private Eye.
- The Evening Press.

Rule 10. **To begin words in the names given to ships, aircraft, trains, clubs, restaurants, etc.**
- Irish Oak.
- Enterprise Express.
- The Pink Flamingo.
- The Little Chef.

Rule 11. **To begin all adjectives which are formed from proper nouns.**
- Irish, European, French, Edwardian, Elizabethan, Georgian.

Rule 12. **To begin the first word of direct speech which is a sentence within a sentence.**
- Peter suddenly remarked, "Fishing is a lazy sport."

Assignment **4**   USING CAPITALS CORRECTLY

In each of the following sentences all capitals have been omitted. Refer to **Rules 1-12** above to rewrite each sentence with capital letters correctly included. After you have rewritten each sentence correctly, list all the words to which you gave capitals. Then write the rule number that made you decide that the word should have a capital.

1. peter donovan spent the first two weeks of june in kerry.
2. my mother has a new phillips washing machine.
3. we have a dog called blackie and she has a sore nose.
4. liam and paul went fishing for trout and salmon in the river liffey.
5. The chef turned to his assistant and said, "too many cooks spoil the broth".
6. the assistant replied "many hands make light work".
7. peter's father used to drive a ford escort but now he has a bmw.
8. the doctor and the priest were sent for when the guards arrived at the scene of the accident.
9. when doctor o' neill arrived at st. anne's hospital, nurse nagle told him that he was to report to the children's ward.
10. findus fish fingers are advertised on television but I have never seen an advertisement for walsh's sausages.
11. peter bought the sunday independent, the sunday mirror and the rte guide but his brother bought irish papers only.
12. the opening of a new production of 'macbeth' by w. shakespeare was attended by mr. and mrs. browne.
13. miss o'brien left cork on tuesday around ten thirty and drove to dublin airport in her toyota starlet.
14. the greek and spanish teams arrived in london airport at around midnight on saturday.
15. american wines are becoming increasingly popular in britain, although french wines are still the most popular wines.
16. when the jet landed, captain connolly, the pilot, relaxed and sat back in his seat.
17. the shop assistant turned to miss naughton, "we seem to be out of daz. can I offer you any other washing powder?"
18. james enjoyed reading 'black beauty'. he thought it was a great book.
19. is the capital of the united states of america called new york?
20. the esb does not generate any electricity from nuclear generating stations.

PET FILE - ONE

Reptiles such as snakes, lizards, tortoises, terrapins, crocodiles and alligators are <u>vertebrates</u> with a hard, dry skin and no fur or (1) _____ . The reason for this is that they do not need a built-in blanket to (2) _____ them against the (3) _____ , since they are cold blooded.

This does not mean that they are always cold, but rather that their body temperature relies on the heat of their surroundings. On a hot day, a lizard or a tortoise will be warm and on a chilly day it will be cold to touch.

It is very (4) _____ to a reptile that it should be warm enough for most of the (5) _____ , for it can only be active and find and <u>digest</u> its food or escape from its enemies when its temperature is fairly (6) _____ . As a result, we find that most of the world's reptiles live in (7) _____ countries and those which are kept here as pets may have to be given (8) _____ heat if they are to (9) _____ .

Tortoises are the most (10) _____ reptilian pets. If properly (11) _____ , they are capable of surviving for many years. When (12) _____ a tortoise, try to find one which feels heavy for its size. It is better to buy a male and a (13) for although they are unlikely to (14) _____ successfully, the presence of a member of the opposite sex will prevent them from wandering from the (15) in (16) _____ of a mate.

Assignment	5		MAKING SENTENCES

1. Fill in the blank spaces with suitable words from the box.

buying	female	weather	important	high	time
extra	search	treated	garden	hot	breed
popular	survive	feathers	protect		

2. Find the meanings of the underlined words and put them into suitable sentences.

3. How does temperature affect reptiles?

SPELLING

- *We hope that when you have worked your way through this book your spelling will have improved. The anagrams, crosswords, wordsearches and other exercises will help. However, you can do much to help yourself.*

- Keep a spelling notebook and write out your own list of difficult or unusual words which you might wish to use more often.

- If you are in doubt about how a word is spelt, consult your dictionary.

- When learning spellings, watch out for a part of a word where you are likely to go wrong e.g. double letters (committee), silent letters (comb, knife).

- Don't worry too much if you are not sure how to spell certain words that you wish to use in a piece of writing. Break them into syllables and spell each part as it sounds. If your handwriting is neat and easy to read, the reader will recognise the word you wish to use. A few misspelt words in an examination will make little or no difference to the result. If you wish to use an interesting word but you are not sure of its correct spelling, use the word and take a chance with the spelling.

SPELLING WORKSHOP — A HUNDRED WORDS TO WATCH

Here are lists of words which you should be able to spell correctly.

1	2	3	4	5
business	guess	thought	below	temporary
foreign	clothes	begin	enough	queue
apologise	argument	cupboard	personally	definitely
beautiful	probably	committee	friend	February
answer	people	saucer	experience	finish
although	might	tough	amateur	beginning
together	always	early	autumn	listen
bicycle	better	both	association	breakfast
secretary	government	notice	particularly	biscuit
children	guarantee	secondary	cried	laboratory

6	7	8	9	10
knock	chocolate	soldier	cousin	newspaper
found	unconscious	recipe	either	those
favourite	neighbour	restaurant	through	caught
receipt	chimney	exhaust	because	holiday
unnecessary	busy	colour	sympathy	these
original	already	tomorrow	purpose	accident
laugh	maintenance	journey	close	every
bought	parallel	immediately	separate	ambulance
wrong	awful	different	surprised	character
rough	brother	around	library	write

SPELL RIGHT!

Similar sounding words (different meanings — different spellings)

Rewrite the sentences below, filling in the spaces with the correct words from the box.

allowed	board	pause	grate	medal	paws
beach	great	aloud	bored	beech	meddle

1. One hot days the _____ is always crowded.

2. He won a _____ in the sports.

3. We enjoyed the football match. It was a _____ game.

4. The dog's _____ were dirty.

5. Peter is not _____ to climb the _____ tree.

6. He spoke for an hour without a single _____ .

7. Anne is _____ with geography.

8. Do not _____ in other people's business.

9. Before setting a fire you must first clean out the _____ .

10. The child spoke _____ in the church.

PUNCTUATION — USING COMMAS

Punctuation marks are used to break up reading material into small parts which can be easily understood. Two of the most frequently used punctuation marks are the **comma** and the **full stop**.

The most important punctuation mark is the full stop. It is placed at the end of sentences. Commas are also important. They break up long sentences and should be inserted where we would pause naturally, if we were reading aloud.

For example:
(i) *When I realised what was happening, I decided to telephone the gardai.*
(ii) *Jane, who won first prize in the competition, was selected to travel.*

Commas are also used to separate items in a list of things.

For example:
(i) *The students were asked to bring a copybook, a pen, a pencil and a ruler.*
(ii) *In Dublin we visited the zoo, did some shopping, met my cousin and went to the cinema.*

In some sentences commas can be very important to express the exact meaning. Never use a comma unless you are sure that it is necessary.

 **Assignment** **6** PUNCTUATION USING COMMAS

Rewrite the following sentences, inserting commas where necessary.

1. Not easily frightened our dog continued to bark at the horses.

2. Although running is a good way of keeping fit one should not overdo it.

3. If I decide to go I will telephone you tomorrow.

4. Never a very reliable car the Model T was still very popular.

5. Two boys none of whom I knew arrived.

6. I decided having thought about it carefully not to travel.

7. I asked him knowing he was a local person the way to the football grounds.

8. Five persons two of them children are still missing.

9. Tom who is five is in Peter's class.

10. Dublin a city I know well has many beautiful parks.

11. Henry Ford the famous car manufacturer had Irish ancestors.

12. In fact nobody turned up to greet us.

13. He knew that even as things were she was far happier in her new school.

14. On the other hand it may be better to travel by train.

15. Two hundred and fifty grams of mushrooms four ounces of flour two ounces of margarine and a stock cube are the ingredients needed to make mushroom soup.

16. Our local pet show was disappointing as only two dogs five cats three guinea-pigs and a goldfish were entered.

17. London Paris Amsterdam and Canterbury none of which I have visited all have famous buildings.

18. A group of us from my old primary school including two teachers visited a model farm in Co. Kildare which had pigs lambs goats calves and rabbits on display.

19. Tidying my room hoovering washing and drying dishes hanging out clothes on the line and ironing are just some of the jobs I hate doing.

20. Some of my favourite occupations include watching television playing with my computer walking my dog playing with my guinea pigs and chatting to my friends on the telephone.

PET FILE - TWO

Almost everybody, at (1)_____ time or other, wants to keep a pet. A pet is a creature with which we share (2)_____ home and our company for no reason other than that we (3)_____ to have it about us. It will need housing, feeding, care and love all through its (4)_____. Even when we are (5)_____ or feeling tired a pet may need <u>grooming</u> or exercising. Yet we do keep pets because, although they need a lot of time and attention, they can give us a great deal of pleasure in return.

Most animals which are kept as pets are (6)_____ and this alone can give us pleasure: the brilliant (7)_____ of a budgie or a lizard may make us feel cheerful on a dull day: the <u>lithe</u> movements of a cat or fish are always pleasing to watch and the amusing <u>antics</u> of most sorts of pets can cheer us up when we are feeling (8)_____.

More important still, a pet can give us <u>affection</u> and loyalty. A dog, or any other sort of pet does not mind about the sort of thing that often bothers people. It doesn't (9)_____ if you are not good at sums, or if you are untidy, for you are its special person whom it can trust and love. To develop this feeling between yourself and any kind of (10)_____ is very exciting and one of the best things that can come from keeping pets.

Pets can (11)_____ us things too. Because they are totally dependant on us, we must (12)_____ remember their needs and this can teach us responsibility for others and self <u>discipline</u>, so that we become reliable people in our general way of life. People who treat animals well are usually (13)_____ to human beings also.

Assignment 7

1. Fill in the blank spaces above with suitable words from the box.

life	like	care	kind	our
teach	busy	beautiful	colours	animal
miserable	some	always		

2. Use your dictionary to find the meaning of the underlined words.
3. List the advantages and disadvantages of keeping a pet.

THE APOSTROPHE

1. The apostrophe is used to show that one or more letters have been omitted from a word. This results in two words becoming one.

For Example: *She's late.*
Here the apostrophe indicates that the letter *i* has been left out. The two words *she is* are changed to one - *she's*.

Assignment	8	USING APOSTROPHES

A. Rewrite these phrases putting in letters in place of the apostrophes.

It's early.   He'd like one.

Don't go.   They're running away.

You're late.   We can't pay.

We've left.   There's one left.

What's the matter?   We'll do it again.

B. Rewrite these phrases, but in shortened forms, by putting in apostrophes where necessary.

Who is walking home?   You are always late.

He is running.   They would never try.

She will go.   I cannot attend.

They have lost.   It is too late.

We are winning.   He will not leave.

That is the house.   I have lost the key.

2. The apostrophe is also used to show **ownership**. It cuts out the need to use clumsy phrases such as "the coat of the teacher" or "the house of the girls". Instead we write *"the teacher's coat"* or *"the girls' house"*.

Remember

1. *If there is one owner*
    - The apostrophe is put in **before** the final "s" e.g. the boy's bicycle, the dog's collar, the company's headquarters, the band's equipment.

2. *If there is more than one owner*
    - The apostrophe is placed **after** the "s" e.g. the house of the boys — the boys' house; the collars of the dogs — the dogs' collars; the equipment of the bands — the bands' equipment.

3. *Certain words change their form completely to make plurals e.g* men, *women, children*
    - In these cases, the apostrophe to show ownership comes before the "s" e.g. the men's club, the women's clothes, the children's toys.

4. *Possessive Pronouns*
    - Possessive pronouns do not have an apostrophe e.g. Its engine is damaged. Yours is not worth it. Theirs is very valuable.

Assignment **9**

Change the following into the possessive form using the apostrophe.

1. The glow of the fire.
2. The house of the child.
3. The cover belonging to it.
4. The lair of the fox.
5. The colour of the boxes.
6. The club of the ladies.
7. The food of the cat.
8. The home of the dogs.
9. The park of the people.
10. The coach of the group.
11. The dismay of the mother.
12. The sizes of the buses.
13. The dog belonging to the brothers.
14. The shoes of the women.
15. The numbers of the houses.
16. The coat of the lady.
17. The owner of the dogs.

CROSSWORD NO. 2

Across

1 Definitely not dear.

7 A very wild and uncivilised person.

9 To drop liquid.

10 Not wet.

12 A message over the wires.

13 A letter (with a sting!)

15 Keep away from.

16 To give counsel.

17 Knots : problems (S _ _ _ _)

Down

2 Occurred.

3 A state in which most people are at night.

4 Friend.

5 Not good!

6 Opens locks.

8 Exciting (story).

11 The car was _____ recklessly.

13 A unit of chocolate!

14 First Woman.

15 Donkey.

THERE   THEIR   THEY'RE
Getting them right!

- **There** occurs most frequently, e.g. There is one sweet left. Tom found the ball over there.
- **Their** means *belonging to them* or *owned by them.*
- **They're** is a short way of saying *they are.*

If in doubt check if *their* or *they're* fit. If not use *there*.

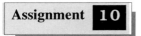

Choose the correct word (**there, their** or **they're**) for each of the spaces below.

1. _____ was no one _____ when we got to the station.
2. _____ house was sold.
3. The boys said that _____ not going to the match.
4. _____ dog was found over _____.
5. _____ are too many passengers travelling on the bus.
6. We saw _____ car in town.
7. _____ were four of us in town.
8. _____ late again.
9. Don't you know _____ running in the second race.
10. _____ is a little hut in the woods.
11. The match is due to be played in _____ pitch.
12. _____ colours are red and white.
13. Yesterday _____ was an accident on our road.
14. _____ going to travel by car to London.
15. _____ comes a time when all young people want more independence.
16. _____ parents will come to collect them and _____ to travel home with them.
17. Here and _____ we found wild strawberries.
18. What's that over _____ ?
19. Was it _____ cat that was killed?
20. _____ are too many boys in our class.

USING THE DICTIONARY

The Alphabet

a b c d e f g h i j k l m n o p q r s t u v w x y z

A B C D E F G H I J K L M N O P
Q R S T U V W X Y Z

Assignment 11

1. List the two letters of the alphabet that come *before* and *after* the following letters:-

    __ s __ ,   __ d __ ,   __ g __ ,

    __ o __ ,   __ n __ ,   __ k __ ,

    __ l __ ,   __ y __ ,   __ h __ ,

    __ v __ ,   __ b __ ,   __ p __ ,

    __ f __ ,   __ t __ ,   __ i __ ,

    __ q __ ,   __ u __ ,   __ r __ ,

    __ m __ ,   __ j __ ,   __ e __ ,

    __ w __ ,   __ c __ ,   __ x __ .

2. Rearrange the following groups of letters in alphabetical order.

    (a) f t e w q a s   (f) p x m o r d

    (b) j i y t v f r d   (g) v r b o w c e m

    (c) n h g v c d s a w   (h) b m x c y i l p u

    (d) p o i u t e q l j g d a m b c z   (i) r p u l t a x i m p n

    (e) q e t u o s f h k x v n c g y   (j) s n a m d b i l j o p s q

2. Dictionary Quiz

(a) Use your dictionary to solve each of the following questions.

1. What colour is amethyst?
2. For what purpose is an anemometer used?
3. Aq _ _ _ _ _ _ : a certain type of bridge. What crosses this bridge?
4. What colour is auburn hair?
5. Are you bilingual?
6. Can a beverage be eaten or drank?
7. Is a biped a living creature or a type of machine?
8. From what word does the word budgie come?
9. Calico - a fruit?
10. Campanology - the study of camping?
11. Do carbohydrates contain oxygen?
12. Does a cedar lose its leaves in autumn?
13. What colour is cerise?
14. Cha _ _ _ _ _ _ : What is unusual about this lizard?
15. Cha _ _ _ _ _ r : This person is paid to do what?
16. Clodhopper - an insect?
17. Symbols or cymbals - Which do drummers use?
18. What two meanings has the word *'invalid'*?
19. Are guinea-pigs docile animals?
20. Would you expect to find a double-bass supporting a large building or in an orchestra?

(b)
1. If a performer got an encore would she be pleased?
2. What type of an instrument is an epigram?
3. Do fastidious people make good company?
4. Are there any fauns in Ireland?
5. Is cotton made from flax?
6. If a man's manner was described as formal would he be warm and friendly?
7. Why would a pair of goloshes be of little use on a dry day?
8. Why do we sometimes gesticulate?
9. Is gingham edible?

10. Was Gorgonzola an imaginary man-eating monster?

11. Would you find a gudgeon in the sea?

12. Is it easy to fool a gullible person?

13. Why would somebody look haggard?

14. Is the haggis a native Scottish animal?

15. Harlequin - another name for a judge?

16. Where would you expect to find a harpy?

17. What is meant by a hereditary talent?

18. Do farmers sometimes export hillocks?

19. Is a hopper a machine?

20. Why should you never cut off a hydra's head?

(c) 1. Ichthyology - the study of skin diseases?

2. Name a well-known fungus.

3. Why would an army officer wear insignia?

4. What makes an invertebrate different from most other creatures?

5. What is the difference between an isobar and an isotherm?

6. In what continent are ivory trees found?

7. Jasmine - a bush, a flower or a tree?

8. Is Juniper a planet?

9. Could a castle be described as a keep?

10. Why would you not go to a Kibbutz for a relaxing holiday?

11. Kittiwake or Kittihawk - a type of bird?

12. If you called somebody a knave would you be praising him?

13. Is a larch a bird?

14. Are you likely to find an orange-coloured larkspur?

15. Limo is short for what word?

16. A loganberry is like which other kind of fruit?

17. Magenta, Magnolia, Madrigal. - A tree, a colour, a ship. True or False?

18. What subjects does a reporter who covers maritime affairs write about?

19. Which falls on the earth - a meteor? a meteorite?

20. Does a millipede have a thousand legs?

(d) 1. Which measures time - a minute or a minuet?

 2. Would a nefarious person be a good companion?

 3. Where would you find an obituary?

 4. Do omniverous creatures eat meat?

 5. What is the difference between a panther and a puma?

 6. A phial and a barrel. Are they similar?

 7. What two different types of activities does the word poaching describe?

 8. Troubadour - a soldier, singer, sailor?

 9. Wombats are found only in Africa?

 10. Which of these words describe a person who is never cheerful - sullen, doleful, disconsolate, discerning?

 11. Which of these words describe a person who is rude:
civil, curt, disparaging, courteous, refined, abusive, churlish?

 12. Complete each of the following words which describe a wicked person:
ras_ _ _ , vi_ _ _ _ _ , sco_ _ __ _ _ , ro_ _ _

 13. Which of the following words mean (i) to clean (ii) to dirty? - contaminate, purge, tarnish, defile, scour, purify, defile?

3. Find the *odd one out* in each of the following.

(a)	lyre, lupin, lute	(k)	onyx, opal, onus
(b)	organdie, osprey, otter	(l)	parakeet, partridge, papyrus
(c)	shrew, sleuth, skunk	(m)	speedwell, spatula, spruce
(d)	toucan, terrier, teal	(n)	tulle, turbine, tunic
(e)	vole, vixen, visor	(o)	whippet, whelk, whey
(f)	xylophone, zephyr, zither	(p)	kittiwake, kiwi, kitten
(g)	magenta, magnolia, marigold	(q)	pugilist, punnet, pullet
(h)	raffia, ragworth, refuse	(r)	rowan, rupee, rosemary
(i)	sham, shamrock, shallot	(s)	stockade, stile, stole
(j)	moccasin, mohair, mollusc	(t)	sonata, regatta, nocturne

PET FILE - THREE

If you live in the country and have enough (1) _____ in which you can keep them, there are several sorts of (2) _____ animals which you could keep as pets.

The animal that (3) _____ children want to keep is a pony. Ponies are grazing animals which (4) _____ a lot of space, usually about one acre per animal, but more if the land is (5) _____ . To (6) _____ one on less space than this will probably mean the ground becomes overgrazed and may become very badly (7) _____ up by the animal's feet.

Ponies are herd animals and may (8) _____ terribly through being alone. Solitary animals try to make (9) _____ with all sorts of other (10) _____ and may run to the edge of their (11) _____ to see any passer-by or even try to break out to be with (12) _____ ponies.

Buying a pony is more difficult than obtaining most other pets. True, there are always lots of ponies for sale, but most of them are fairly expensive. Be honest about your own abilities and think very hard about the time, effort and financial commitment involved with keeping a pony.

A beautiful, highly strung pony may be what you are after, but unless you are a good rider, it may be (13) _____ for you to manage. Do not go to a sale by yourself; you could buy a pony which was quite unsuitable in a number of ways. The best way to go about getting a pony is to make friends with the owners of a reputable local riding school. They will be able to help you choose a suitable animal, with which you will have lots of fun.

Orphan lambs make friendly pets while they are (14) _____ , but there are few households which could tolerate a grown sheep living indoors. Their hooves are surprisingly (15) _____ and having been petted when they were (16) _____ , they will grow up attempting to butt or bully their way to getting what they want. Most lambs (17) _____ up as pets end up unhappy for they find it difficult to mix with other (18) _____ once they have become (19) _____ to being members of a human family. Until they have lambs of their own, they tend to be outcasts from the flock.

Assignment **15**

1. Fill in the blank spaces with suitable words from the box.

keep	cut	difficult	young
small	suffer	brought	need
poor	space	paddock	sheep
sharp	creatures	used	many
friends	other	large	

2. Find the meanings of the underlined words and put them into suitable sentences.

3. Write a short paragraph about (a) Ponies and (b) Orphan lambs.

SPELL RIGHT!

Rewrite the sentences below, filling in the spaces with the correct words from the box.

scent	seem	sow	past
site	sole	sight	seam
sew	passed	sent	soul

1. I intend to _____ some lettuce seeds this week.
2. _____ music is played mainly by black musicians.
3. The _____ from daffodils is very faint.
4. The builder said that the _____ for the new house was very reasonably priced.
5. The men _____ to be fishing from the boat.
6. Angela's jacket ripped at the _____ .
7. James came to Galway for the _____ reason of meeting Jane.
8. He _____ the money by post.
9. The car _____ out the bus on a bend.
10. David offered to _____ Angela's jacket.
11. Some dogs have very sharp eye _____ .
12. We drove _____ the school.

IDIOMS

An idiom is an expression whose meaning is not immediately clear from the actual words. If a teacher tells a parent that Johnny has been *swinging the lead* since September he does not mean that Johnny has been literally swinging a lump of lead for a few months! The teacher means of course, that Johnny has not been studying since September.

People often use idioms in conversation and writers often use them when writing dialogue for characters. Idioms can add life and colour to a conversation or a piece of written dialogue.

Idioms often present problems to foreigners who are learning to speak English. Can you suggest why?

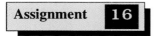

Assignment 16	COMMON IDIOMS

1. Match each of the idioms in **List A** with the correct meaning in **List B**.

List A	**List B**
1. to have an axe to grind	(a) to behave unfairly towards somebody
2. to have a bee in one's bonnet	(b) to have something to gain by an action
3. to hit below the belt	(c) to be obsessed by a particular idea
4. to be a wet blanket	(d) to be a spoilsport
5. to have a bone to pick with someone	(e) to pay too much
	(f) to exaggerate
6. to draw the long bow	(g) to take on a problem boldly
7. to make a clean breast of it	(h) to suspect something
8. to take the bull by the horns	(i) to have a complaint to make
9. to paddle one's own canoe	(j) to do things without depending on others
10. to put the cart before the horse	
11. to pay through the nose	(k) to confess to something
12. to smell a rat	(l) to do things in the wrong order

2. Match each of the idioms in **List A** with the correct meaning in **List B**.

List A	**List B**
1. to let the cat out of the bag	(a) to keep it secret
2. to be under a cloud	(b) to reveal a secret
3. to keep it dark	(c) to deny something to others that is of no value to yourself
4. to be a dog in the manger	(d) to be under suspicion
5. to make both ends meet	(e) to boast
6. to have a feather in one's cap	(f) to show fear
7. to show the white feather	(g) to make friends after a quarrel
8. to sit on the fence	(h) to refuse to take sides in an argument
9. to play second fiddle	(i) to have achieved something worthwhile
10. to bury the hatchet	(j) to stand back while someone else leads
11. to give a person the cold shoulder	(k) to live on what you have
12. to blow one's own trumpet	(l) to make somebody feel unwelcome or disliked

3. Match each of the idioms in **List A** with the correct meaning in **List B**.

List A	**List B**
1. to hang one's head	(a) to make small problems seem like big ones
2. to live from hand to mouth	(b) to spend all you have got without being able to put some by for the future
3. to flog a dead horse	(c) to look after yourself at the expense of others
4. to strike while the iron is hot	(d) to suggest that an idea is of no value
5. to swing the lead	(e) to put an effort into something which is unlikely to pay off
6. to turn over a new leaf	(f) to be ashamed
7. to be at loggerheads	(g) to act while conditions are in your favour
8. to make a mountain out of a molehill	(h) to dodge work by pretending to be sick
9. to face the music	(i) to be quarrelling
10. to feather one's nest	(j) to get into trouble
11. to get into hot water	(k) to face punishment or criticism without complaint
12. to throw cold water on something	(l) to lead a better life

CROSSWORD No. 3

Across

3 Get bigger.

6 You run for this when the bullets are coming thick and fast.

8 Governing (R _ _ _ _ _)

9 Payment for work done.

13 Perfect.

15 A supporting part of a building.

16 Not ever.

17 The stories of some rich people are _ _ _ _ to riches stories.

Down

1 The _ _ _ _ _ Island - a famous adventure book.

2 In this place.

4 An unexpected attack.

5 What a dog does with its tail.

7 Someone from Russia.

10 Large beast of the desert.

11 Worn on a cowboy's heel.

12 One that is incorrectly wired is very dangerous!

14 The past tense of draw.

PET FILE - FOUR

The golden hamster is a popular pet. In the wild, golden hamsters (1) _____ in a territory big enough to provide food for only one animal and any (2) _____ will be driven out. In <u>captivity</u> their nature does not change and, although there may be (3) _____ of food, the hamster cannot stand others of its own kind living with it. Even males and females cannot be put together (4) _____ . If you wish to (5) _____ hamsters, the male has to be brought briefly to the female and removed again once mating has taken place.

Since the hamster leads a (6) _____ life you should give it as large a cage as you can with plenty of toys such as cotton reels or pine cones to chew and cardboard rolls for it to run through. Although the (7) _____ should be made of wood, it should be as smooth as possible, or the hamster will (8) _____ it badly. A (9) _____ will give the animal the exercise it (10) _____ , for although the hamster is <u>sluggish</u> in the daytime it becomes very active at (11) _____ .

Hamsters can be fed a single meal each day. A cereal mixture is the basic food but this can be <u>supplemented</u> with porridge oats, an occasional dog (12) or even a small piece of cake. In the wild, hamsters probably eat some insects and a little animal <u>protein</u> is (13) _____ to keep them in really good health. A little hard boiled egg, cheese or tiny scraps of lean cooked meat will give them the essentials which they (14) _____ .

If you put your hamster's food in a dish, do not be surprised if it vanishes very quickly. This is not because the hamster is a very rapid eater, but because it has large <u>pouches</u> inside its mouth and it stuffs all the food into these and (15) _____ it off to its own secret larder. When you clean out your hamster's cage, you may find that it has in fact not eaten all the food which you have been giving it, but <u>caching</u> quite a lot of it away.

Hamsters come from a hot part of the world and should therefore be kept in a fairly warm atmosphere. If the (16) _____ of the room in which they are housed falls too low, particularly in the winter time, they may <u>hibernate</u>.

Assignment ▮ 17 ▮

1. Fill in the blank spaces with suitable words from the box.

night	carries	temperature	chew
solitary	breed	safely	biscuit
need	wheel	necessary	plenty
needs	invaders	cage	live

2. Use your dictionary to check the meanings of the underlined words and put them into suitable sentences.

3. What surprising habits do hamsters have?

THE ALPHABET QUIZ

A _ _ _ _	The seed of an oak tree.
B _ _ _ _ _	Gets you across.
C _ _ _	Not a musical bird.
D _ _ _	Pull.
E _ _ _ _	Majestic bird.
F _ _ _ _ _	Many trees.
G _ _ _ _ _	Not innocent.
H _ _ _	Stringed instrument.
I _ _ _ _ _	Surrounded by water.
J _ _ _	A funny story.
K _ _ _ _	It cuts.
L _ _ _	Bread.
M _ _ _ _	Soldier's walk.
N _ _ _	Bird's home.
O _ _ _	Egg shaped.
P _ _ _ _ _ _ _	Gift.
Q _ _ _ _ _ _ _ _	Ask.
R _ _ _ _ _	Manlike machine.
S _ _ _ _	Nettles do it.
T _ _ _ _	A game fish.
U _ _ _ _ _ _ _ _	Useful in rain.
V _ _ _	Very big.
W _ _ _	Small bird.
X _ _ _ _ _ _ _ _	Musical instrument.
Y _ _ _ _	A sailing boat.
Z _ _ _	Nil.

PROVERBS

Proverbs are sayings that contain sound advice or wise observations on life.

| Assignment | **18** | COMPLETING PROVERBS |

1. In each of the following proverbs a word has been omitted. Find the correct word in the box below to complete each proverb. When you have this completed state briefly, in your own words, what each of the proverbs mean.

   Example: *Birds of a feather **flock** together.* This proverb means that people with the same interests or attitudes enjoy each other's company.

   1. Birds of a feather _____ together.

   2. Absence makes the heart grow _____ .

   3. Actions speak louder than _____ .

   4. As you make your bed so must you _____ on it.

   5. _____ must not be choosers.

   6. The _____ bird catches the worm.

   7. A bird in the _____ is worth two in the bush.

   8. Once _____ , twice shy.

   9. Blood is thicker than _____ .

   10. You cannot get blood out of a _____ .

   11. When the cat's away the mice will _____ .

   12. _____ begins at home.

   13. Don't _____ your chickens until they are hatched.

   14. Every cloud has a _____ lining.

   15. Cut your _____ according to your cloth.

   16. Too many cooks _____ the broth.

   17. _____ costs nothing.

   18. Barking dogs seldom _____ .

   19. _____ dog has his day.

A bird in the hand is worth two in the bush.

207

20. Let sleeping dogs _____ .

21. A drowning man will clutch at a _____ .

22. Don't put all your _____ in one basket.

23. _____ is as good as a feast.

24. Where there's _____ there's fire.

25. A fool and his money are soon _____ .

26. A friend in _____ is a friend indeed.

27. _____ fruit tastes sweetest.

28. God helps those who help _____ .

29. Grasp all, _____ all.

30. More _____ , less speed.

fonder	words	courtesy	bite	hand
spoil	flock	bitten	water	every
play	straw	enough	themselves	coat
early	lie	beggars	stone	lie
charity	eggs	count	haste	parted
need	forbidden	silver	lose	smoke

2. One word is omitted from each of the following proverbs. This time *no dashes* have been included to indicate where the missing word should go. Complete each of the proverbs. The missing words are in the box below. When you have this completed, state briefly, in your own words, what each of the proverbs means.

1. Make while the sun shines

2. Two are better than one

3. Honesty is the policy

4. Hunger is the best

5. A hungry man is an man

6. A leak will sink a great ship

7. Least said soonest

8. Half a loaf is better than bread

208

9. Look before you

10. One man's is another man's poison

11. Is the mother of invention

12. Look the pence and the pounds will look after themselves

13. He who pays the piper calls the

14. Any in a storm

15. Practice makes

16. Of sight, out of mind

17. A stitch in time saves

18. One swallow does not make a

19. Set a thief to a thief

20. Time and tide for no man

21. Will out

22. Vessels make most noise

23. Waste, want not

24. We never miss the water till the well runs

25. Leave enough alone

26. Where there's a will there's a

27. It's an ill wind that blows any good

28. When the wine's in the wit's

29. Words butter no parsnips

30. What's worth doing is doing well

When the cat's away the mice will play.

necessity	mended	tune	catch	well
out	heads	no	port	wait
hay	nine	best	leap	perfect
small	after	not	sauce	meat
way	nobody	summer	fine	angry
truth	empty	worth	dry	out

209

PET FILE - FIVE

Having decided that you really do want a pet, you must (1)_____ what sort of animal would be best for you. Lots of people think that it would be (2)_____ to have a really unusual pet.

The (3)_____ animals which are really suitable as pets are those which have been bred in <u>captivity</u>. They will not have suffered the stress of having been captured and <u>transported</u> far from their real (4)_____. They will be used to seeing people and being touched by them from the beginning of their lives, but you will still need a certain amount of skill and a great deal of care to handle them or make them (5)_____. If you go to a breeder or to a good pet shop to get your pet, the animals should be healthy in themselves and less likely to <u>pose</u> a human health risk.

Remember when making (6)_____ choice that small pets are often better than large ones, especially if you have never had a pet before. There are lots of (7)_____ for this - usually they cost less to buy in the first instance and that is likely to be an advantage in itself. A small pet will almost certainly need (8)_____ room than a big one and if you live in a flat, or a house without much garden, this can be important. Its cage can be smaller and (9)_____ to construct. A small pet will eat less than a big one, so it should cost less to <u>maintain</u>.

It will also probably be easier to handle. If you fall for a Great Dane puppy you may (10)_____ find that he is taking you for a walk rather than the other way around. It (11)_____ not take long for him to grow to be much heavier and stronger (12)_____ you are.

A very tiny or fragile animal may not be suitable either, for you want to have a pet which you will not hurt accidentally when you are handling it. Creatures which might easily be damaged are likely to feel frightened of you, so they will not be so tame or friendly as animals which do not fear you.

Assignment 19

1. Fill in the blank spaces above with suitable words from the box.

only	decide	tame	less	soon	your
will	fun	home	cheaper	than	reasons

2. Use your dictionary to find the meaning of the underlined words.
3. Explain why animals born in the wild do not make good pets.
4. Give five reasons why small pets can be more suitable than large ones.

HANDWRITING

It is always pleasing to get a postcard or a letter written in neat handwriting. It is easy to read and you get the feeling that the writer took a little extra care.

Nowadays computers and printers are widely used in both the workplace and the home. Producing a neatly printed document was never so easy.

Nevertheless neat handwriting is a very important skill. In primary school you will have been taught the basics of good handwriting. As you begin the next stage of your education you should continue to aim for a high standard of handwriting in all subjects. A high standard of handwriting will work to your advantage in all your future examinations. Nothing is more annoying for a teacher or examiner than page after page of untidy handwriting where almost every word presents a difficulty.

The most common cause of poor handwriting is hurrying to get a passage written. When handwriting is rushed it usually results in one or more of the following:

When the cat's away

— Individual letters badly formed.

Too many cooks spoil the broth

— Letters bunched too closely together.

mary Had a little lamb

— Letters which are the wrong size or height in relation to other letters.

A bird inthe hand is worth

— Incorrect spacing between words.

Alls well that ends well

— Words that wander above or below the line.

She He has who ~~His~~ hesitates ~~was~~ is

— Many words and letters crossed out.

How to Improve your Handwriting

Everyone, by taking a little care and attention, can write in a neat and readable style. The basic rule is to slow down to a pace where each word can be clearly read. Practise this and you will find that your writing speed will gradually increase without losing its quality

Here are the basic shapes of the letters of the alphabet. Note that not all letters are the same height. (Some letters such as **f** and **r** have more than one form. You should continue to use the form that you were taught in primary school.)

SMALL LETTERS

a b c d e f g h i j k l m n o
p q r s t u v w x y z

CAPITAL LETTERS

A B C D E F G H I J K L M...

You may wish to use the following forms of capital letters to achieve a more decorative effect.

A B C D E F G H I

All letters can be written in one stroke except **f**, **t** and **x** which require two strokes.

fox   tea   fist   other

All letters begin from the top except **d** and **e** which begin from the centre.

JOINED WRITING

The disadvantage of 'printing' is that you have to lift the pen off the paper after writing each letter. This is both time-consuming and tiring. Joined writing allows you to write most words without lifting the pen from the paper.
'Joined' writing - also called cursive writing - simply involves joining up letters with slopes, loops and curves.

The letters **a c d e h i k l m n t u** and **x** all finish on up-strokes and this can be extended to join with any letter that follows, e.g. el ch of sk st cb

art cat duck oxen evening hat ink

Never join a letter to the top of any of the tall letters - **b d f h k l t**. You should make the join at the halfway point of the tall letter.

habit ball

This is a common alternative method of joining any of the letters **a c d e h i k l m n t u** and **x** to a tall letter.

pal duck ink ball

Letters that go below the line may remain unjoined.

join queen gate job

Alternatively **g** and **y** may be joined with a loop to a letter that follows.

goal yacht

The letters **f o v w** are joined to letters by a short cross-join that is slightly curved.

fox van following

Not all letters join smoothly. In the case of **b p q** and **s** for example it may be necessary to lift the pen off the paper before beginning the following letter.

By writing slowly and neatly you will gradually develop your own individual writing style.

CROSSWORD NO. 4

Across

1 Not blunt.

5 Sometimes confused with too!

7 What attracts a moth.

10 The writing part of a pen.

11 "Goodnight _ _ _ _ _" - a well-known song.

12 A type of poem (O _ _)

13 A tool used by leather workers.

14 A steep-sided valley.

16 To colour cloth.

18 To give way.

19 A cutting tool.

20 A meal to celebrate a special event.

Down

2 What all schoolchildren look forward to.

3 Capital of Italy.

4 When a book belongs to you, you _ _ _ it.

6 Where the oil comes to the surface.

8 Present tense of *were*.

9 Many teenagers do not ____ classical music.

13 Ninety could be regarded as a ripe old ____.

15 Travel by horseback.

17 We do this to satisfy our hunger.

PARAGRAPHS

Examine any piece of writing—a newspaper, magazine or book—and notice how the print is divided into paragraphs. Each paragraph begins on a new line and often a little way in from the margin. Dividing material into paragraphs makes the task of reading the material easier.

Most paragraphs are made up of a **main sentence** - which tells us what the paragraph is about - and a number of **supporting sentences** which support or back up the main sentence with extra details. The first sentence of a paragraph is usually the main sentence.

Assignment **20**	IDENTIFYING THE TOPICS OF PARAGRAPHS

(a)   Study each of the paragraphs below and give the topic of each one, using a single word or short phrase.

(b)   Each of the paragraphs contains a sentence which is out of place. Identify the sentence in each case and explain why it doesn't belong.

Example

Assignment

(i)   Water is the oldest means of transport. Deep rivers and lakes are natural inland waterways, which for centuries man has used for travelling and trading. Where rivers and lakes did not exist, canals were built. Canals are man-made ditches or channels filled with water. They were often built to link two or more cities. Today many people enjoy fishing in canals. Sometimes they connected inland cities with the sea. In areas with few rivers they provided inland waterways for transport and communication.

Answer

(a) Topic of the paragraph:- *Why canals were built*

(b) The sentence that does not belong is the one about fishing. The paragraph is about how canals were used long ago to transport goods and not how they are used nowadays.

(ii)   Our world is a far noisier place than it used to be. Long gone are the days when the loudest sounds in a neighbourhood were those of children, barking dogs or the clip-clop of horses' hooves. Gone also are the days when all trains were drawn by steam engines. Noise seems to be part and

215

parcel of modern life, with motor and air traffic, radios, televisions and all kinds of household gadgets causing wear and tear on our ears — and our nerves.

(iii)   Lions only kill for food. When they make a kill the lions in the hunting party feed on the carcass for several days. When it is finished they go hunting again. The lion is often called the king of the jungle. Many young animals know by instinct how to hunt for their food, but lion cubs are an exception—they have to be taught by their mother.

(iv)   A tiger's colouring depends on the region in which it lives. In colder regions, tigers have pale coats. In warmer jungle areas their coats are brighter. The tiger's stripes are a good disguise. Household cats are descended from the tiger family. In the forests where it lives the stripes break up the animal's shape, making it look like shadows cast by the trees. In this way the tiger blends with its surroundings. Albino (all-white) and all black tigers occur from time to time, but they are very rare.

(v)   The leopard is smaller than the lion or the tiger, but it moves more quickly than either of them, and is more savage by nature. It lives in tropical forests, open grasslands and in dry regions at the edge of deserts. Last summer visitors flocked to Paris Zoo to see two leopard cubs that had been born there. It is equally at home at sea level or at high altitudes. Because it can live almost anywhere, the leopard is much more widespread than the lion or the tiger. It is found throughout Africa and Asia.

(vi)   All ice-hockey players wear protective clothing, including shin-guards, elbow-pads, hip-pads and thick gloves. Goalkeepers also wear chest protectors and large leg-pads. Most goalkeepers protect their faces with masks made of rubber and plastic. Soccer players do not wear protective clothing. Many ice-hockey players also wear helmets.

(vii)   After dinner all the gang turned out to hunt for turtle eggs on the bar. They went about poking sticks into the sand, and when they found a soft place they went down on their knees and dug with their hands. Sometimes they would take fifty or sixty eggs out of one hole. They were perfectly round white things, a trifle smaller than an English walnut. English walnuts were too expensive to buy. They had a famous fried-egg feast that night, and another on Friday morning.

PARAGRAPH BUILDING 1

Each of the sentences below is the topic sentence of a paragraph. Read them carefully and consider the type of sentences that might follow them in the paragraph.

Topics:
(a) Cycling has become very popular for a number of reasons.
(b) John caused the accident.
(c) A torch can often come in useful.
(d) It was a beautiful morning to be out in the countryside.

Now read each of the sentences below (**1-21**) and indicate to which paragraph, (a), (b), (c) or (d), they belong. Write each paragraph into your copy, putting the sentences in the best order.

Sentences:
1. He came speeding down the avenue and on to the main road.
2. However sheep and cows do not give birth to their young during daylight hours only.
3. Through the winter it is dark from five onwards.
4. A bike is a faster and a cheaper way to get around a city or a town.
5. The new mountain bikes with their many gears allow you to go places where it would be impossible to go in a car.
6. The sun was shining from a clear blue sky.
7. It was lucky that none of the Sheehans was in their garden.
8. Swallows skimmed over the treetops.
9. He was doing daring tricks, like wheelies, on his mountain bike to show off to the girls.
10. He was looking back to see if he was being noticed.
11. The driver escaped injury.
12. In the garden by the rose bush the dog dozed in the sun.
13. This is particularly true if you live on a farm like I do.
14. Many nights I walked the darkened fields with my father searching for a sheep that was due to have lambs or a cow that was due to calf.
15. It is a good way of keeping fit and healthy.
16. He didn't see the truck coming and it had to swerve to avoid him.
17. It went right through Sheehan's hedge and ended up in their back garden.
18. He remembered walking the same fields with his father and only a smelly oil-lamp to show the way.

19. Below, the fields of lush grass rippled in the morning breeze.
20. Cycling in the country is a good way of seeing things which you wouldn't be able to notice from a car.
21. From the hawthorn bushes, now covered in white blossoms, small birds chirped happily.

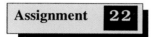

Assignment 22   **PARAGRAPH BUILDING 2**

The following sentences come from **three separate passages**, each dealing with a separate topic. However they have been mixed up.

(a) Read all the sentences carefully to discover the topic sentence of each of the three passages. Write these down.
(b) Next list, after each topic sentence, the sentence numbers which you think belong to that particular topic.
(c) Finally, in the case of each topic, put the sentences in the order that you think is best and write them into your copy. You may need to divide some passages into two paragraphs.

1. It was probably by accident that some early hunter overcame his fear of fire and learned how to use it.
2. Man knew only that fire was hot and could kill him if he stayed in its path.
3. The land shakes and buildings tremble; cars collide in the streets; fires break out; trees and telegraph poles collapse; and everywhere there is panic.
4. And they are trained to charge at a waving cape.
5. He saw it in its most terrifying forms, in red-hot lava that spurted from volcanoes and in forest fires started by lightning.
6. It melts metals so that they can be moulded into useful shapes.
7. Earthquakes are very common.
8. It is very difficult to be quite sure of the answer to this question.
9. So a bull would probably charge at the cape no matter what colour it was.
10. Long ago, before history began, man feared fire just as the wild animals did.
11. Most victims find themselves quite helpless in the face of this gigantic force.
12. It made steam pressure to turn the wheels of industry.
13. We still do not know whether bulls are colour blind, or not.
14. If bulls are colour-blind, the colour red would certainly not be irritating to them.

218

15. There are around a half-million earth movements every year but only one-hundred thousand of them are large enough to be felt, and only a few hundred of these are big enough to cause any damage.

16. Does the colour red irritate a bull?

17. Anybody who has lived through an earthquake will never forget it.

18. A bad earthquake can seem like the end of the world to the people caught in it.

19. The results have not given us a definite answer.

20. Fire is a useful servant, but if carelessly handled, it can become a dangerous master.

21. Fire keeps us warm and still cooks food in many countries.

22. Experiments have been made on hoofed animals, such as the bull, to find out if these animals can see colour and if they can tell one colour from another.

23. We do know, however, that bulls will rush at a moving object.

24. Perhaps on a cold day he came upon the dying embers of a forest fire.

25. He felt and enjoyed the fire's warmth.

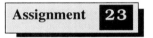 **Assignment 23** CREATING PARAGRAPHS

The extract below was originally divided into paragraphs. Rewrite it dividing it into **three** paragraphs. (Remember that you begin a new paragraph on a new line and about two inches in from the left-hand margin.)

Some people became known by the area they ruled. Other people took their names from their trades, or the place where they lived, or from some personal quality. Because few people could read or write, the same name was often spelled in different ways. Two brothers might write their names as Sharp and Sharpe. Many people took their names from the kind of work they did. Shepherd comes from sheep-herd, the man who looked after the sheep. The Norman-French word for someone who made fine clothes was *tailleur.* He became known as Taylor. Spinner and Weaver were the names of people who provided material for the *tailleur.* Coward originally meant cow-herd. Smith is the most common surname in the English-speaking countries of the world and forms of it are found in other countries. The German name Schmidt and the Italian name Ferraro both mean Smith. The craft of the smith goes back through the ages. At his forge, he shod horses and made armour and swords. Today, we have surnames such as Blacksmith and Goldsmith.

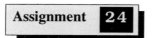

PARAGRAPHS AND PUNCTUATION

The passage below describes a young man breaking into a museum. All capitals, full stops and commas have been removed.

Rewrite the passage (i) dividing it into 5 paragraphs and (ii) putting in capitals, full stops and commas correctly.

(N.B. It is worth remembering that, when writing passages that describe exciting action writers frequently use very short paragraphs. A paragraph can consist of a single sentence.)

it was midnight an old red ford van pulled into the empty car park and stopped the driver got out he was a young man about twenty dressed in a black overall he was carrying a small rucksack he stood by the van listening across the car park some steep stone steps led up to a large building the building was in darkness except for one lighted window it was the security guard's office the young man left the van and ran silently up the steps and round to the back of the building there was a very tall jacaranda tree close to the building its scented blossom looked like a cloud of purple smoke in the moonlight the young man climbed the tree and swung across onto the roof he took a large screwdriver out of the rucksack and levered open a skylight he looked at his watch once inside once his feet touched that polished floor he would have just four minutes he put on the rucksack again and gripped the edge of the skylight he swung down into the blackness and hung there for a second or two listening he let go knowing exactly where he would land four metres below

SPELL RIGHT!

Similar sounding words (different meanings — different spellings)

Rewrite the sentences below, filling in the spaces with the correct words from the box.

ate	bawl	layer	eight	knew	new
lair	hole	ceiling	whole	ball	sealing

1. Helen _____ a _____ bowl of bran.
2. The baby started to _____ when we put her into her pram.
3. He paid _____ pounds for a _____ pair of shoes.
4. I _____ my history today.
5. There is a _____ of mud on your shoes.
6. The tiger returned to his _____ .
7. The boys dug a _____ in the sand.
8. He needs a step-ladder to paint the _____ .
9. The _____ needs to be pumped before the match.
10. Wax is sometimes used for _____ knots in string.

CROSSWORD NO. 5

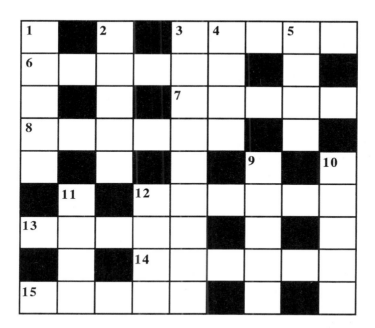

Across

3 Milk is delivered on a ___ basis.

6 A craftsman who works with clay and a wheel.

7 You would not be surprised to find a cow in one.

8 Summoned

12 Ultimately responsible for the contents of a newspaper.

13 Backbone.

14 He has _____ from Cork to Limerick in only two hours.

15 You're in one now, most likely.

Down

1 Gives foods that little extra.

2 The crooked sixpence was found on one!

3 They come to the defence.

4 A desert is a very ___ region.

5 A quiet spell or a pause in the fighting.

9 Useful for cooking and heating.

10 Quenches thirst.

11 A valuable stone.

12 Finishes.

PREFIXES

The opposite in meaning to many words can be found by putting a *prefix* in front of the words e.g. *correct* and *incorrect*; *perfect* and *imperfect*.

| Assignment | 25 | FORMING OPPOSITES |

1. Form the opposite to each of the following words by using the prefix **un-**, **in-** or **im-** and put each into a suitable sentence.

1. direct	**6.** possible	**11.** known	**16.** capable
2. movable	**7.** signed	**12.** passable	**17.** wanted
3. done	**8.** wrap	**13.** broken	**18.** roll
4. invited	**9.** easy	**14.** polite	**19.** necessary
5. caring	**10.** pleasant	**15.** proper	**20.** steady

2. Form the opposite to each of the following words by using the prefix **un-**, **in-**, **mis-**, **ir-**, **dis-** or **il-** and put each into a suitable sentence.

1. use	**6.** employment	**11.** regular	**16.** do
2. happy	**7.** certain	**12.** informed	**17.** appear
3. expensive	**8.** legal	**13.** cover	**18.** decided
4. accurate	**9.** convenient	**14.** honest	**19.** selfish
5. correct	**10.** respect	**15.** skilled	**20.** helpful

DIALOGUE

Note how conversations are set out in the short stories in this book. When a passage gives us the exact words spoken by characters in a story it is called **dialogue**.

Quotation marks are used to show where the words spoken by a character begin and end.

Example 1.

"I have lost my pen!" said David.

Example 2.

"When is the next bus due?" the lady asked.

Example 3.

'Pat, I want you to do a message,' said his mother.

Example 4.

"Did you bring some lunch?"
the teacher asked Nuala.

- Note in the examples above that two types of quotation marks may be used:
  double " _____ "
  single ' _____ '

In novels and short stories you will find examples of both types. However, it is recommended that you use double quotation marks in your own writing as they will stand out more clearly.

- Note that **question marks (?)** and **exclamation marks (!)** go inside the quotation marks.
  "What time is it?" asked Anne.
  "It is after nine!" exclaimed Jim.

- An exclamation mark placed after a piece of dialogue shows that the words were spoken in a loud or excited manner. This could show anger, fear, surprise, joy, danger, disappointment or a warning.

- These are general guidelines on writing dialogue. You will find they vary a little in some books. By noting carefully how dialogue is laid out in novels and short stories you should quickly master the technique of writing dialogue.

Assignment **26** W**RITING** D**IALOGUE USING** Q**UOTATION** M**ARKS - 1**

Write out these sentences in your usual handwriting, inserting quotation marks, capital letters and other necessary punctuation marks (full stops, question marks, apostrophes etc.) in their proper places.

In all these sentences the spoken words are at the start of the sentence. Study the example carefully before beginning.

> **Example:**
>   i think that peter will be picked for the team said jane
>
> **Answer:**
>   "I think that Peter will be picked for the team," said Jane.

(a)   today is my mother's birthday she said
(b)   will this rain ever stop sighed the farmer
(c)   you need a proper haircut said peters mother angrily
(d)   i'm telling my mammy on you wailed denis
(e)   i bought this in london said keith
(f)   follow me please said the nurse
(g)   this is a new type of engine announced the salesman
(h)   are you being looked after asked the assistant
(i)   maybe mother said when i asked her if we were going to the cinema
(j)   dont ever try that again snapped the teacher after he saw me melting my pen with a lighter
(k)   where were you all morning enquired the manager when i arrived

Assignment **27** W**RITING** D**IALOGUE USING** Q**UOTATION** M**ARKS - 2**

Write out each of the following passages in your usual handwriting inserting quotation marks, capital letters and other necessary punctuation marks (full stops, question marks, apostrophes etc.) in their proper places.

In all these sentences the spoken words occur at the end.
Study the example carefully before beginning.

> **Example:**
>   he went up to the policeman and said i think im lost
>
> **Answer:**
>   He went up to the policeman and said, "I think I'm lost."

(a)   he looked at the boy and said you broke my window
(b)   ann walked into the shop and asked how much are the brown boots in the window
(c)   father often says every cloud has a silver lining
(d)   she thought for a few moments and then remarked i have decided to travel after all
(e)   the teacher came into the room and shouted who's responsible for this
(f)   andrew replied i think you may be right
(g)   i said is there a museum in this town
(h)   whenever i meet the principal on the corridor she always says why are you wandering about miss collins
(i)   my dad often says when i was your age things were different
(j)   i asked him if he was sorry and he answered not really

Assignment **28** WRITING DIALOGUE USING QUOTATION MARKS - 3

Write out each of the following passages in your usual handwriting inserting quotation marks, capital letters and other necessary punctuation marks (full stops, question marks, apostrophes etc.) in their proper places.

The spoken words are interrupted.
Study the example carefully before beginning.

Example:
>   we leave the school at nine sharp said the teacher those who are not here by nine will be left behind

Answer:
>   "We leave the school at nine sharp," said the teacher. "Those who are not here by nine will be left behind."

(a)   meet at the pitch ten minutes before the game said the captain ive a few words to say to you
(b)   well andrea said the teacher i don't believe that the dog ate your maths copy
(c)   put out the dog said david's mother he is not to be fed in the house
(d)   if i see peter in town i'll tell him the good news said fiona if not i'll ring him tonight
(e)   i am not worried about myself said the politican i am more worried about my family

(f)   close the gates after you warned the farmer the cattle might wander on to the road if you don't

(g)   this is my garden said the man my grandfather planted the apple trees over twenty years ago

(h)   i was not asleep replied Paul the thunder has kept me awake

(i)   im shocked he answered i was talking to him only yesterday is he badly injured

(j)   are you angry Una asked i did not mean to hurt your feelings

Assignment 29   LAYING OUT DIALOGUE FOR TWO SPEAKERS

Write out each of the following passages in your usual handwriting inserting quotation marks, capital letters and other necessary punctuation marks (full stops, question marks, apostrophes etc.) in their proper places. There are two speakers in passages **A**, **B**, and **C** but there are more than two speakers in passage **D**.

Remember:

1.   Follow the layout of each passage by beginning a new paragraph for each speaker.

2.   Some paragraphs may consist entirely of dialogue - i.e. it is not necessary to identify the speaker after each piece of dialogue, particularly when only two people are talking. The paragraphs in each passage have been numbered to help you.

3.   Quotation marks should enclose spoken words only. Read the passage carefully a number of times to work out who exactly is speaking and what words they actually speak.

Passage A

1.   i was thinking about this old dog the other day helen its not only that hes just about blind but did you notice that when we drove up today he didnt even bark said henry

2.   its a fact he didnt henry replied helen

3.   no not much good even as a watch-dog now

4.   poor old fellow its a pity isnt it

5.   and no good for hunting either and he eats a lot i suppose

6.   about as much as he ever did henry

7.   the plain fact is the old dog isnt worth his keep any more its time we got rid of him

8.   its always so hard to know how to get rid of a dog henry said helen sadly

Passage B

1. Mavis and i entered a small dark clearing in the forest totally hidden from the road
2. well wheres the surprise
3. right here i said and i threw her books on the ground
4. what did you do that for mavis asked
5. i got tired of carrying them i said
6. is this what you brought me all the way down here for well you just pick em up again
7. make me l said quietly
8. what the shock on her face was almost comical
9. you heard make me

Passage C

1. back in the changing-room james collins started going on about my football kit he egged everybody else on
2. listen collins this jersey belonged to my uncle and he scored hundreds of goals i said
3. collins just laughed
4. your uncle - your auntie more like you look like a big girl
5. everybody laughed
6. listen collins - you dont know who my uncle is
7. i was sick of james collins i was sick of his bullying and his shouting and i was sick of him being a good footballer
8. my uncle is roy keane i blurted out
9. it was a lie of course to make matters worse roy keane was coming to the town on the following day to open a new shopping centre

Passage D

1. my pimple was just above the knee as ive said - easy to fiddle with while i was watching television
2. i do wish youd stop picking at that david my mother prodded my shoulder as she passed youll get them all over your hands if youre not careful
3. what do you mean i asked
4. warts david
5. warts i havent got warts
6. only one at the moment dear but if you go on messing it about itll get bigger and spread
7. like mushrooms man my elder brother said with a laugh you should only pick them first thing in the morning after the rain
8. dont be disgusting jim my mother said

CROSSWORD NO. 6

Across

1 Favourite season for most.
6 Prayers' last word!
7 Cinderella's sisters.
9 Should not be confused with sea.
10 A type of fishing boat.
13 Sounds like Dep-oh! A base or storehouse.
16 Night bird.
18 She made five famous.
19 Look over something quickly.
20 Tom _____ too much time listening to the radio.

Down

2 To encourage.
3 A good month for trout fishing.
4 Where jars of spice are stored.
5 Found on trees.
7 When my grandad was a boy he _____ to walk barefoot to school.
8 Jump.
10 A command for a dog!
11 A strong metal.
12 Often necessary to do so to put a letter in an envelope.
14 Apples 10p ____ . Twelve for £1.00!
15 Possesses.
17 Uncontrolled, not tame.
18 Essential for seeing.

PICKING THE RIGHT ONE

Who's: A short way of saying "who is . . .".
The apostrophe is in place of the letter "i".
Examples: Who's going to the match? Look who's running towards us. Do you know who's playing in goal?

Whose: Indicates or questions ownership.
Examples: Whose coat is this? I don't know whose pen it is.

To: Opposite of "from"
Examples: I walk to school. I am going to my piano lesson. I am going to my home.

Too: Use instead of "also" or "more than required".
Examples: Too big, too young etc. Will you come too? Too many drivers speed on our roads. My shoes are too small.

Two: The number.
Examples: The lion had two cubs. David will be back in two or three minutes.

Theirs: Indicates ownership.
Examples: That cat is theirs. Is the red car theirs?

There's: A short way of saying "There is . . .".
Examples: There's a big crowd gathering. There's little point in going any further.

We're: A short way of saying "We are . . ."
Examples: We're late again. When we're early the teacher is surprised.

Were: Past tense of "are".
Examples: Were you at the cinema last night? Where were you? The dogs were barking all night.

Where: To question or indicate a place.
Examples: Where is the book? Do you know where I left my pen?

Assignment **30**

Fill in the blanks in the sentences that follow using the correct words from the box below.

1. _____ making that noise?
2. The boy, _____ dog died, was crying.
3. _____ is this coat?
4. That house is _____ .
5. _____ a small dog in the garden.
6. We travelled to _____ the accident happened.
7. _____ is the schoolbag?
8. We _____ in France on holidays.
9. He spends _____ much time reading.
10. The dogs _____ barking.
11. _____ all going to see the film.
12. If _____ going to Cork, we should leave before six o'clock.
13. _____ girls from our school won prizes.
14. The dog was _____ big for the kennel.
15. Mr. and Mrs. O'Neill are going to Spain and their children are going _____ .
16. Do you know _____ bike that is?
17. _____ house is the one with the red door?
18. If you want _____ play the piano well, you must be prepared _____ practise hard.
19. The lady _____ smiling won the Lotto.
20. Thunder storms do not occur _____ often in Ireland.
21. The band had _____ records in the charts.
22. We decided _____ walk _____ town.
23. The Byrnes live there and the field opposite the house is _____ .
24. _____ no point crying over spilt milk.
25. Where _____ you this morning?
26. Do you know _____ the key is kept?
27. _____ travelling by coach.
28. _____ is the pencil case?
29. Do you know _____ the referee?
30. _____ all very happy.

Who's	Whose	Too	Two	There's
Theirs	We're	Were	Where	To

PET FILE - SIX

Pets' Menu

(1) _____ if you can, what sort of food the pet you think you want is going to eat. Although all animals have their food preferences, (2) _____ are much choosier than (3) _____ . It is far (4) _____ to keep an animal which will feed on a lot of different things than one which will eat only one thing, for if you run out of it, your pet would (5) _____ .

Food bills for pets can become quite a <u>burden</u>, so you must remember this when you are trying to (6) _____ what sort of pet to keep. You (7) _____ feed some pets quite largely on table scraps, but you should always check first what sort of <u>diet</u> they need. For instance, it would be useless if you and your family were <u>vegetarians</u> to expect to feed a cat on table (8) _____ , for cats and dogs must have meat in their diet and they would become (9) _____ without it.

Always give your pets their own separate food (10) _____ , otherwise you will have problems with <u>hygiene</u> and health.

Assignment 31

1. Rewrite the above piece, filling in the blank spaces with a suitable word from the box.

easier	scraps	ill	suffer	check
dishes	decide	some	can	others

2. Find out the meaning of each of the underlined words and put each one into a new sentence.

3. List three things we should remember about feeding pets.

NOUNS

brakes	radiator	
gears	spark plugs	
exhaust	camshaft	

sail	rudder	
hull	mast	
compass	deck	

scale	beat	
octave	key	
note	harmony	

All activities have their own sets of words. A mechanic understands clearly what a radiator is for, a sailor knows what a mast is and a musician is familiar with the word 'octave'.

The study of English - or any language - is an activity that involves working with words. Therefore this activity has its own set of technical terms or special words to describe different kinds of words, different groupings of words and different punctuation marks.

You have come across many already, such as: -

• Full stop	• Sentence
• Question mark	• Paragraph
• Comma	• Phrase

Here are four new terms with which you may not be familiar.

• Noun	• Verb
• Adjective	• Adverb

NOUNS:

There are three kinds of nouns.

1. Common Nouns

The name *'dog'* (i.e. the noun *'dog'*) is common to all dogs. Equally the noun *'chair'* is common to all chairs.

2. Abstract Nouns

These are also a type of common noun. *'Anger'* is a noun that names something we all understand. We cannot touch *'anger'*, yet it names something important. Examples of other abstract nouns are *honesty, love, envy, danger, kindness.*

3. Proper Nouns

As we pointed out above, the name 'dog' (or the noun 'dog') is common to all dogs.

However, the noun *'Rover'* is only common to some dogs i.e. it is the *property* of only some dogs.

Likewise, the word 'boy' is a name that refers to all boys. However, *'Daniel'* is a word that names only certain boys - i.e. it is the *property* of only some boys.

'Daniel' and *'Rover'* are examples of *proper* nouns. Proper nouns are always spelt with a capital letter.

Assignment 32   **IDENTIFYING NOUNS**

1. What type of noun is each of the following?

• Animal	• Tree	• Computer
• Evil	• Henry	• Orange
• Football	• Pete	• Africa
• Happiness	• Dave	• River
• Sorrow	• Typewriter	• Ashtray
• Fear	• Pencil	• Fire
• Dundalk	• Field	• Galway

2. In the case of each of the proper nouns below, give the equivalent common noun e.g.   Liffey - river

    (Some may have *more than one* answer)

• Liffey	• Jane	• O'Brien
• Newbridge	• David	• Mentor Ltd.
• Lough Neagh	• John	• Murphy
• Dublin Bay	• Blackie	• Kelloggs Cornflakes
• Cork Harbour	• Opel	• Nissan

3. In the case of each of the common nouns below, supply an equivalent proper noun: -

• city	• bicycle	• politician
• village	• football team	• television
• street	• river	• province
• writer	• ocean	• horse
• musician	• country	• county
• actor	• zoo	• park

SPELL RIGHT!

Rewrite the sentences below, filling in the spaces with the correct words from the box.

principals	steak	sale	scene
rose	wringing	sail	stake
seen	principles	rows	ringing

1. He is a scoundrel with absolutely no _____ .
2. Jason's clothes were _____ wet.
3. The pupils sitting in the first two _____ could see as far as the gate.
4. The _____ of the three school in the town meet regularly.
5. Dingle Bay at sunset is a beautiful _____ .
6. The yacht's _____ is damaged.
7. The church bell is _____ .
8. David replaced the_____ when the fence was broken.
9. The sun _____ this morning at six o'clock.
10. My dad bought a new car and our old one is for _____ .
11. The robbers were _____ entering the building.
12. The _____ from the new butcher's shop was very tasty.

CROSSWORD No. 7

Across

1 A type of corn.

6 Below the mouth.

7 Mix ingredients as they cook.

8 Popular citrus fruit.

11 Centre of a wheel.

13 Snakelike fish.

14 Builds up.

16 For walking on.

17 Ball used in hockey.

18 Heavenly messenger.

Down

2 Famous king of the Round Table

3 Nil.

4 The sun will _____.

5 You do this to pray.

9 Not a popular rodent.

10 Soft and kind.

11 Assists.

12 Place to sit in a park.

15 To revolve rapidly.

ADJECTIVES

A word which gives us more information about a noun (or a pronoun) is called an **adjective.**

In the sentences below the words in bold print are adjectives.

1. The *small* boy got a *new* ball.

2. The *red* car won the *last* race.

3. *That* film is a *good* comedy.

4. The *last* song was an *old* favourite.

5. John is a *better* player than Peter.

6. The *red-haired* man was a *nervous* wreck.

7. The *old* house had *many broken* windows.

8. The *Irish* team enjoyed a *splendid* victory.

9. When the *final* whistle blew, the *large* crowd cheered.

10. The *American* ship was an *enormous* battleship.

 **Assignment 33** | MATCHING ADJECTIVES

Each of the adjectives in the left-hand box has a synonym in the right-hand box. A **synonym** is a word which has the same - or almost the same - meaning as another. For example *'to hide'* and *'to conceal'* are synonyms.

1. In your copy, list all the words in the left-hand box in alphabetical order and leave a space after each word.
2. When you have this completed find the synonym in the right-hand box for each of the words in your list and write them in the spaces that you left. Try to complete the task without using a dictionary. The first word is *awkward* and its synonym is *clumsy.*

A

awkward	clumsy
accurate	short
aggressive	friendly
cautious	plentiful
abrupt	yearly
anonymous	quarrelsome
amiable	sufficient
brief	careful
avaricious	sudden
annual	haughty
ample	nameless
arrogant	correct
abundant	greedy

B

indolent	outstanding
courteous	horrible
drowsy	active
insane	shining
celebrated	brave
grave	famous
eminent	sleepy
infuriated	lazy
industrious	polite
gleaming	angry
energetic	mad
gruesome	serious
courageous	busy

C

obstinate	quick
invincible	careful
jovial	jolly
perpetual	weak
intoxicated	unending
motionless	high
lofty	stubborn
peculiar	dumb
pathetic	still
meticulous	sad
melancholy	odd
mute	pitiful
prominent	priceless
invaluable	outstanding
puny	unbeatable
prompt	drunk

D

reluctant	enough
sufficient	empty
robust	slim
valiant	waste
rare	isolated
secluded	strong
wealthy	calm
squander	rich
wretched	unwilling
vacant	miserable
sly	still
slender	rash
reckless	cunning
stationary	rotten
peaceful	brave
putrid	scarce

| Assignment | 34 | ADJECTIVE ANAGRAMS |

1. Each of the following adjectives below are followed by a number of synonyms - but the letters have been mixed up. For example *ugeh* becomes *huge* which is a synonym of *large*. Unscramble each of the jumbled words.

large	ugeh	menseim	ganticig
happy	huefcler	dencenott	htelidegd
sad	doartheewnd	jeteedcd	oworfulsr
fast	seydpe	piadr	twifs
dull	slislest	lcolesours	naitf
funny	cocialm	gaminus	ilusahori
new	fhesr	naligori	nelov
weak	gilfrae	faril	lictedea
dirty	fitlyh	oluf	elploutd
nice	ligdehfult	nidk	aplentas

2. (a) Form one adjective from each of the nouns below by adding one of the following endings (*suffixes*). In some cases you will have to make some spelling changes. Use your dictionary to check your answers.

- y	- ful	- ish	- ly
- like	- less	- ent	- ic
- ous	- ed	- ible	- able

(b) Now put each adjective into a sentence.

• noise	• saint	• doubt	• heaven
• danger	• care	• hero	• scenery
• snob	• wood	• life	• magnet
• God	• glory	• sun	• plenty
• paint	• volcano	• style	• mud
• beauty	• Ireland	• Britain	• Denmark
• ice	• pass	• apology	• fool
• leaf	• value	• violence	• drama
• talent	• Spain	• sense	• cloud

PET FILE - SEVEN

Guinea Pigs

Guinea pigs - sometimes known as cavies - are perhaps the best of all animals for your first pet, as they are gentle and undemanding, yet have a lot of character, which makes them interesting to keep.

The breeds fall into three main groups depending on coat type. The one which is probably the best for a (1) _____ pet is called the *Smooth-haired or English Cavey*. As its name suggests this cavey has a close coat which is either single or <u>multicoloured</u>. The coat is easily (2) _____ with a soft brush, such as the type used for very young children.

A second breed is called the *Abyssinian*. In these animals, the fur is coarse and in various parts of the body grows "against the grain", forming upstanding <u>tufts</u> called rosettes. The Abyssinian's coat is easy to keep in good (3) _____ . A toothbrush does the job very well since a stiff bristle is needed.

The third type of cavey is the *Peruvian Guinea Pig* where the fur grows enormously long. This sort of coat requires a lot of (4) _____ and effort to keep it in good condition, and, therefore, Peruvian Guinea Pigs are not really suitable as household pets.

Guinea Pigs are <u>sociable</u> animals so, if (5) _____ , you should keep more than one. If you do not wish them to breed, two or more females will live happily side by side. Otherwise, you may put a male to (6) _____ with one or several females. On no account, however, put two males with a female for the mild guinea pigs will suddenly change, and will (7) _____ to the death for sole possession of the female.

You may keep guinea pigs in a cage (8) _____ , but it is better to give them more room in a shed or outhouse. In summer take their cage outside and run on the grass in the garden, although you must have the cage raised slightly from the (9) _____ . They should have plenty of sweet hay for bedding. This also forms an important part of their diet. Cavies spend much of their time eating and hay gives them the bulk that they need.

As well as this they should have a cereal mixture which you can get from your (10) ____ _____ and, as a treat, brown bread squeezed out in a

(11) _____ milk. Many garden weeds make a good addition to a guinea pig's (12) _____ , but you must be careful that they have not been sprayed with weedkiller or <u>insecticide</u>, and that you know which plants you are (13) _____ to them. Guinea pigs, unlike most other animals, cannot make their own vitamin C, so you must make (14) _____ that they have food which is rich in it. An evening meal of greens will supply the vitamin C and carrot and raw beetroot will provide vitamin A.

Assignment 35

1. Find suitable words to fill each of the spaces in the passage above. Now compare your answer with the original words in the box below. (The letters have been mixed-up but they are in the correct order.)

1. ISFRT	2. ROEGOMD	3. NDIOCOTIN
4. IETM	5. LOIPSSBE	6. IVLE
7. IGHFT	8. DRINOOS	9. UNGORD
10. TEP HOPS	11. TLLITE	12. IEDT
13. EDIFEGN	14. URSE	

2. Find out the meanings of the underlined words and put each one into a new sentence.

3. Name three guinea pig breeds and write a sentence about each breed.

4. What must you avoid if you wish to keep more than two guinea pigs?

5. Imagine that your friend has agreed to mind your guinea pigs while you are on holidays. Write out a set of guidelines to help him/her do so.

6. Rewrite each of the following anagrams of animals' names.

ETOTR	OSMUE	RADBGE
QIERSURL	EDGHOGEH	TOSTA
BABRIT	EAVBRE	KMNI

CROSSWORD NO. 8

Across

3 Worth three points in Gaelic.
5 A policeman's nickname.
7 Make a knot.
8 Among; in the middle of . . .
9 A vessel driven by steam.
13 German christian name (OT . .)
14 To make a mistake.
16 One is one!
17 Flies over buildings - not a bird, not a plane . . .

Down

1 Not cold by any means!
2 An intelligent creature of the jungle.
3 It makes the countryside green.
4 When somebody charged with a crime can prove that he was elsewhere, then he has an A _ _ _ _ .
6 Used for smoking plug tobacco.
10 This is what you get when everything is added up.
11 "A _____ those girls and boys, are some very hardworking students."
12 Plant used for medicine or for flavouring food.
14 Strange bird (E _ _).
15 Dangerous colour.

VERBS

Words that describe actions or the state or condition of a person, place or thing are called verbs.

- The dog *bit* the postman.
- The car *crashed* into the wall.

- The man *shouted* at the referee.
- The swimmer *dived* into the pool.

The words in italics in the above sentences are all verbs. They describe different kinds of action.

Sometimes two words are needed to form a verb.

- The day *became sunny.*
- The people *were happy.*
- The boy *was late.*

- The book *was on the table.*
- The girl *felt frightened.*

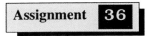 **IDENTIFYING VERBS**

Pick out the verbs in each of the following passages.

1. It was morning. Jane and Michael climbed the hill to the castle. The old man from the cottage had already unlocked the door, so they crept down the winding stairs and peeped round at the old bed with its carved wooden post at each corner. There they saw a man asleep! He had a small, dark beard, black hair, and ragged clothes. "A tramp!" gasped Michael, surprised.

2. The men gave a great pull. Slowly the wooden ship moved. It creaked and scraped, and its big square sail fluttered in the wind. With all their strength the men pulled at the ropes, dragging the ship across the strip of land, until they reached the sea on the other side. Down into the green-grey water went the ship again. Magnus laughed, for he had sailed around the island.

TENSES OF VERBS

The *tense* of a verb tells us when the action took place. The three most common tenses are the ***future*** *tense*, the ***present*** *tense* and the ***past*** *tense*.

The Future Tense

We *will arrive* at seven o'clock and we *will have* a light snack. Afterwards we *will meet* Peter and Brian and then we *will play* a game of squash.

The Present Tense

McCarthy *has* the ball. He *passes* it to Donovan. Donovan *is tackled* by O'Shea. O'Shea *gets* the ball and *passes* it to Spillane. Spillane *kicks* and he *scores*.

Newspaper Headlines

Newspaper headlines are often written in the present tense even though they are about the events that have happened in the past. This gives readers an impression that the stories are happening almost as they are reading them - e.g.

'Bus Crashes into Bridge'

sounds more exciting than

'Bus Crashed into Bridge'

Assignment 37

Rewrite each of the following headlines in the present tense.
1. Trainer Caught Escaped Lion.
2. Budgie Flew from Tralee to Cork.
3. Gardaí Arrested Bank Robber.
4. Portlaoise Boy won Lotto Prize.
5. Pop Singer Told All.
6. Football Manager Lashed Out.
7. Miracle Baby Went Home.
8. O'Brien Took Control of the Company.

The Past Tense

Almost all stories are written in the past tense as they tell of events that have happened.

Assignment 38

1. Rewrite the following extracts in the past tense.

   (i) Soon everything is ready. The man holds a big bag of food under his cloak. His son carries a lantern and a bundle of pine logs. Out into the dark night they walk, past the great heaps of snow at the side of the path and over the hill at the edge of the forest. The air is full of whirling snowflakes and a bitter wind blows.

   (ii) Three weeks pass. During the first week the doctor comes twice a day and the tramp tosses and turns and sleeps and wakes and understands nothing. During the second week he grows better bit by bit. He begins to wonder where he is and to ask questions about how he has come here. He says his mother is the most beautiful person he has ever seen. The children come to visit him and he tells them interesting things and wonderful stories.

2. **Sounds of Nature**

   Each of the words below is the present tense form of a verb which describes the sound made by different creatures. Change each of these verbs into the past tense and put them into sentences, e.g. *"Bark"* becomes *'barked'*; *The dog barked at the postman.*

hum	bellow	bark	purr	croak
cackle	bleat	roar	squeak	hoot
squeal	grunt	chirp	hiss	howl

3. **Everyday Sounds**

   Each of the words below is the present tense form of a verb which describes the sound which certain objects make. Make up sentences using the following form of the words '. . . was _ _ _ _ ing' e.g. *The clock was ticking loudly in the hall.*

clang	tinkle	rattle	tick	click
clatter	rattle	slam	splutter	creak
rustle	buzz	wail	rumble	drone

245

CROSSWORD NO. 9

Across

1 Don't say 'growed', say _____ .

7 Working clothes.

8 A trainee officer.

10 The early bird catches the _____.

12 Behaving like another character.

14 To trim a shrub or cut off.

15 For the want of a nail the _____ was lost.

17 Small mountains.

19 I will en_ _ _ _ _ the winner's name on the trophy.

20 The poacher _____ the traps nightly.

Down

2 A fishing implement.

3 Flat (surface).

4 Nobody likes a _____ day.

5 A Christmas hymn.

6 Round and fat.

9 The curved support of a bridge or doorway.

11 List of names.

12 Posed a question.

13 "When the going gets rough, the _____ get going."

16 Place where honey is made.

17 She _ _ _ no money.

18 To allow or give permission.

PET FILE - EIGHT

Making a Bird Table

Wild birds can be attracted by putting out (1) _____ for them on a bird table. You can (2) _____ these, but if you have woodwork classes at (3)_____, you (4) _____ make one. The best kind has a cover and a tray with drain holes in it, so that if it rains the food will not get (5) _____ . It should be on a firm stand placed in the open, which is too high for (6)_____ or (7) _____ to reach the food.

Some birds will be (8) _____ by almost any kind of food (even white bread crusts, (9) _____ these are not very good for them), but if you want to see as many different (10) _____ of birds as possible you should put out a variety of different things to eat.

Many sorts of table (11) _____ are good food for birds. They include bacon rinds, preferably cooked, and small pieces of fat (12) _____ or bones with a bit of meat on, which can be (13) _____ from the bird table. Birds which eat (14) _____ will find this a very attractive addition to their diet and you can watch them from some kind of hide or through (15) _____ from your house.

Brown bread or perhaps partly stale white bread, biscuit or cake scraps or crumbs will be (16) _____ by the seed-eating birds such as the finches.

Even if you live in a flat, you can make a tray bird table to (17) _____ to a window sill and many wild birds may (18) _____ it, though you may live several floors above the ground.

(19) _____ way of attracting birds is to put up nest boxes. The best ones are for titmice and other hole-nesting birds, but all sorts of birds will use <u>artificial</u> nest boxes provided that they are the right shape and (20) _____ . It is a lot of fun watching a (21) _____ of birds bring up their (22) _____ and once they have reached this stage, you have very little to do, for most <u>fledglings</u> are fed chiefly on insects, which the parents will find for them. Baby birds grow very (23) _____ and, in some cases, they outgrow the nest before they are really ready to leave it. Usually they (24)_____ in thick bushy places and the parent birds continue to feed and (25) _____ for them but sometimes they do come to the ground.

Assignment 39

1. Fill in the blank spaces with suitable words from the box.

meat	family	hung	pair	insects
soggy	binoculars	cats	attracted	food
although	sorts	buy	another	size
fast	eaten	perch	care	visit
scraps	school	fit	could	dogs

2. Check the meanings of the underlined words and put them into suitable sentences.

3. Write a set of accurate instructions on how to keep a bird-table.

SPELL RIGHT!

Rewrite the sentences below, filling in the spaces with the correct words from the box.

there	tide	peal	flour
tear	their	pail	flower
pale	tied	they're	peel

1. _____ all running away.
2. It is easy to slip on a banana _____ .
3. He _____ his laces.
4. The lady looked very _____ .
5. The boys ran over _____ .
6. The _____ is due in at eight.
7. I heard the bells _____ .
8. _____ is the main ingredient of bread.
9. Don't _____ up the paper.
10. _____ dog is called Blackie.
11. I'll fetch a _____ of water.
12. He picked a _____ in the garden.

ADVERBS

Adverbs tell us more about verbs. They frequently end with the letters - *ly*.
  e.g. • The train passed *slowly.*
        • The dog barked *loudly.*
        • The robber *savagely* ordered the staff to lie on the floor.

Adverbs can also tell us more about adjectives.
  e.g. • The film was *exceedingly* long.
        • The drummer is *exceptionally* good.

Adverbs can also tell us more about other adverbs.
        • He drove *incredibly* quickly.
        • He spoke *very* loudly.
        • She sang *quite* well.

Assignment 40   **BUILDING ADVERBS**

(a) Change the following phrases to single adverbs e.g. *with kindness* becomes
    - *kindly.*
    In the case of some of the adverbs you may need to use one of the
    following *prefixes:* **un -   im -   dis -   in -**.

(b) Now put each one into a suitable sentence.

1. with kindness	**2.** with caution	**3.** with care
4. with speed	**5.** with happiness	**6.** with precision
7. with humour	**8.** with triumph	**9.** with sense
10. with skill	**11.** without happiness	**12.** without truth
13. without accuracy	**14.** without perfection	**15.** without respect
16. with envy	**17.** just a little	**18.** at once
19. without patience	**20.** without wisdom	

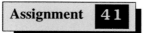

ADJECTIVES TO ADVERBS

(a) Change each of the following adjectives to an adverb.

1. bitter	**2.** sensible	**3.** patient	**4.** angry
5. responsible	**6.** scornful	**7.** graceful	**8.** dutiful
9. tidy	**10.** honest	**11.** careful	**12.** new
13. hopeful	**14.** cautious	**15.** frequent	**16.** quick
17. improper	**18.** feeble	**19.** kind	**20.** rapid
21. close	**22.** frantic	**23.** cool	**24.** brave
25. busy	**26.** regular	**27.** secret	**28.** harsh

(b) Put each one into a suitable sentence e.g. *bitter - bitterly.*

SPELL RIGHT!

Rewrite the sentences below, filling in the spaces with the correct words from the box.

praise	currant	checks	layer	cruise	cereal
crews	lair	cheques	prays	serial	current

1. "Glenroe" is a popular _____ .
2. The tiger has returned to his _____ .
3. The _____ from the two ships decided to have a football match.
4. Tom never eats _____ for breakfast.
5. My dad regularly _____ the brakes of his car.
6. The old lady _____ in the church every evening.
7. In winter, the _____ in the river is very powerful.
8. The boots were covered with a _____ of mud.
9. It is important to _____ and encourage young people.
10. Mrs. Donovan, who won the Lotto, is going on a world _____ .
11. Catherine complained that there was not a single _____ in her bun.
12. The bank manager put the _____ in the safe.

CROSSWORD No. 10

Across

5 Mended.

6 Unused.

7 Pick.

9 Perform on stage.

11 Spoil (M _ _).

12 Speckled bird.

13 Big, well-known London timekeeper.

14 Copied.

Down

1 Not many.

2 Man with a yacht.

3 Witch transport.

4 Mathematical snake.

5 Stretch out.

8 Rescued.

9 Top of the house.

10 Teach an animal.

13 He was prepared to _____ , steal or borrow to get a ticket.

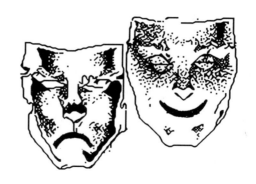

III - DRAMA

INTRODUCTION

Drama is written to be performed - either on stage or on screen. When we see a play on stage or on screen, the actors, their costumes, the scenery, the props and special effects all help to bring the play to life. However, it is not necessary to see a production of a play to enjoy it. Reading plays can be enjoyable. Pay attention to the dialogue and stage directions and your imagination will bring the events of the play to life.

Costume is the word used to describe the clothes a particular character wears. The costume of a character in a play helps the audience to understand the kind of person that the character is. The costumes play an important part in a play. They make it immediately clear who each character is - a nurse, a doctor, a policeman, a soildier etc. All can be identified immediately by their costume. Ordinary clothes can even tell something about a character such as whether that character is rich or poor.

Scenery, or set, is a word that describes the painted backdrops and other objects on the stage which show the audience where the action of the play takes place. It can be elaborate and detailed or very basic. The set in *The Coming of the Kings* does not change throughout the play.

Props (short for 'properties') is the term given to items which the actors will need to use during a performance, i.e. a telephone, a gun, a tray, etc.

Special effects: Many playwrights make use of lighting and sound effects. Lights can be used to mark the change from day to night or from night to dawn. Effects such as snow falling or lightning can also be achieved using lights. In the past, sound effects all had to be created backstage. The sound of galloping horses was created with coconut shells and the sound of thunder by sheets of tin foil. However, since the advent of recorded sound, an endless supply of realistic sound effects are available.

LAYING OUT DRAMA

In plays, dialogue is laid out very differently from the way it is laid out in novels and stories. The main difference is that quotation marks are not used in plays to mark off dialogue. Note also how stage directions are in brackets and the names of the speakers appear on the left-hand margin.

The following examples show the difference in layout between novels and plays.

Layout used in Novels

"What's the matter, Karen? Do you not feel well?" Miss O'Neill asked in a gentle voice.
 Karen began to sob.
   "I've lost my money, Miss" she replied.

Layout used in Drama

| Miss O'Neill: *(gently)* | What's the matter Karen? Do you not feel well? |
| Karen: *(sobbing)* | I've lost my money, Miss. |

FAWLTY TOWERS

by
John Cleese/Connie Booth

INTRODUCTION

Here are three short extracts from one of the most popular television comedy series ever - *Fawlty Towers*. The series is unusual in that it was written by the actors John Cleese and Connie Booth, who both play leading roles in the series.

John Cleese talks about Basil

Speaking of the character, *Basil Fawlty*, whom he plays, John Cleese commented:

"... then I became Basil Fawlty. Now I'm a bad-tempered, angry man, who insults people and hits small foreigners. Whatever I do next, people will characterise me as that. And that's perfectly fair. That's how they see me. They don't have dinner with me every night, so they have to characterise me. But what IS funny about Basil is that he's such an awful man ... record-breaking awful ... and people love him ... they feel warm to him. They wouldn't, if they met him! ... "

Note how the stage directions, the characters names and the dialogue are laid out in the following extracts. All twelve episodes of *Fawlty Towers* are available on video.

Extract 1: *Basil changes his attitude towards a guest ...*

*(**Basil** hurries bad-temperedly into the lobby. **Melbury** is standing there.)*

Basil: Yes, yes, well, yes?

Melbury: ... Er, well, I was wondering if you could offer me accommodation for a few nights?

Basil: *(very cross)* Well, have you booked?

Melbury: ... I'm sorry?

Basil: Have you booked, have you booked?

Melbury: No.

Basil: *(to himself)* Oh dear!

Melbury: Why, are you full?

Basil: Oh, we're not full ... we're not <u>full</u> ... of course we're not <u>full</u>!!

Melbury: I'd like, er ...

Basil: One moment, one moment, please ... yes?

Melbury: A single room with a ...

Basil: Your **name**, please, could I have your name?

Melbury: Melbury.

*The phone rings; **Basil** picks it up.*

Basil: *(to **Melbury**)* One second please. *(to phone)* Hello? ... Ah, yes, Mr O'Reilly, well it's perfectly simple. When I asked you to build me a wall I was rather hoping that instead of just dumping the bricks in a pile you might have found time to cement them together ... you know, one on top of another, in the traditional fashion. *(to **Melbury**, testily)* Could you fill it in, please? *(to phone)* Oh, splendid! Ah, yes, but <u>when</u>, Mr O'Reilly? *(to **Melbury**, who is having difficulty with the register)* there - there!! *(to phone)* Yes, but when? Yes, yes ... ah! ... the flu! *(to **Melbury**)* <u>Both</u> names, please. *(to phone)* Yes, I should have guessed, Mr O'Reilly, that and the potato famine I suppose ...

Melbury: I beg your pardon?

Basil: Would you put both your names, please? ... *(to phone)* Well, will you give me a date ?

Melbury: Er ... I only use one.

Basil: *(with a withering look)* You don't have a first name?

Melbury: No, I am <u>Lord</u> Melbury, so I simply sign myself 'Melbury'.
There is a long, long pause.

Mr Leeman: The continental.

Basil: You wouldn't care for kippers?

Mr Leeman: Oh … fine, kippers, yes, thank you.

Basil departs resignedly.

Sybil: Toast, butter, marmalade …

Mr Leeman: Yes, thank you.

Sybil: Tea or coffee?

Mr Leeman: *(not feeling at all well)* Yes, er … tea, thank you.

Sybil: A newspaper?

Mr Leeman: Er … *Telegraph.*

Sybil: Thank you … Good night.

Mr Leeman starts to move off: *Sybil* goes into the office; *Basil* comes back in.

Basil: Rosewood, mahogany, teak?

Mr Leeman: … I beg your pardon?

Basil: What would you like your breakfast tray made out of?

Mr Leeman: I don't really mind.

Basil: Are you sure? Fine, well you go along and have a really good night's sleep then - I'm hoping to get a couple of hours later on myself … *(shouting after Mr Leeman as he goes up the stairs)* but I'll be up in good time to serve you your breakfast in bed. *(Leeman has now gone)* If you can remember to sleep with your mouth open you won't even have to wake up. I'll just drop in small pieces of lightly buttered kipper when you're breathing in the right direction, if that doesn't put you out. *(imitates Sybil)* Basil! *(slaps his own wrist).*

? Questions and Assignments

1. Imagine that Manuel discovers Mr. Leeman dead in bed on the following morning. He rushes down to break the news to Basil. Write the dialogue that you imagine would take place between Basil and Manuel.

2. Basil goes to investigate and finds that Manuel was telling the truth. Write the dialogue that you imagine would then take place between Basil and Sybil.

THE COMING OF THE KINGS
by
Ted Hughes

INTRODUCTION

Acting, like storytelling, is as old as mankind. Although we don't know for certain, it is likely that stone-age people acted out scenes from, perhaps, a hunt or a battle to entertain each other around a fire at nightfall.

In Europe, around one thousand years ago, priests and nuns acted out scenes from the life of Christ as part of church services. Sometimes these scenes were performed in market-places and the townsfolk also took part. These early plays were called miracle plays and were put on to mark major religious feasts such as Christmas and Easter.

The people of the town - all amateur actors - enjoyed acting in these plays and took great pride in giving a good performance. The first professional actors did not appear until around four hundred years ago in Britain. Today some professional film actors are very well known and earn very large amounts of money.

The tradition of amateur drama is still very much alive today. Most towns in Ireland have amateur drama groups where local people enjoy performing in plays. Plays are also staged by pupils and teachers in many schools.

Often one of the highlights of the school year is the Christmas concert. Frequently a *nativity play* - a play depicting the events surrounding the birth of Jesus - is produced as part of the concert.

The Coming of the Kings is a nativity play. It is like the miracle plays of old in many ways. Extra characters, not found in the original gospel story, are put in by the dramatist to give added interest; sometimes the characters speak in verse; the play has funny scenes as well as solemn ones and it helps us to understand, perhaps, the Christian message a little more clearly.

I

The road leads in from the right-back, towards the audience, dividing the Inn, on the left, from the tumbledown animal shed on the right. The Inn is red, with white door and window frames. Out over the door hangs a large sign: The Emperor's Head, *from which dangles a giant reproduction of a Roman Coin, with a head crudely painted on it. The cottage is black, with loose sacking over the windows and the door which, lifted aside, would reveal most of the interior:*

A cock crows.

The Fortune-teller appears, trudging down the road towards the audience. He stops, yawns, shifts his pack. At that moment, deafening commotion from the shed on the right: kicking sounds, violent bangs, and the prolonged lusty braying of a donkey. Fortune-teller drops his pack in surprise, stares at the shed in amazement. Bedroom window of the inn slams open, Innkeeper's Wife's head appears: she yells at the top of her voice.

Wife: All night long you've been at it!
When will you shut up your racket!
Shut up, you ugly brute, you!
Or I'll get my husband to shoot you.

*The donkey is silenced. Her head disappears and the window whams shut.
The **Fortune-teller** looks to and fro between the shed and the inn. He tiptoes
towards the shed, listens. An ox lows. The fortune-teller starts, listens again.*

Fortune-teller: What's that?

What did you say? *[Ox lows.]* What? Here? Today? *[Ox lows.]* That's
what I thought you said. *[Ox lows.]* Oh, my poor head! But that's
incredible! *[Cock crows.]* What's that? You say it's true? *[Dog barks.]* You
too? You too? Oh, now what shall I do!

*Donkey begins to bray and kick up a tremendous din. Inn door opens, and
out comes the **Innkeeper** in his nightcap and nightshirt, waving a thick stick.
Bedroom window opens and his **Wife**'s head sticks out.*

Wife: Batter the brute with your stick.

Till where he's thin he goes thick.

And where he's thick he goes thin.

Silence the monster's din.

I haven't had a wink all night ...

No wonder I look such a sight.

Fortune-teller: Stop! What will you do?

Innkeeper: I'll hammer the donkey black and blue

And the ox I'll hammer pink.

All night we've not had a wink

For their mooing and creaking

and braying ....

Fortune-teller: But don't you hear what they're saying?

Innkeeper: Saying? Are you right in the head?

Fortune-teller: Didn't you hear what the donkey said?

Innkeeper: Now you're a peculiar feller!

Wife: Is that that fortune-teller?

Fortune-teller: Madame, at your service.

If you've a wrinkle in your palm, I'll read it: there's health, wealth and
beauty in wrinkles, if you get the right man to read them. The more
wrinkles you have, the more there is to read for your fortune, so the more
fortune for you. That's a lucky face, lady.

Wife: I've heard of you. Wait. I'll be down.

Her head disappears.

| ? | **Questions and Assignments** |

Most of the following questions can be answered in a few sentences. Write your response to each one in complete sentences. For example, your response to Question 1 should begin ***The wife was angry with the donkey because ...*** Never begin an answer with the word 'because'!

1. Why is the wife angry with the donkey?

2. When the fortune-teller speaks for the first time it is clear that he has an unusual power. Explain this power.

3. *'No wonder I look such a sight'*. What do you think the wife means by this statement?

4. *'Are you right in the head?'* Why did the innkeeper say this to the fortune -teller?

5. Why does the wife want to meet the fortune-teller?

Innkeeper: Have you just arrived in town?

Fortune-teller: I know where the money lies.

Innkeeper: Well, this town has plenty of flies. But money? Think again. I have to scrape like a hen. I've had to sell my brother for a slave. It's so difficult here to save.

*Enter **Wife** from inn.*

Wife: Fortune-teller!

Fortune-teller: Madame!

Wife: Oh, please read my palm. What does it say, quick? Oh, I feel funny.

Fortune-teller: First, you cross my palm with money.

Wife: How much?

Fortune-teller: Let it be silver.

Innkeeper: Stop!

Wife *turns on her husband furiously, while **Fortune-teller** holds and inspects her palm.*

Wife: Have you mended my wobbly mop?
Have you nailed the carpet down?

Or flattened the nail that catches in my gown?
Or oiled the door and the kitchen pump?
What are you standing there for, you lump?

Innkeeper: Week in, week out, and never a guest,
And you give silver to this pest?

Wife: Then why did you want to keep an inn?
Think of the lady I might have been
If you'd had guts enough to launch
That pudding barrel elephant paunch
Into some trade with better …

? Questions and Assignments

6. Which of the following words describe the innkeeper and his wife - happy, lazy, greedy, contented, cruel? (You may choose more than one word.) Give reasons for your answer.

7. Is there evidence in this section that the innkeeper and his wife love and respect each other? Briefly explain your answer.

8. *'Week in, week out, and never a guest,/And you give silver to this pest?'*. Explain what the innkeeper means by these lines.

Fortune-teller: Money!
Wife: What?
Innkeeper: What's that?
Fortune-teller: I read here
That the greatest good luck in a million year
Is coming your way.
Innkeeper: What? Where? When?
Fortune-teller *[still studying the Wife's palm]*: Today.
Wife: Today?
Fortune-teller: The King of Men is going to visit your inn - today.
Innkeeper: What? What's that? What do you say?
Fortune-teller: Be prepared.
Innkeeper: A king?
Fortune-teller: Three kings.
Innkeeper: Beyond my wildest imaginings! To stay with us here?

Fortune-teller: To visit this inn.

A new age is going to begin

From what occurs at this inn today.

And you will be famous for ever.

Wife: Forever!

Innkeeper: Now who's stupid?

Now who's clever?

I bought this inn ten years ago

For this moment. What else do you know?

Fortune-teller: Prepare.

Wife: Three kings!

Innkeeper: When we've had them,

Every night after, we'll be crammed full,

We'll be on the map, the fashionable

Most famous Inn in Bethlehem.

We'll make a fortune!

Wife: *[in great excitement]*:   Get the place clean.

Some of those rooms aren't fit to be seen.

Scrub them, sweep them, quick, quick, quick, and

Get the flea-powder.

Innkeeper: Get the chickens

Out of the bath.

Wife: Get all the dogs

And their pups out of the beds and the hogs

And the hoglets out of the cupboards and scatter

Disinfectant. What's the matter?

Innkeeper *[standing almost in a trance]*:   This is the greatest day of my life!

Wife: And as usual you've to thank your wife.

Get a move on.

*They dash into the inn. Through what follows the **Wife** is throwing bundles of rags, broken chairs, picture frames, etc out of the windows.*

?   **Questions and Assignments**

9. What does the fortune-teller tell the wife?

10. Why were they happy when they heard what he forecast?

11. What clues can be found in this section of the play which indicate that it is a *nativity* play?

*Soon the **Innkeeper** re-emerges dressed and begins to carry the junk into the shed. But first:*

Fortune-teller: I told them no more than is true.
But I have not told it all.
A cloud wrote on the blue
That a world is about to fall
Out of mind and care;
Along with the rest, these two:
This penny-shoveller,
His ghost shall be trapped in the bell
Of a Grocer's till, and shall cry
Every sale with a yell
Of envious agony!
Throughout eternity
That shall be his Hell.
And his grasping wife
Who would have beaten the ass,
She shall stare eternity out
Trapped in a looking-glass!

*Exit the **Fortune-teller**.*
*Enter the **Innkeeper**, loads himself with flotsam.*

Innkeeper: The lazy dog will miss his chance
But the ambitious dog will dance
And so will I. When luck arrives
It's a ready man who thrives.
Others awake when it's flown past ...
But I'm the ready man at last.
I shall not miss it, I shall not miss it!
I'll catch it by the wings and kiss it.

***Wife** throws down a basketwork cradle from the bedroom; it hits him.*

Wife: Dump this old cradle into the shed.
Have you fixed the attic bed?
[She continues until he has flung all the rubbish into the shed and scurried back into the inn.]

Have you polished the brass door-knobs?
There are about a thousand jobs.
Have you scrubbed the table-top?
A new hinge on the cellar-drop?
Have you brought the barrels up?
Hurry up! Hurry up! Hurry up! Hurry up!

Innkeeper: Yes, yes, yes . . .

*[He is about to re-enter the inn when he stops, stares. A **Priest** in sumptuous robes enters.]*

Er — your majes — er, your Lordship — er, your honour . . .

Priest: Your Grace.

Innkeeper: Your Grace?

Priest: As you see, I'm a high priest of the temple,
My means and my spirituality are equally ample.
That is to say ... I'm a power on earth, and in heaven.
That is to say ... do you follow me? Yes?

Innkeeper: Your Grace.

He bows, he kneels, he bumps his forehead on the ground.

Priest *[pompous]***:** No need to bang your
        head so hard on the street.
It's quite enough if you kneel.
        Both knees, I repeat:
When you look at me, do you feel
        yourself quake?
That's the devil in you.
        I'm more than he can take.
You know the most evil things in this world,
        what they are?
They are troublesome new religious ideas.
        Heavens! I could swear.
I could curse the ears off an elephant,
When I think of the wickedness of people! *[He grows enraged.]*
I will not permit them to think whatever
        they want,
I want their souls, I tell you, tethered to
        my steeple.
I want them in my fold. In my power.

269

I will not let them out of my grasp. I want

    to see them cower

Under the purity of my glare

When I see them sitting so wicked there!

Oh!

Innkeeper: Yes, your Grace.

Priest: And now you know what's come to my ear?

An illegal religious festival is going to be held. Here.

Well?

Innkeeper: Your Grace, I—

Priest: The wickedness! The wickedness!

People think they can have heavenly

    happiness

Without my permission. They want to be

    able to pray

Without paying me money! Though my

    money's all taken away

By Great Herod to pay for his army.

Innkeeper: Your Grace —

Priest: Where are the vandals? Don't deny it to my face.

Innkeeper: Your Grace — I don't know what you're talking about.

Priest: You say so. Very well. I shall stay.

    I shall sit them out.

I'll stay here in your inn till I hear their revels,

Then I'll descend in the Hand of God and cast out their devils

And deliver them over to Herod who knows full well

That these new religions come from Hell.

Lead me to a room.

Innkeeper *[scrambling up]*: Your Grace.

Priest: And bring me wine.

And bring me roasted quails. I might as well dine.

Priest *follows the* ***Innkeeper*** *into the inn.*

?	**Questions and Assignments**

12. At the beginning of this section the fortune-teller speaks to us - the audience - and lets us in on a secret. What is the secret?

13. Why do you think that he described the innkeeper as a *'penny shoveller'* and the wife as a *'grasping wife'*?

14. How, according to the fortune-teller, are the innkeeper and his wife going to spend eternity?

15. At this point in the play we are waiting for certain events to happen. Our expectations are being built up. What are your expectations at this point?

16. How does the priest treat the innkeeper?

17. Why did the priest come to the inn?

18. What do you understand by the term *'an illegal religious festival'*?

19. What does the priest plan to do at the inn?

20. What information in this section tells us that the play is set around the time of the birth of Jesus?

21. Do the words 'humble' 'pious' and 'gentle' describe the priest? Give a reason for your answer.

*Enter, in a bowler, and humming 'Three Blind Mice', a **Businessman**. He studies the inn. Re-enter **Innkeeper** and **Wife**, in great excitement.*

Wife: What's he talking about?
Innkeeper: I don't know.
Wife: Illegal religious festival?
Innkeeper: He says so.
Wife: But whatever can he mean?
Innkeeper: That's it. What can he mean?
Wife: And is he paying for the wine?
Innkeeper: We'll send him the bill.

Wife: But he's a great man. He'll advertise us, he will.

I mean, just by being here. Get him his quails.

Innkeeper: I've sent. We must put on a great banquet, for if today's fails—

Wife: Don't you see? It's beginning.

Our luck's begun.

Innkeeper: O let me be wealthy for ever before today's done.

Wife: Get about it, you idiot.

She goes, he stands, calculating on his fingers the items he needs to remember, flustered and pressed.

Businessman: So this is 'The Emperor's Head'. Then this is the one.

Innkeeper *[startled]***:** Your Grace?

Businessman: What?

Innkeeper: I mean, sir, is there—

Businessman: Tell me, my good man,

I've heard there's going to be a world-famous magician

Performing an earth-shaking exhibition

Of miracles here today. Have your heard?

Innkeeper: Magician? Here? Today? Not a word.

Businessman: One of those Holy Men who walk on fire,

Tie venomous snakes in knots without any fear,

Turn a sardine into a cartload of cod,

Bring the rain down like Almighty God,

Convert a crust of bread into a whole field of barley—

One of those Holy wonders. Maybe I'm a bit early—

Innkeeper: I've heard nothing about it, sir.

Businessman: Come, come,

Some rival interest's paid you to keep mum.

Eh?

Innkeeper: Rival interest?

Businessman: Well, well, well.

Don't think I'm going to be fooled.

It's valuable—

A show like this. I sign him on, see?

Wait a minute, maybe you don't know me.

Innkeeper: I'm afraid, sir, er, I ....

Businessman: Socrates D. Conkhorse.

I'll sell anything—reasonable of course.

I don't try to sell the moon, though some would buy.

You must understand, I'm a plain honest guy.

I sell untried gladiators by tens,
Rope-sandals by millions, dwarfs with wens
By the brace. Would you like a crocodile
Or a beautiful slave-girl plus the coconut isle?
Cash down and it's yours.

Innkeeper: As a matter of fact, my sandals are a bit frayed —

Businessman: And with this miracle-worker, I'm made!
A man who can raise the dead!
That's really new!
I sign him on at forty per cent and — Phew!
It makes me sweat to think of the fortune going.
Look, five per cent for you, just for showing
Where he's lodging

Innkeeper: But I don't quite see —

Businessman: Look: ten pounds, and he'll raise your aunt or your uncle
Agree?
A hundred pounds to raise a grandad. Three
Thousand to raise a father.
There's no limit!
Don't you want to make a fortune, dammit?
Where is he? O.K. You're going to play dumb?
Well, I'll stay here in this hotel till he's come.
I'll hear him by the crowd.

Innkeeper: You can stay gladly.

Businessman: But understand I think you've served me badly.
Bring me some beer in, and I'd like some beef.

Innkeeper: Straight ahead, sir.

? **Questions and Assignments**

22. The innkeeper and his wife talk about the priest. What do they think of him?

23. Why does the businessman come to the inn?

24. *'Maybe I'm a bit early - '* Is the businessman speaking a truth here without realising it? Explain.

25. *'Some rival interest's paid you to keep mum.'* What does the businessman mean when he says this?

26. What kind of 'business' does Socrates D, Conkhorse do?

*As the **Innkeeper** and the **Businessman** enter the inn a **Police Inspector** saunters up, stops, surveys the shed and the inn, consulting his notebook. Re-enter the **Innkeeper** and his **Wife** talking together excitedly.*

Wife: It's beyond belief.

Innkeeper: We've never had such guests in our lives.

Wife: Fortune comes to the one who believes
All that the fortune-teller says.

Innkeeper: I'll have to run down into the town.
We need more food. Oh, day of days!
Hurry up and get it, you clown!

***Wife** re-enters the inn; the **Innkeeper** is about to dash off when he sees the **Police Inspector**.*

Police Inspector: The Emperor's Head, Hm! *[Consulting his book.]*
Opposite, a shed
Of god-forsaken ruinous aspect. The shed!
This must be the place. Hm! *[Shuts his book.]*
And you're the proprietor?

Innkeeper: That's right, Inspector.
Anything wrong?

Police Inspector: We haven't met before?

Innkeeper: No.

Police Inspector: Sure?

Innkeeper: Yes.

Police Inspector: What are your politics?

Innkeeper: I haven't any.

Police Inspector: Be careful.

Innkeeper: I agree with all tax.

Police Inspector: Good for you. Well, well, and who'd have thought!

Innkeeper: What's wrong, Inspector?

Police Inspector: Who's staying with you? Straight out.
Don't stop to invent a lie.

Innkeeper: Guests?

Police Inspector: Who?

Innkeeper: A high priest of the Temple. And a businessman. Just two.

Police Inspector: And what do you know about this demonstration?
Don't put on that dumbfounded, ox-like expression.
It's been brought to our notice that today
A Political Agitator is going to say his say

274

Here at 'The Emperor's Head', and threaten our state
With red-hot ideas, turbulence of passion
To shake our law and order out of fashion,
Make people discontented with their noses,
And shoot at policemen, and trample the palace roses
With peering in at the windows carrying knives.
Herod's court are in terror of their lives.
What have you to say?

Innkeeper: Me? I'm just an innkeeper.

Police Inspector: Politically, you're a dangerous sleeper.
It's men like you who let the matches catch,
Who let the fireflies of rebellion hatch.

Innkeeper: I don't know what you're talking about.

Police Inspector: Well then,
Where is the crowd assembled to hear this man?

Innkeeper: Which man?

Police Inspector: This revolutionary with his message for the people which
Is going to shake Herod and cause a hitch
In the smooth running of great Caesar's lands?
I've got to catch him. Stop wringing your hands.

Innkeeper: I just don't know what all this is about.

Police Inspector: Haven't you seen some bearded ferocious figure
With a dagger like a bread-knife only bigger,
Whispering to a dozen like himself?
He wants to topple Herod off the shelf.
I can't decide whether you're innocent
Or only bluffing.

Innkeeper: Please, Inspector, don't.
I don't know what's come over me today.
I hardly understand what people say.

Police Inspector: All right then, I'll stay here, in your pleasant inn.
And when this fellow's followers begin
To gather to hear him speak—I shall be peeping.
Today, the State's safety is in my keeping.
Show me a room.

Innkeeper: Certainly, Inspector.

Police Inspector: If this man's the disease, then I'm the doctor.
Bring me a barrel of wine and a boar's head.
I'll fix a hundred of them when I've fed.

*Exit the **Innkeeper** with the **Police Inspector.***

> ## ? Questions and Assignments
>
> **27.** Now that things are looking up for the innkeeper and his wife, does she treat her husband any better than before?
>
> **28.** In what way does the police inspector behave like a typical policeman?
>
> **29.** Why do you think that the police inspector asked the innkeeper what his politics were?
>
> **30.** The innkeeper tells the police inspector that he believes in all tax. Do you think that he is telling the truth? Why do you think he said this?
>
> **31.** The police inspector describes the *'Political Agitator'* (a political agitator is one who stirs up people's feelings against a government).
> (i)   What does he expect him to look like?
> (ii)   What does he expect him to do?
> (iii)   Will the police inspector eventually be proven right? Explain.
>
> **32.** The policeman says *'If this man's the disease then I'm the doctor'*. What do you think he means by this?

Enter the **Wandering Minstrel,** *in beggarly raiment. He stands looking at the shed. He lifts the sacking and peers in. Re-enter the* **Innkeeper** *and his* **Wife,** *excited as before.*

Innkeeper: It's beyond me.

Wife: Three of them!

Innkeeper: The Great of Jerusalem!

Wife: But *three.*

Innkeeper: Yes, and the greatest!

Wife: *Three.*

Innkeeper: This Inspector, the latest,

He fairly made me sweat!

Now they're downing all they can get.

The High Priest's drunk a crate.

He's joined with the businessman.

But what do they all mean?

What are they waiting for?

One man, or three, or more?

An illegal religious meeting?

A fire-walking, fire-eating

Magician, or a revolt?

I'm sure it's not my fault.

Wife: I've got it!

Innkeeper: What?

Wife: Three!

Innkeeper: What do you mean? I don't see.

Wife: The three kings are these three.

The fortune-teller told

There would be three, and—behold.

Innkeeper: These three are Kings?

Wife: Aren't they?

Innkeeper: Disguised, do you mean to say?

Wife [*dancing*]: Kings, Kings!

What wonderful creatures are Kings!

Innkeeper [*still incredulous*]: And we've got a houseful?

Wife: Isn't it blissful?

Innkeeper [*suddenly going wild*]: We shall make a fortune! We're made!

They'll say: 'That's where *They* stayed.'

Both: Kings! Kings!

O Wonderful things ...

They dance around together; but break apart seeing the **Minstrel**.

| ? | Questions and Assignments |

33. What does the innkeeper mean by *'The Great of Jerusalem'*?

34. The innkeeper and his wife dance with joy at the end of this section of the play. Why?

Innkeeper: Who's that? What's he doing peering into my old stable?

*The **Minstrel** comes forward, as if not seeing the two.*

Minstrel: The hills were against me.
The sharp, peevish edges of the road-stones were against me,
And the thorns were against me,
But I made my way.
The dogs were with me; one brought me a ham-bone.
The birds were with me and showed me fresh eggs,

And the stream, the stream

Came out of its way to clear itself at my feet.

By these signs a traveller knows

The moving spirits are friendly.

And here is the place: the Emperor's Head.

The Emperor's Head that spoke to me in a dream—

Innkeeper: Hey, you, rags, what do you want?

Minstrel: Food and a bed.

I have come a long way with a fever in my head.

Innkeeper: Do you know where you are?

Minstrel: I am under the sun, the god- given day-star.

Innkeeper: Don't you know where you're standing?

Minstrel: On an earth of the Creator's making and lending.

Innkeeper: Do you know who you're speaking to?

Wife: Yes, just whose pig-keeper are you?

Your toes are insulting the sky.

The birds have slept in your hair.

Your trousers are ready to die,

Your coat's only just there.

You're like a rat's nest walking.

Are you begging or hawking?

Minstrel: Any bed and a slice of bread.

To keep the soul in my body, lady.

Wife: Away with you, you rubbish heap.

This is an Inn where Great Kings sleep.

He's one of those disreputable minstrels.

?   **Questions and Assignments**

35. The minstrel speaks of his journey to Bethlehem.
   (i) What made it difficult?
   (ii) What made it easy?

36. (i) What do we learn of the minstrel's appearance from the wife?
   (ii) What is her attitude towards the minstrel?

*Upper window opens. **Priest's** head appears.*

Priest: More wine up here! Service! Do you hear?

***Businessman's** head appears.*

Businessman: Get more beef up and more beer.
Wife: Coming, sir.

She runs into the inn.

Innkeeper: Well, you heard that.
Now what are you staring at?
Minstrel: Look at that star.
Innkeeper: It's only a star.
Minstrel: But it's shining by day.

*Upper window opens again and the **Wife's** angry head sticks out.*

Wife: There you still are!
Hurry up, man. More food and more drink.
Don't stand gaping like the kitchen sink.
The head vanishes and the window bangs.
Innkeeper: You'd better be off.
And I'd better hurry.
As you see, we're full up. I'm sorry.

***Innkeeper** runs off. **Minstrel** stands as he was.*

Minstrel: What a King of Men is Greedy!
Penny calls to penny, stronger than a man.
Floors call to carpets, stronger than a man.
Tables call to linen, stronger than a man.
Walls call to paintings, stronger than a man.
For a man's mind is money's slave.

The poor torn coat calls to the silk lining,
The old split bowl to figured silver.
The dirty dry glass to the vineyards
The rough bread calls to the sturgeon—
And a man goes running their errands
For a man's mind is money's slave.

Bow down, bow down and worship

The big belly of the cash-bank

That has swallowed so many slaves.

May you all go to the heaven

Of a crumbling junk-heap.

? **Questions and Assignments**

37. Describe the behaviour of the priest and the businessman in this section.

38. The minstrel draws an unusual sight to the innkeeper's attention.
   (i)   What is this?
   (ii)   How does the innkeeper react?
   (iii)   Is this sight important in the play as a whole? Explain.

39. This section closes with the minstrel talking about greed. Some of the lines may puzzle you at first and will require a little thought to work out their meaning. Say briefly, in your own words, what you think these final seventeen lines mean.

[During this the stage has darkened: he turns to the shed.]

Now night falls on the mountain valleys and in the gardens.

Now the cold comes down

Murdering the small birds in their feathers as they sleep.

The fish in ponds lose consciousness with the cold.

I'll creep in here and the breath of an ox and a donkey

Will do me for blankets. These are hard times

For those who cannot persuade themselves to rob.

He goes into the shed. The three guests are singing 'Three Blind Mice' as a round-song. **Joseph** *and* **Mary** *come up the road and stop in front of the inn.*

Joseph: We have come a long way. We can't go farther tonight, in the cold. The snow is beginning to prickle our faces. If this inn's full up, the Lord knows what we shall do. I'll knock.

Joseph knocks. The Innkeeper comes scampering up, returning from his errand of ordering more food. He doesn't notice that Joseph has knocked.

Innkeeper: Brrr! What a night! Hello—is your wife ill? She looks as if she might need a doctor. You ought to look after her, old man.

[He speaks to audience.]

These people who wander about the roads are terrible. They treat each other like rats and mice: no feelings at all. Brr!

He goes in, shuts the door.

Joseph: I'll try again.

[He knocks. Wife looks out.]

We need a room. And my wife here needs a bed.

Wife: Sorry, full up.

She bangs the door to.

Joseph: Now what shall we do?

Door opens. The Innkeeper comes out.

Innkeeper: I'm terribly sorry. I think I ought to explain.
You see that sign: it says 'The Emperor's Head'.
That is to say, it's a hostel for Emperors—Kings.
Kings as Kings, or incognito Kings.
Those three fine voices come from the throats of Kings
Who may well be pretending not to be Kings.
And I'm reserving three rooms for three Kings
Who whether they come disguised or else as Kings
Who still demand I treat them all as Kings.
And can a man of my sort deny Kings?
Kings made me, and Kings keep me.
I am the King's.
You understand? You can sleep in that shed.
You do understand that I can't do differently?

He runs back into the hotel.

Joseph: We're out of luck. Go in.

They go into the shed. 'Three Blind Mice' rises and falls away. 'We Three Kings' heard faintly in the distance. 'Three Blind Mice' rises again, falls away behind what follows.

? **Questions and Assignments**

40. In the opening lines of this section the minstrel continues speaking. Say in your own words what he is describing.

41. As Joseph and Mary stand outside the inn the innkeeper speaks to the audience about *'these people'*.
    (i)   Who are *'these people'* he speaks about?
    (ii)   What does he say about them?
    (iii)   Would you agree that it is a little odd to hear such words coming from the innkeeper? Explain your answer.

42. The innkeeper explains why Joseph and Mary cannot stay. What reasons does he give?

---

*Enter **Innkeeper** and his **Wife**, arguing.*

Innkeeper: But if these are Kings we could be renting
The three empty rooms. Two here were wanting
A room just now, and they'd have paid.
Wife: And if they're not Kings, but just what they said?
Then the three Kings will be coming tonight.
The fortune-teller's proving right
In everything else, so why not in this?
We can't afford to miss what we'd miss.
Those three rooms must be kept for the Kings
Who will be coming if these are not Kings.
I'm freezing. Anyway you're wrong. These *are* the Kings.
Innkeeper: They don't behave much like Kings.

Wife: Do you mean because they're blotto?
'The Customer's always right' is my motto.
Bring up more wine, in case more Kings come.
You are so unbelievably dumb.

She goes in. **Innkeeper** *runs in after.*

Innkeeper: I'm only afraid I'm losing money!

> **?** **Questions and Assignments**
>
> **43.** The innkeeper is having second thoughts about his three guests. Explain why.

'We Three Kings' is now quite loud. **Minstrel** *comes staggering out of the shed, shaking his head, rousing himself. He stands, collecting his wits. Something amazing has happened to him.*

Minstrel: I've just had an astounding dream as I lay in the straw.
I dreamed a star fell on to the straw beside me
And lay blazing. Then when I looked up
I saw a bull come flying through a sky of fire
And on its shoulders a huge silver woman
Holding the moon. And afterwards there came
A donkey flying through that same burning heaven
And on its shoulders a colossal man
Holding the sun. Suddenly I awoke
And saw a bull and a donkey kneeling in the straw,
And the great moving shadows of a man and a woman—
I say they were a man and a woman but
I dare not say what I think they were. I did not dare to look.
I ran out here into the freezing world
Because I dared not look. Inside that shed.

As he turns to look at the shed, he sees something down the road where before he had seen the star by day. The Innkeeper comes out of the inn, pausing in the open doorway.

Innkeeper: What do you say?

Wife: I said get more logs.

Innkeeper: I heard. I have only a man's legs.

I don't have a stag's or a running dog's.

[Now to the minstrel]

What's the matter with you?

You look so white you look blue.

What are you staring at?

Minstrel: Look.

Innkeeper follows the direction of Minstrel's finger, stares, then drops the log basket he is carrying and bolts into the inn.

Innkeeper: Wife! Wife! Quick! Look at this!

Minstrel: A star is coming this way along the road.

If I were not standing upright, this would be a dream.

A star the shape of a sword of fire, point-downward,

Is floating along the road. And now it rises.

It is shaking fire on to the roofs and the gardens.

[Star appears, suspended, rising slowly from behind till it comes to rest directly over the animal shed.]

And now it rises above the animal shed

Where I slept till the dream woke me.

And now

The star is standing over the animal shed.

During this speech, as the star rose to its position, a light kindled within the shed, and now light is beaming from every crevice. 'We Three Kings' at full volume, so much as may not drown the speech.

Re-enter, from the inn, Innkeeper and Wife. He points not at the star but down the road up which it has come.

Innkeeper: Look, if those are not three Kings, I'm a turnip.

Wife: Oh, bless that fortune-teller. It's the Kings.

Enter majestically, fully arrayed, the three Kings. Innkeeper and his Wife fall on their knees.

Innkeeper: This way, your Majesties.

Everything's prepared for your ease.

A banquet to tickle your eyes.

Wife: We're roasting a dozen sucking pigs.

Innkeeper: We're basting them with brandied figs.

Wife: We've hired a little orchestra

To help you down the vintage-jar.

Innkeeper: Our motto is 'Guests, stuff your gullets

Till your buttons fly like bullets'—

Er—your Majesties—this—this

This is the inn. Your Majesties!

That's only a horrible old place where I keep my donkey and my old bull
and my rubbish—your Majesties.

*The three **Kings** ignore the inn and the **Innkeeper**; their attention is on the
stable.*

First King: We have followed the star over mountains

Where the stones cried and the thorns were broken.

We have followed the star over deserts

Where the rocks split at the touch of the night cold,

We have followed the beckoning of that star

Till it stands where it stands.

We have arrived.

Second King: He will be born to the coughing of animals

Among the broken, rejected objects

In the corner that costs not a penny

In the darkness of the mouse and the spider.

*The third **King** has lifted aside the sacking front of the shed.*

Third King: He is here. The King of the Three Worlds

Has been born and is here.

*The three **Kings** enter the shed, leaving the sacking wide, the light blazing
out from the interior. Snow has started to fall and is now coming down in thick
windless flakes. 'Once in Royal David's City' begins softly, taking over from
'We Three Kings' which faded as they spoke. **Innkeeper** and his **Wife** are still
kneeling.*

Innkeeper: What? What are they saying?

Where are they going? Who's been born? What's happening?

Why are the three great Kings going into my old stable?

Why is that star standing over the roof of my old stable?

Who has lit that great light inside my old stable?

What is happening? Why doesn't somebody tell me? What's going on in my old stable?

'Once in Royal David's City' now loud. **Minstrel** *stands in stage-centre, under the thickly falling snow.*

Minstrel: Listen. The snow is falling.

Snow is falling on all the roads.

Falling on to the hills, on to the eyelashes of sheep.

Slowly the heavens are falling,

Every snowflake is an angel.

The angels are settling on the world.

The world will be white with angels.

The world will be deep in angels.

'Once in Royal David's City' now very loud. The **Minstrel** *stands in the large falling flakes. The* **Innkeeper** *and his* **Wife**, *as they were, bewildered and overawed, kneel in the snow. The manger scene is silhouetted in the great golden light beaming from the stable under the large bright star.*

? Questions and Assignments

44. What do you think caused the minstrel to leave the shed?

45. Why does the innkeeper drop the log basket?

46. What caused the innkeeper and his wife to drop to their knees?

47. What did the innkeeper and his wife offer the kings?

48. What do we learn about the kings' journey?

49. The innkeeper's final speech is one of puzzlement. Explain why he is puzzled.

50. To what does the minstrel compare the snowflakes?

? General Questions and Assignments

51. (i) Make a list of all the characters needed to stage the play.
(ii) Describe how you would dress each one. (You may like to sketch and colour each costume.)

52. What props would be needed to stage this play?

53. What special effects - lights, sounds etc. - would be needed?

54. What characters did you (i) like? (ii) dislike? Explain your choices in each case.

55. (i) What scene in the play did you find funny?
(ii) What scene did you find most moving and solemn?

56. Tell the story of the play in your own words.

57. Describe the scene you enjoyed most. Give a reason for your choice.

58. What do you think is the main message of this play?

YOU, THE JURY

by
Paul Groves/Nigel Grimshaw

Mr. Healy
Miss Keegan
Miss O'Reilly   *the finalists*
Mr. McNamara
Mr. Miller
Mrs. Wise
Mr. Quinn   *a millionaire*
Clerk
The jury   *(the rest of the class)*

Scene I
(a room in the town hall at Ballyford)

Clerk   Good morning. You are the six finalists picked out by Mr. Quinn. May I wish you all well in presenting your worthy cases. This could take a long time, though Mr. Quinn does want a decision today. You, the jury, please listen attentively to all that is said by the finalists. Perhaps you would all stand when Mr. Quinn comes in. Ah, here he comes, precisely on time.

(**Mr. Quinn** *enters. They all stand*)

Clerk   Good morning, Mr. Quinn.

Mr. Quinn   Good morning. Can we begin right away?

Clerk   Would you like to open the meeting with a few words?

Mr. Quinn   It will be a few. I'll get quickly to the point. As you all know I was born in this city. I love it. I made my first pound here. It means a great deal to me. In honour of my son, who was so tragically killed last month, I have decided to give a sum of money to the city.

Clerk   If we could offer our sympathy and condolences . . . .

Mr. Quinn   Thank you. I have, therefore, decided to give twenty million pounds to the most worthy cause.

Clerk   Twenty million! I thought it was ten million.

Mr. Quinn   My wife and I discussed it again last night. We wish to double it.

Clerk   It is the most generous offer I have ever heard of.

Mr. Quinn   I want a really fitting memorial to my son.
Can we begin at once, please?

Clerk   You six finalists know the rules, though you may have to adjust your case because of the increased offer. Each of you will have one chance only to state your reasons for receiving the twenty million. After you have all spoken the jury alone will decide which cause is the most deserving. Mr. Quinn may question you but he will not vote in the final decision. You have all drawn lots for speaking order. Mr. Healy, please begin.

Mr. Healy   I represent the town council. I would like to thank Mr. Quinn for his most generous offer. I must bore you first with a little history — essential history, though.

Mr. Quinn   Don't be too long.

Mr. Healy   I won't. This city was nothing but a village before the Industrial Revolution. Then came the machines, and the cotton that made this city great. The main part of the city was built in Victorian times. You can see this in a walk round the city square. It still looks a grand town.

Clerk   We all know that. Please get on with your argument.

Mr. Healy   I am coming to the main point. Mr. Quinn says that he loves this city. I wonder if he would love what is behind the face of the city square: rotting roofs, crumbling plaster, woodworm. Our national heritage — the town centre — is in danger of falling down. And now that another ten million has been added we could have new amenities — a theatre and concert hall, with an art gallery. We could also have a public garden with a piece of sculpture in remembrance of Mr. Quinn's son. We would call it the Quinn Centre.

Mr. Quinn   Cannot the Government and the Arts Council help?

Mr. Healy   The Government says it is the town's problem and the Arts Council will pay only part.

Mr. Quinn   Why not raise the rates?

Mr. Healy   I have left the most important part to last. Underneath the town centre the sewers are crumbling. Only last month, as you know, a hole the size of a double-decker bus appeared in the square. We will have to put the rates up considerably to repair the sewers. We cannot have a new centre as well. If the sewers are not rebuilt there could be a serious outbreak of disease — perhaps cholera. It makes sense to do both schemes together.

Clerk   I think you have made your point.

Mr. Healy   I do not think any of the rest of you can have a better case than this.

Clerk   We shall see. Miss Keegan, please.

Miss Keegan   You all know that for a town of our size the hospital accommodation is a disgrace. I represent the hospital board. There is not enough accommodation and what there is, is falling down. Some patients are in huts put up as a temporary measure in the last war. A surgeon told me this week that he had to stop a delicate eye operation because of rain falling through the roof. I also feel sorry for the children. A girl having her tonsils out could be in a bed next to an old lady dying of cancer. It's a disgrace.

Mr. Quinn   What about the Health Board? Can't they rebuild?

Miss Keegan   We are not at the top of the list. We may have to wait five years.

Mr. Healy   You will have even more serious cases if the sewers are not repaired.

Clerk   Please, Mr. Healy, you have had your say.

Mr. Quinn   Would my son have been saved if you had had more life-support machinery?

Miss Keegan   We would have stood a better chance. We want to do more research on the care of people injured in road accidents. The extra ten million would provide a research unit. We would call it the Quinn Accident Research Unit.

Mr. Quinn   Thank you.

Clerk   Miss O'Reilly, please.

Miss O'Reilly   You all know about the unemployment situation. You have seen the young people hanging around the streets of Ballyford with nothing to do. Cotton no longer makes this town prosperous, so why do we need a grand town centre? I think the money should be spent on youth by providing leisure and sporting facilities throughout the city. We could build several free leisure and sporting centres and buy a supply of equipment to last for years. We could have swimming pools and ice rinks. The extra ten million could provide training centres for the unemployed. We must not make our schoolchildren or our youngsters feel useless. Many people now in employment could be put out of work by computers, so the problem will grow. Miss Keegan mentioned physical illness. What about mental illness caused by having nothing to do and feeling useless?

Clerk   Have you finished?

Miss O'Reilly   There's much more I could say.

Mr. Quinn   I had very little as a boy. Don't you think children of today are spoiled?

Miss O'Reilly   Don't blame the youth of today for the age they live in. Come with me into the cafés and listen to them as they try to pass the time. I don't find them spoiled.

Mr. Quinn   Thank you.

Clerk   Mr. McNamara, please.

Mr. McNamara   I think we must look a little wider than Ballyford. The country desperately needs modern factories that can export. I have invented a new lightweight material for space research. Here on earth it could replace asbestos. It needs developing fast before the Japanese do it. I need money to build a factory and set up production lines. Twenty million would provide five hundred jobs, perhaps even more. We would not need all the things Miss O'Reilly asks for if the young people are usefully employed. And the town would be richer and able to pay for better medical treatment. Perhaps we could even make enough money to help the council with the sewers.

Mr. Healy   I doubt it. I have heard of these fancy space schemes before. Most of them go bankrupt. My scheme would give the town a new heart and employ three hundred men.

Clerk   Please, you have had your say.

Mr. McNamara   Men, you say. What about women? I would employ women as well.

Mr. Quinn   What is your business experience, Mr. McNamara?

Mr. McNamara   I have worked for ten years in industry as a manager. I know a good thing when I see it. The export potential is tremendous.

Mr. Quinn   You expect to make a large profit?

Mr. McNamara   The factory could be a co-operative. The workers could share in the profits and therefore the town would, too. It would be called the Quinn Space Research Co-operative.

Clerk   That you. Mr. Miller, please.

Mr. Miller   All these plans seem deserving. But before anything else people must live somewhere. I'll be frank: the council made a mistake in the building of the Fore Street high-rise flats. The concrete is crumbling. The flats are damp and cost too much to heat. We want to pull them down at a cost of four million. Then we could use the rest of the money to erect new two-storey dwellings with small gardens. They would be for the whole community, but particularly the old and the newly wed. We would call it Quinn Way.

Mr. Quinn   What about the Government?

Mr. Miller   They say it must come from the rates. We can't go on putting up the rates.

Mr. Quinn   Is there any guarantee you won't make another mistake?

Mr. Miller   We have learnt our lesson as far as housing is concerned.

Mr. Quinn   Thank you.

Clerk   Mrs. Wise, please.

Mrs. Wise   I have listened to all the others and I must say that they have good cases. But, by and large, the people of this country are well housed, well-fed and have good medical and sporting facilities. I have been to many eastern countries where millions have no proper water supply. This causes dreadful disease and early death. If only you had seen the thin, wasting children. If only you had heard their cries and screams. If only you had seen the blindness and the look of hopelessness. I propose, Mr. Quinn, that we set up an organisation to fight this problem, with its headquarters here in Ballyford. It would be called the Quinn Water for the World Project.

Mr. Quinn   Do you not believe that charity begins at home?

Mrs. Wise   Charity does not. Charity begins where the human need is greatest. I can never forget what I have seen. Try drinking filthy muddy water for a week.

Mr. Quinn   Thank you.

Clerk   Have you finished?

Mrs. Wise   I would like to show my slides.

Clerk   No, we have not allowed the others to show slides or film.

Mrs. Wise   But you should see them.

Clerk   No. You have all had your time. Well, members of the jury, you have heard of six deserving causes. Which one should have the money? Mr. Quinn, do you want a further word?

Mr. Quinn   I do not want to influence the jury in any way.

Jury leader   The jury would like to ask if it is possible to divide the money.

Mr. Quinn   No, it is not. A condition of my giving this money is that the most deserving cause gets it all.

Clerk   Jury, you must make your decision.

You, the class, must now act as the Jury and give your verdict.

? Questions and Assignments

1.   (i)   Why does Mr. Quinn make a donation of £20m?
     (ii)   Do you admire him? Why?

2.   Comment on the cases put forward by each of the candidates. Which of them have something personal to gain if their case is accepted?

3.   Which candidate do you think should have won the prize?

4.   (i)   Do you think that the money should have been divided? Why?
     (ii)   Do you think it is right that Mr. Quinn had twenty million pounds in the first place?

5.   If you had an opportunity to present a case to the jury, what case would you present?

6.   Write out the speech the winning candidate might have made.

7.   Imagine that you are producing the play for a school performance. Describe, in detail, the setting and the costumes you would have.

V - Writing Skills 2

PERSONAL WRITING — ESSAYS

Introduction

We all like to talk about things that happened to us, particularly if they were exciting or interesting. Talking about things comes easy to us and yet writing about the same things often appears to be a much more difficult task.

Have you ever chatted to your friends or family about a time when you got into trouble; your part-time job; a person you admire; the difficulties you face in school; the school bully; how you spent the week-end; what happened on Christmas Day in your home; your favourite teacher or your favourite pop group? Clearly your answer will be 'Yes'.

You will be interested to know that all these topics were essay titles set in the Junior Certificate examination over the past few years. Students doing the exam are required to write between one and two pages on topics such as these - topics that come up again and again in their everyday conversation. This section of the examination is called **Personal Writing** because - as you can see from the above - all the topics relate to the kind of things that young people like you will have experienced personally.

Ten Tips for Better Essays

| 1. | Getting Ideas |

Never begin an essay without first **thinking about it** and **planning it**. For this you will need a blank page. Use this to jot down all the ideas you have on the topic. Try to represent each idea with a few words. Write without stopping for **two or three minutes**, putting down every idea that comes into your head. This is called 'brainstorming'.

Example (i) — *The School Bully*

- sneers, really a coward, greedy, sneaky, her/his 'gang', picks on certain people (who? - names); Murphy's big brother; licks up to teachers, slags, mocks, why does she/he bother?; 'ratting' on her/him; your worst experience........etc.

Example (ii) — *Christmas Day at Home*

- no batteries; waking up; uncle Tom singing; dog gets sick; brother's new electric guitar; presents - good and not so good; awful telly programmes; phone relatives abroad; unexpected visitors....etc.

Ten Tips for Better Essays

2. Planning

This stage again should only take a few **minutes**. Go back through all your ideas in stage one; consider each one and cross out those which you think are are not worth following up. In the case of the remainder, decide on the **order** in which you are going to present them.

On essays such as *"Christmas Day"* or *"My Weekend"* the most straightforward and effective way is to follow the natural time sequence. Don't try to cover every single moment - concentrate on the interesting episodes. If the essay does not break up naturally into blocks of time, concentrate on five or six interesting aspects of the topic. When you have this stage completed the rest of the job will be easy - the essay will almost write itself!

Example (i) — *The School Bully*

Paragraph 1.	*Appearance; habits; build; face; clothes; sayings.*
Paragraph 2.	*How she/he 'licks up' to teachers; give example or two.*
Paragraph 3.	*Describe how she/he picks on other students.*
Paragraph 4.	*The problem of telling ...*
Paragraph 5.	*Her/his 'gang'.*
Paragraph 6.	*The day she/he met her/his match.*
Paragraph 7.	*Your experience.*
Paragraph 8.	*How you would end bullying if you were in charge ...*

Example (ii) — *Christmas Day at Home*

Paragraph 1.	*Early Morning: opening presents - surprises.*
Paragraph 2.	*Mid-Morning: meeting your friends - comparing notes.*
Paragraph 3.	*Afternoon: phoning your brother in London.*
Paragraph 4.	*Christmas Dinner: grandad remembers.*
Paragraph 5.	*Evening: Visitors - relations - uncle playing with computer game, party sing-song.*
Paragraph 6.	*Bedtime: Your thoughts as the day draws to a close.*

Ten Tips for Better Essays

3.	Beginning Writing

When you have completed stage two you will have worked out the number of paragraphs for your essay and the topic of each of these paragraphs. Now, on a new page, you simply begin writing.

At this stage some students seem to seize up: *"I can't get started"* - *"I don't know what to write"* - *"I'm not able to think of a good opening sentence"* - *"I can't think of anything to write"* - *"I'm stuck"*. These are some of the more common complaints that teachers frequently hear.

A useful **'trick'** to get over these difficulties is to imagine that you have made a 'new' friend, who is anxious to get to know you. This imaginary friend is very inquisitive. She is asking you about the topic of the essay. Imagine the questions that she would ask. Then compose a complete answer in your head.

Each answer should be a **complete sentence**. 'Listen' to each sentence in your head. Make sure the words flow easily and that they get across each idea clearly. Then write it down.

Remember to follow your plan and to write in paragraphs. Paragraph lengths can vary from one or two sentences to six or seven, depending on the topic.

Example (i) — *The School Bully*

Here are some questions your imaginary friend might ask:
Does he look like a bully? What does he look like? Is he strong and tough looking? What does she/he dress like? Does she/he have any noticeable habits or sayings?

The answers give you the first paragraph of the essay:

If you saw Brian Triggs you would never think that he was a bully. He is small for his age and has a pointed face a bit like a rat. He walks with a swagger and always has his thumbs hooked in his trouser pockets ...

Ten Tips for Better Essays

Example (ii) — *Christmas Day at Home*

Here are some questions your imaginary friend might ask:
Who awoke first? When did you get up? Where were your presents? How many did you get? What was the best thing you got? What was the most unusual thing you got and what was the dullest thing you got? Did any members of your family get unusual presents? How did they react?

Essay ...
Deirdre, my little sister, woke me at seven with squeals of excitement. When I realised what day it was, I hopped out of bed too. The presents, all wrapped in fancy paper, were stacked at the foot of the Christmas tree . . . . .

If you are still getting 'stuck':

1. Consult your plan again.

2. Read over the last sentence you have written and consider the questions that would follow it, e.g. *Who? What? When? Where? Why? How?*

Ten Tips for Better Essays

4. | Using Dialogue

Good writing is less about 'telling' the reader and more about helping him or her 'see' and 'hear'. Readers enjoy a conversation much more when they can 'hear' it, rather than just being told in broad terms what it was about.

One of the best ways to let a reader 'hear' a conversation is by using dialogue. Instead of telling the reader that somebody praised you, blamed you, advised you, threatened you or mocked you, let the reader hear the actual words that were said.

It also helps to tell the reader how the words were spoken. Try not to depend on the verb 'said'. Think of suitable alternatives such as

> *shouted,*   *hissed,*
> *warned,*   *snapped,*
> *cried,*   *smiled,*
> *yelled,*   *snarled,*
> *roared,*   *bellowed etc.*
> *whispered,*

Be clear on adverbs such as *angrily, quietly, jokingly, softly, nervously* etc. also helps the reader to 'hear' the tone of voice in which a piece of dialogue was spoken.

Use the rules for punctuating and laying out dialogue. These start on p 223.

The basic rules for dialogue are:

1. Only spoken words should be enclosed in quotation marks - "_____"

2. Begin a new line for each speaker.

3. In a conversation between two speakers it is not necessary to keep identifying the speaker.

Ten Tips for Better Essays

The following two examples show the importance of laying out dialogue correctly. In the first example quotation marks are used incorrectly and new pieces of dialogue do not begin on new lines. The result is confusing and difficult to follow. Note how easy it is to read and understand the corrected version.

(i) The *Wrong* Way

Over dinner my grandad talked about his favourite subject - the Good Old Days. "Christmas was much different when I was your age," said Grandad. "We know. You keep telling us," muttered my brother. We had no such things as computer games in those days "continued Grandad" what kind of presents did you get when you were my age Grandad asked my young sister Oh an apple and an orange if we were lucky . . .

(ii) The *Right* Way

Over dinner my grandad talked about his favourite subject - the Good Old Days.

"Christmas was much different when I was your age," said Grandad.

"We know. You keep telling us," muttered my brother.

"We had no such things as computer games in those days," continued Grandad.

"What kind of presents did you get when you were my age, Grandad?" asked my young sister.

"Oh, an apple and an orange if we were lucky."

Finally, remember to use dialogue sparingly. One or two short pieces of dialogue can add variety to your essay. Don't include it just for the sake of including it - try to write dialogue that is a little dramatic. Everybody enjoys hearing a good argument but not a conversation about the weather.

Ten Tips for Better Essays

5.	Setting the Scene

The **setting** is where an event in a story takes place. It could be anywhere - the principal's office, a park at night, outside a take-away on a frosty night, a derelict house etc.

Always include a sentence or two to let the reader 'see' where the action is taking place. Don't try to give a detailed description of a setting. Try to select one or two details which will help the reader to imagine the entire scene.

Examples:

(i) *Rain. Rain. Rain. Was it ever going to stop? The sky was a mass of grey clouds. It was raining in a slow, lazy sort of way as if it was going to go on forever. An old lady pushed by and jabbed me in the leg with her shopping bag. People never look where they are going when it's raining.*

(ii) *The park was a bit creepy. The rain dripped through the tall trees. Shivering, I picked my way along the path. My eyes got used to the gloom, and I began to make out the swings and the roundabout.*

(iii) *I picked my way over the rotten floorboards and stood in the hall, or at least what was left of it, and shone the torch upwards. There were holes in the ceiling. Big beams of wood were hanging down. Most of the stairs were missing. It wouldn't be safe to try upstairs.*

(iv) *The small back room was empty. No furniture. No cupboards. I bent down and looked at the floorboards. It was difficult to tell if anything could be hidden under them. And I didn't fancy looking. I didn't like rats.*

Ten Tips for Better Essays

6. | Describing People

Again, it adds to the reader's enjoyment to let him or her 'see' the people you encounter in your essay. As in the setting, avoid long detailed descriptions. One or two interesting details of a person's appearance is sufficient.

The following are some adjectives which you might find useful for this task:

Build: *lanky, tall, short, stout, thin, frail, muscular, weedy, brawny.*

Face: *wrinkled, tanned, long, pointed, fat.*

Hair: *neat, curly, long, tangled, grey, brown, red, balding, bald.*

Eyes: *clear, bright, innocent, shifty, large, small, sly, merry, twinkling, beady.*

Clothes: *shabby, smart, fashionable, grubby, drab, gaudy, worn, threadbare, neat.*

Voice: *low, gentle, friendly, soft, sharp, hoarse, deep, harsh.*

Character: *friendly, snobbish, kind-hearted, greedy, lazy, cheerful, miserable, gloomy, honest, blunt, charming, spiteful, loyal, generous, sincere, detestable, timid.*

Many writers use **similes** in order to give a more colourful description of the person in question.

Example (i)

My father once told me that Doc Spencer had been looking after the people of our district for nearly forty-five years. He was a tiny man with tiny hands and feet and a tiny round face. The face was as brown and wrinkled as a shrivelled apple. Nobody feared him. Many people loved him, and he was especially gentle with children.

Example (ii)

Lankers, our teacher, was a horrid man. He had carrot-coloured hair, a little clipped carrotty moustache and a fiery temper. Carrotty-coloured hairs were also sprouting out of his nostrils and his earholes. We were all terrified of him. He sat at the top of the class making snuffling grunts like a dog sniffing at food.

Ten Tips for Better Essays

7. | Describing Action

When you want to capture an exciting piece of action stick to short sentences, short paragraphs and short pieces of dialogue. Also try to select a few good descriptive verbs - *sprinted, raced, grabbed, slammed,* etc. to describe particular actions.

Example (i)

Suddenly he said, 'I see you play chess. Would you like a game now?' Well, I had to smile! He wanted to play. I had set the trap and he couldn't wait to fall into it. It was all so easy. I made the first move and sat back. It would all be over soon.

He played slowly. He wouldn't rush. He stopped to think about every move. I was getting fed up. The game would go on forever at this rate.

---

8. | Write about the World you Know

Personal Writing gives you the opportunity to write about events of which you have first-hand personal experience. It is a chance for you to write about places you know and things that happened to you or to your friends and family. Making up stories about people and places you saw on television or read about in novels is a difficult task and such stories rarely have a 'ring of truth' about them.

Even if you want to write a ghost story, a horror story, a science fiction story, a love story or a crime story, why don't you make it happen in your own street, your own town or school?

Ten Tips for Better Essays

9.	Be Sincere

One of the great pleasures of reading is learning about how other people cope with the ups and downs of everyday life. When you are writing about a personal experience don't be afraid to reveal your feelings. If something delighted you, amused you, saddened you, angered you, made you feel guilty or made you look silly, don't be afraid to say so. It will add interest and depth to your work.

10.	Neat Handwriting and Presentation

No matter how original and interesting an essay is, it will not make a good impression on the reader if she or he has to struggle from word to word trying to make out bad handwriting. Remember that clear, legible handwriting and neat layout always make a good impression on the reader.

Assignment **1** | PERSONAL WRITING — ESSAYS

1. My earliest memories.
2. My pet.
3. An argument with a friend.
4. The funniest thing that ever happened in school.
5. An adult - not a relative - whom I admire.
6. My views on sport.
7. Learning a new skill.
8. School is not easy.
9. A school outing.
10. The most terrifying experience of my life.
11. Looking after a young child.
12. If I won the Lotto …
13. Ghosts - do they exist?
14. How I see myself in ten years time.
15. What I would like to be good at - and why.
16. A true friend.
17. Monday mornings at home.
18. Neighbours - good and bad.
19. Songs that bring back memories.
20. My unhappiest day at school.
21. My favourite television programme.
22. My hobby.
23. Saturdays - how I spend them.
24. Things that make me angry.
25. My friends.
26. A row that I witnessed.
27. A sad occasion.
28. My favourite place - and my least favourite place.
29. A time when I was treated unfairly.
30. My town.

LETTER WRITING

Formal and Informal Letters

In general, informal letters are those which you would write to people with whom you are on first name terms, while formal letters are those to people with whom you are only distantly acquainted or not at all.

Informal letters are friendly, chatty letters which you would write to friends and relatives. Occasionally, though, you might have to write an informal letter in less than friendly terms.

Formal letters include those to organisations or businesses seeking information, making complaints or suggestions and applying for work.

Layout of Letters

Informal   **Formal**

A. The **address** from where you are writing. Addresses can either be written with a vertical *or* with a sloped margin.

e.g.   13 Oakfield Rd.,   27 Greendale Ave.,
         Perrystown,   Coolara,
         Dublin 12.   Co. Kildare.

Each word in an address begins with a capital letter. Any shortened words are followed by a full stop. Each line of the address ends with a comma except for the final line, when a full stop is used.

B. The **date** on which the letter is being written.

e.g.   15/3/1998   *or*   15 March 1998

C. The **name** of the person (if known), their **title** e.g. Manager, Secretary, etc. and the **address** of the organisation to whom you are writing. ***(This applies to formal letters only and should not be included in informal letters.)***

D. The **greeting**. In informal letters you can be quite casual e.g. *Dear Anne, Hi Anne* or simply *Anne* are all acceptable. However, in a formal letter never use the first name of the person to whom you are writing, even if you know it. You will generally use one of the following :

Dear Mr. Murphy, Dear Mrs. Murphy, Dear Miss Murphy, Dear Ms. Murphy.

    If you are writing to a large organisation and you do not know the name of the person who will deal with your letter, then you begin with *Dear Sir/Madam.*

E. The **body** of the letter. Unless your letter is very short you should divide it into paragraphs.

F.   The **complimentary close** and **signature**. Again formal and informal letters differ here.

e.g.   **Informal**

Best wishes/Lots of love/
See you soon/Regards
are just some of the many
phrases that can be used here.

Formal

(i) If you used Dear Sir/Madam
in your greeting:
Yours faithfully,
Peter Murphy

or

(ii) If you used an actual name
in your greeting:
Yours sincerely,
Peter Murphy

(If your signature cannot be read easily, write your name in block capitals underneath it).

Assignment **2**   **LETTER WRITING**

In the case of each of the following assignments you must firstly decide if they are formal or informal letters and then use the correct layout for each one.

In each case when you have completed the letter draw a rectangle to represent an envelope in your copy and in it write the name and address as you would on a real envelope.

Example:

```
                                    ┌──────┐
                                    │ ÉIRE │
                                    └──────┘

            Ms. Angela Davis
            13 Gardener's Hill,
                 Cork
```

1. Your godmother Angela Davis, who lives in 13 Gardener's Hill, Cork, sent you twenty pounds for your birthday. Write and thank her. Tell her how you spent your birthday and what you intend to do with her present.

2. Write to the manager of a local bank or building society seeking support for a sponsored cycle in aid of Gorta Famine Relief. You do not know the manager's name.

3. Your brother is in college in Dublin. He is a bit lonely. Write a letter to him telling him the latest family news and try to cheer him up. He lives in Flat 4, 34 Upper Rathmines Road, Dublin 6.

4. Write to the controller of television programmes in RTE explaining why you think that *The Late Late Show* should be broadcast on Monday evenings instead of its usual slot.

5. Write to the presenter of a local radio show that you enjoy. You may have a few suggestions to improve it.

6. Mrs Donavan, a neighbour of yours, is spending a few weeks with her daughter Emma who lives at 34 Willow Park, Jordan Hill, Oxford OX2 8EJ in England. Write to her with the news that you accidentally broke the roof of her greenhouse.

7. You are secretary of your local youth club. Write to the secretary of your local G.A.A. club asking for the use of their pitch for your club's annual sports day.

8. Your uncle, Tom Browne, who lives at 3 Avondale Drive, Bray, County Wicklow, invites you to go on a camping holiday with his wife and children to France. Their children are aged five and seven and you have always found them difficult to get along with. Write to your uncle declining the invitation.

9. You are on holiday with your cousin in a different part of the country. Write home, telling your parents the good points and the bad points about the holiday, as well as some reminders about those things which you asked them to look after while you are away.

10. You had arranged to meet your cousin Andrew O'Neill, who lives in 3 Curragh Close, Newbridge, County Kildare, in Dublin on Saturday last.
    (i)   You didn't turn up. Write and explain why.
                                        or
    (ii) He didn't turn up and has not contacted you. Write to him on the matter.

11. Novelists, poets and dramatists like to receive letters from children who enjoy their work. Write to a writer whose work you enjoyed, telling her or him why you enjoyed it. You may also wish to find out something about the author. (You can address the letter to the publisher e.g. Tom Elliot, c/o Apple Publishers, 34 Grafton Street, Dublin 2. *(c/o - this stands for* 'care of'…)

12. A sign at the entrance to your local park reads *'No ballgames, no picnics, no bikes, no radios, all dogs on leads'*. You do not agree with some - or all - of these rules. Write a letter to the Parks' Superintendant of your local county council or corporation. State the reason why you are complaining - (you may have a dog, like mountainbiking, football etc). Try to make a sensible suggestion for solving the problem.

REVIEWS

Writing about Books, Plays and Films

- Begin with the title of the book, play or film and the name of the author. Make sure to use capital letters correctly here.
- Describe, in a sentence or two, the subject matter of the story.
- Tell briefly when and where the events of the story take place and the time span which the story covers.
- Describe the most memorable incident in the story.
- Write a little about the main characters in the story and what they did. Describe those you like and those you dislike. Explain why.
- Say what you consider to be (i) its strong points and (ii) its weak points.
- Finally, say if and why you liked or disliked it.

1. Write a review of a video, play or film you have seen recently.

HOW TO WRITE CLEAR INSTRUCTIONS

- Well-written instructions will never confuse the reader. As you write, it should be helpful to imagine someone asking you about the process, step by step.
- Give a clear title to your instructions e.g. *(How to ... mend a puncture ... record a tape ... care for a puppy ... make an omelette etc.).*
- Now list the things that are needed and the quantities.
- Number each instruction and make sure they are laid out in the correct order.
- Draw the reader's attention to any stage of the instructions where particular care is needed or to any stage which could be potentially dangerous.

Give clear instructions for each of the following:
1. How to mend a puncture.
2. How to iron a garment.
3. How to make a tasty snack.
4. How to get to the local post office from your school or home.

KEEPING A DIARY

People keep diaries to help them to remember events dating back over months or years. Many diaries, written by both famous people and 'ordinary' people, have been published over the years and they provide interesting information about the day-to-day lives of their authors.

Assignment 5

Keep a diary for a week. Write about the things which were important to you. It might provide interesting or exciting reading in a few years' time. You can write phrases rather than long sentences. The extracts below may be useful to help you to get started. The first two are fictitious and the remaining three are from the diaries of actual people.

Monday 1 March Got up. Went to school. Came home. Had fishfingers. Went to bed. Started to count up to a billion but only got up to 7,643 because my father made me stop. He said that if he had to come up to my bedroom once more, that he would strangle me. This man is dangerous.
— K. Waterhouse

Monday January 19th The dog is back at the vet's. It has got concrete stuck on its paws. No wonder it was making such a row on the stairs last night.
— Diary of Adrian Mole

---

23 May 1800 Ironing till tea time. So heavy rain that I could not go for letters.
— Dorothy Wordsworth

March 10 1904 Sixteen hrs march, the hottest day we have had ... No water ... Nearly drank from a green stinking puddle, but refrained ...
— Aubrey Herbert

---

6 January 1663 Myself somewhat vexed at my wife's neglect in leaving of her scarf and waistcoat in the coach today that brought us from Westminster, though I confess she did give them to me to look after - yet it was her fault not to see that I did take them out of the coach.
— Samuel Pepys

VI - Reading & Media Studies

Biography and Autobiography

An **autobiography** is the story of a person's life written by that person. The word comes from three Greek words '*-auto*' meaning '*self*', '*-bios*' meaning '*life*' and '*-graphein*' meaning '*to write*'. A **biography** is a person's life-story written by someone else.

In 1960, a young woman died in a house in St. John's Park in Waterford. She was survived by her husband and four children. Seán Dunne was one of those children. In 1991 he wrote the story of his childhood and teenage years in a book entitled In My Father's House. *The book tells the gripping and often hilarious story of how a family survived against all odds. Seán Dunne now lives in Cork where he works as a journalist with the* Cork Examiner, *a local newspaper.*

In this extract from his autobiography he tells of an unusual event that happened in the local shop ...

The strangest creature ever seen in John's Park turned up in Jackie O'Regan's shop. Jackie was opening a wooden box of bananas on his counter one morning when he heard something stir in the straw in which the fruit was settled. He looked in through a slit, saw nothing only bananas and thought he must have been imagining things. He kept opening the box, prising out nails and finally forcing open the top.

The straw stirred again. He took the cigarette from his lips and looked in. There, looking up at him from the green-skinned bananas, he saw the beady eyes of a snake. He was too shocked to speak. When he had regained his composure, he started to shove people out of the shop, hurrying out the women waiting for potatoes and the children leaning over the counter with pennies.

'Get out, get out!" he shouted. 'There's a snake in the banana box.'

The shop was cleared in no time and the customers stood outside. Quickly, a large crowd gathered as news of the snake spread. With the shop to itself, the snake hissed its way along the counter.

'Motheragod, it's a rattlesnake,' said a woman.

'It'll poison everything,' said another.

It was decided to send for Peery Power, who lived just a few houses away from the shop. A middle-aged, muscular man whose hair was cut in an American-style crew-cut, Peery was famous for his bravery and toughness. Tessie said that when bodies went missing in the river, Peery, who was a diver, was sent to get them out. His courage knew no limits. A snake would be nothing to him.

He strode up to the shop with the sleeves of his jumper rolled up. The women gathered around him. 'Jesus, Peery, you're wicked brave,' they said to him. He went into the shop with the swaggering confidence of a sheriff entering a saloon. He looked at the snake. The snake looked at him. He went over to it as if it was a relative with whom he was about to shake hands. He put out his hand. In seconds, he had the snake by the throat and held it in such a way that it was immobilised, stuck there in his grip with its eyes out on stalks and half the women of John's Park looking in at it. He held it like that until the guards arrived and took it away in a container. Peery was the hero of the day and found no shortage of free drink in the pub that night.

Assignment   1

1. What was the first sign that there was a snake in the box of bananas?

2. What did Jackie O'Regan notice first about the snake?

3. Who was in the shop at the time?

4. How did Jackie O'Regan react when he realised that there was a snake in the box?

5. In your opinion, did the women who commented on the snake know much about snakes? Explain.

6. The author says of Peery Power - *'His courage knew no limits'*. What evidence is there in the extract to suggest that this was true?

Vampires

Bram Stoker

Did you know that Dracula's creator was an Irishman? Bram Stoker (Bram is an unusual short form of Abraham) was born in Dublin and educated there. In 1866 he joined the Irish Civil Service. It must have been a rather dull life, but nevertheless he was interested enough to write some reports and books on subjects such as the work of the law courts. In 1878 he left the civil service and became Henry Irving's agent. Irving was the most outstanding figure in the London theatre in the second half of the nineteenth century. As well as acting, he also produced many plays. His favourite plays were those by Shakespeare. Henry Irving was famous for his Shakespearean roles such as Hamlet from the play of the same name, Shylock from *The Merchant of Venice* and Malvolio from *Twelfth Night*. But he also enjoyed producing and acting in melodramas. Melodramas are plays with exciting and sensational events, and which generally have a happy ending.

Perhaps that is where Bram Stoker first discovered his interest in the vampire myths. Bram Stoker's book *Dracula* was first published in 1897. It aroused great public interest at a time when the subject of the supernatural - ghost stories and accounts of events that cannot be explained - had come into fashion. It was an immediate success, and it was followed - and continues to be followed, thanks partly to cinema and television - by very many other stories about vampires and other supernatural creatures. *Dracula* was not the first story to feature vampires but it certainly is the most famous, and today the name 'Dracula' is known in nearly every part of the world.

Dracula

The Dracula story is told through the diaries of a young solicitor, Jonathan Harker, his fiancée Mina, her friend Lucy Westenra, and Dr. John Seward, the superintendent of a large lunatic asylum in Essex in England. It begins with Harker's journey from his native England to Count Dracula's eerie castle in

Transylvania. He went there to help arrange the Count's purchase of Carfax, an ancient house close to Dr. Seward's asylum. After various horrifying experiences as a guest at Dracula's castle, Jonathan makes his way back to England. Dracula, however, manages to get there ahead of him. The rest of the book tells of the attempt to save Mina from Dracula's advances and their subsequent pursuit of him. The evil Count escapes back to Transylvania where, after a thrilling chase, he is beheaded and stabbed through the heart, at which point his body crumbles to dust.

Vampires

The belief in vampires is a very ancient one, most of all in places such as Transylvania. In the stories, the vampire was the ghost of a dead wrongdoer. The ghost returned from the grave in the shape of a huge bat and fed on the blood of sleeping people. These people usually became vampires themselves. So long as it could get human blood in this way, the vampire would never die. But people believed in the protective power of fire, crosses and certain plants, especially garlic. They believed that the only way to kill a vampire and set its spirit free was to cut off its head and drive a sharpened length of wood through its heart.

Transylvania

The name *Transylvania* comes from Latin meaning 'beyond the forests', but it is, in fact, a real place, not an imaginary one. It is located in present-day Romania, lying between western Romania and southern Hungary. It is a mountainous country, enclosed to the east and south by the Carpathian Mountains and the Transylvanian Alps, and to the west by the Bihor Mountains. Gypsies, who are among the inhabitants of the area, play a significant part in the story.

Assignment   2

1. (i)   What was Bram Stoker's first job?
    (ii) For how many years did he have this job?

2. When was *Dracula* first published?

3. Who was Henry Irving?

4. What kind of work do you think Bram Stoker had to do as Henry Irving's agent?

5. In which Shakespearean plays did Irving act? What parts did he play?

6. (i)   Why was the book *Dracula* so successful?
    (ii) Name some characters from *Dracula*.
    (iii) In which countries does the action of the story take place?

7. Write down three facts about Transylvania.

8. What beliefs are associated with vampires?

Ghosts and Hauntings

The banshee, the coach drawn by headless horses, phantom monks, dark figures flitting through the ruins of old houses, eerie events in old graveyards, strange death warnings and terrible sounds in the dark - such are the ghosts of every parish and every townsland of Ireland.

Of them all, the banshee (in Gaelic, *bean-sidhe*, or *fairy woman*) is most particularly associated with Ireland. Rarely sighted but frequently heard wailing in a most doleful way, she was widely accepted as being a sign of impending death, if not of those who heard her, then of some close relative or neighbour.

Before the days of radio and television, storytelling was the main form of entertainment. Ghost stories, in particular, were favourites and, on dark winter evenings, stories of local ghosts were told and retold around the firesides of the district.

Here is one that comes from the town of Celbridge in Co. Kildare.

A Guest at Castletown

William Connolly, said to have been the richest man in Ireland at the time, built Castletown House in Celbridge in 1722. When he died he left the house to his favourite nephew, Thomas Connolly, who lived in nearby Leixlip Castle.

One cold and wet November day in 1767 Thomas Connolly, who was known as Squire Connolly, joined the Kildare Hounds for a day's fox-hunting at Garanagh Cross, two miles from Celbridge. It was a wild, wet and windy morning after a storm that had lasted most of the night. Only a handful of the toughest huntsmen followed the first fox through Garanagh Woods. The fox proved to be as tiresome as the weather, doubling, and redoubling, on its tracks until the hounds were dizzy. As darkness approached, the cold, driving rain added to the discomfort of the hunt. One by one the huntsmen went home to dry clothes and warm fires until, by late afternoon, there were no more than five or six of them left straggling across the fields by Rantully Hill.

As darkness fell Squire Connolly noticed, for the first time, a man riding a lively black horse. The squire looked hard at the rider but could not recognize him as being one of the huntsmen that morning. He turned in his saddle and called out a greeting, asking whether the huntsman was a stranger to Kildare as he did not recognize him. The tall stranger smiled or rather grinned, disclosing abnormally long and yellow teeth, but did not reply. Instead he pointed ahead of him, turned his horse sharply and set off at a canter up the steep hill. At the same time the hounds over the hill began barking fiercely. Connolly knew that they were about to make a kill.

Without a second thought, for he did not want the whole day to be a wasted one, the squire set off in pursuit, determined to be in at the kill himself. As he reached the top of the hill, he stopped in surprise at the sight that met his gaze. The stranger had dismounted from his horse and was standing a little distance away, his feet firmly apart and holding above his head with both hands, a bloody fox, oblivious of its blood dribbling down from his grey beaver hat onto his grey hunting jacket and thigh boots. Still grinning, the man bit off the fox's tail with his sharp teeth and offered it to the squire. Puzzled, the squire looked about him; the stranger's horse stood proudly nearby but otherwise the hill was deserted. The hounds had fled. Hounds  deserting a kill? It was impossible. Squire Connolly sensed that something strange had happened.

As Squire Connolly turned away from the sickening sight, the man called out to him in an unpleasant voice 'Connolly, if you will not accept the tail, will you offer me a cup of something hot at your great house - Castletown?'

Squire Connolly never refused hospitality to anyone and, unattractive as he found the man and his manners, he could not refuse such a request. He told the man to follow him. When they reached Castletown House several of the squire's friends were already seated about the hall, warming themselves with hot drinks while servants busied themselves removing the men's wet boots. As a servant approached the stranger, stretched out now in a comfortable chair, he was rudely ordered away.

'I'm tired. Don't disturb me!' the stranger snapped in a rude voice. For the first time, as the man's eyes closed, Squire Connolly looked hard at him and he now saw in the well-lighted hall that the man was as hairy as a dog. Long, stiff hairs sprouted from his nostrils and great curling tufts of hair hung out of his ears. Even his hands, long-nailed and with tapered fingers, were matted with hair! An awful suspicion crossed the squire's mind and, as the stranger slept, he ordered a servant to carefully remove one of the man's boots. As the boot was drawn from the man's foot a hairy hoof was revealed, black and cloven! Squire Connolly hastily sent a servant to Celbridge to fetch a priest. Just as the priest arrived, the stranger woke up. As soon as he saw that his boot had been removed, he leapt to his 'feet' and limped towards the fireplace. There, spreading his arms on the mantlepiece, he laughed at the priest and dared him to do his worst.

Angered by this behaviour, the priest called out to the creature, 'Be gone in the name of the Lord!' The creature just laughed mockingly. This was too much for the priest, who threw his prayerbook at the sneering face. The book missed its mark and smashed the mirror hanging over the fireplace. As it did so the creature leapt high into the air and disappeared in a cloud of fumes. All that remained was a blackened crack in the marble fireplace. It still remains to remind successive occupants of Castletown House of the strange happenings there on one bleak November night in 1767.

Assignment 3

1. What evidence is there in the passage that the weather was unpleasant on the day of the hunt?

2. Why does the author compare the fox to the weather?

3. What kind of horse did the stranger ride?

4. What was it about the stranger's appearance that struck Squire Connolly when he first caught sight of him?

5. Why was Squire Connolly surprised when he reached the top of Rantully Hill?

6. *'Squire Connolly sensed that something strange had happened'*. Describe the strange thing that had happened.

7. Why did the stranger refuse to let the servant remove his boots?

8. Why do you think the squire called a priest?

9. Describe what happened when the priest arrived.

Visions of the Future - as seen in 1979

*In 1979 Christopher Evans wrote a book called **The Mighty Micro** in which he forecast some of the ways in which computers were likely to change our lives. He believed that books printed on paper would be replaced by computer 'books' ... and that driving would be much safer.*

I

The computer 'books' of the late 1980s will be about the size of the average book today. The screens on which the text is displayed will vary in size depending on what is required. There will be page-size screens for the hand-held computer book, wristwatch-size screens for dictionaries or telephone directories and a ceiling projection for reading in bed in <u>absolute</u> comfort (at last!).

The reader will be able to <u>vary</u> the speed at which the text appears. Different colour displays could also be offered. For children, those with poor vision or for anyone learning to read, the print could be made bigger.

These computer books are not just science fiction dreams. Computer books of this kind, using TV sets as their displays instead of printed pages, are already being built and tested. The first of them may be on sale early in the 1980s. Later years will see a reduction in their price and an enormous spread of their use.

The objection can be raised that computer books, although marvellously cheap and <u>convenient</u>, have none of the satisfying qualities of traditional printed books - the attractive cover or the pleasant touch of paper pages. This problem will be overcome by making the computer books themselves pleasant to look at and to touch. They could be covered in leather with gold lettering. The programs themselves, each containing the text of a book or set of books, will be as easy to change as a battery.

II

The work of the police will be much eased by a reduction in motoring offenses of all kinds. In the late 1980s people will be amazed at the amount of <u>aimless</u> driving that was done in the 1970s.

Furthermore, every car will come with <u>built-in safety features</u>. Even now the world's biggest automobile companies are carrying out tests with 'collision-proof' cars. These cars have many microprocessors capable of sensing 'danger' from other vehicles travelling too close or approaching too quickly. The sensors will be extremely cheap and by the late 1980s these sensors could be standard, or even compulsory, equipment in all cars, together with other safety devices such as microprocessors which would check tyre wear, brake power, faulty lights and so on. They may even be able to shut off the car's engine if they sense that it is being driven dangerously. A car that refuses to start when its driver has drunk too much alcohol has often been joked about, but it could well be the only type on the road in the late 1980s. By then most cars will be <u>virtually theft-proof</u>.

Assignment 4

1. Explain in your own words what the author means by a computer 'book'.

2. Why do you think a reader of a computer book might want to vary the speed at which text appears?

3. What is your opinion on computer books?

4. What changes did the author forecast for cars of the 1980s?

5. Explain the underlined words and phrases.

6. Was the author correct in his forecasts? Explain.

Coca Cola - How it Began

John Styth Pemberton is hardly a household name. But just 100 years ago today, this obscure American chemist came up with two things which have changed the world's drinking habits. They were Coca Cola . . . and a taste for secrecy.

From humble beginnings in Atlanta on May 8, 1886, Coke has developed into the world's top-selling non-alcoholic drink. And the mystery that shrouds its popularity has spread to thousands of other household products. Like Coke, almost every big-selling food and drink these days is based on a formula known only to a handful of people and kept under lock and key in conditions of utmost security. But it was Coca Cola which started it all. It was originally made by melting sugar with water in a brass kettle over an open fire and adding certain ingredients. These were the coca leaf and the kola nut - hence the name.

But the rest of the recipe was secret, passed down by word of mouth so that only two top executives knew it at any one time. They were not allowed to travel together, or even stay in the same house, in case of accident. In 1909, a United States Government inspector analysed all the ingredients - except for the secret component called 7X. Today there are still only two bosses who know the full recipe - but, as a safeguard against unforeseen tragedy, it has been written down and locked in a vault at the Trust Company of Georgia Bank in Atlanta, not far from where the first kettleful was made.

Assignment   5

1. Who 'invented' Coca Cola?

2. What was his profession?

3. How did Coca Cola get its name?

4. What is the mystery that shrouds Coca Cola?

5. What measures have been taken to keep this a mystery?

Virgin Cola

Is there even one snippet of knowledge about the extraordinary billionaire Richard Branson that the public does not know? Everything from his collection of 300 jumpers to his preference for a sensible Rover rather than a Rolls Royce to what he had for breakfast this morning is known.

But making himself available to the media is his business. After all, it's cheaper than spending millions on glossy ad campaigns. In Dublin to oversee the official launch of his latest venture, Virgin Cola, Branson spent most of his time in the public arena, doing interviews and drinking cans of cola. He was scheduled to finish his week with a spot on Pat Kenny's TV show. It is well known that you will meet very few friendly billionaires but Branson appears to be an exception. Politeness is his trademark, along with his woolly jumpers.

But for a man with so much money and power, Branson presents himself as just your ordinary Joe Soap, who happens to have been lucky in life.

Branson, who founded Virgin Airways, Virgin Records and Virgin Megastores, likes to keep busy. In October 1994 he not only launched Virgin Cola but Virgin Vodka and Virgin Computers. He is worth nearly £1 billion, which makes him one of the 10 richest people in Britain. He owns two mansions in London, a country house in Oxfordshire, a holiday home in Minorca, and a private island in the Caribbean. But he wants more.

His latest target is the massive Coca Cola company, the world's leading soft drinks company. He is using the expertise of the Canadian drinks company Cotts, which claims to have cracked the secret recipe so closely guarded by Coca Cola for almost a century. Branson assumes a laid-back style when discussing the background to his new cola. He says he initially blind-tested the recipe for Virgin Cola against Coca Cola on his kids. Then he tried it out on 800 pupils in his children's school. The results showed that 8 out of 10 preferred Cotts' recipe to Coke's. He struck a 50-50 partnership deal with Cotts and forged ahead, guns blazing, to tackle Coca Cola's domination outside his kids' school playground.

He expects to sell over £50 million worth of Virgin Cola in England alone and make £5-£6 million profit.

Within weeks of its launch in Britain last autumn, Virgin Cola had secured 10 per cent of the British market. Ninety million cans have been sold so far. Branson believes he can overtake Coke in Britain within three years.

Coca Cola denies it is worried. But market share has dropped below 50 per cent for the first time and now the company has doubled its advertising for 1995. Branson accepts he will never topple Coke from its number one position in the US. But everywhere else in the world, he says, Virgin Cola will overtake Coke within 10 years.

Emphasising Virgin Cola's success so far, Branson tells a story of a shop in London that was broken into last week. The whole front window had a display of Virgin Cola. Behind it were the cans of Coca Cola. All the Virgin cans were stolen and the Coke was left behind.

Assignment 6

1. What personal details about Richard Branson are revealed in the first paragraph?

2. How does Branson make sure that the general public learn about his products?

3. What is meant by the phrase *"your ordinary Joe Soap"*?

4. List some of Branson's achievements.

5. Explain how he tested Virgin Cola.

6. Why did Branson go into partnership with Cotts?

7. What signs are there that Virgin Cola is likely to capture Coca Cola's share of the British market?

8. If you were interviewing Richard Branson what questions would you put to him? Write out the answers which you feel he would most likely give.

First Train Ever to Fly The Atlantic

The world's first flying train - a 112 tonne, 3,200 horse-power Iarnród Éireann locomotive, mounted on its own rails in the cargohold of a Ukrainian Antonov 124 Russian aircraft - became the first train ever to fly the Atlantic when it landed at Dublin Airport at 0730 hrs this morning with the heaviest load ever flown in Irish aviation history.

When the cargo door at the nose of the aircraft opened it revealed a 60 ft. long locomotive in shining new Iarnród Éireann colours and the most dramatic air cargo ever landed at an Irish airport.

The locomotive is the first of 10 ordered by Iarnród Éireann from General Motors of Canada.

Delivery of the first 201 Class locomotive is being made by air in advance of the remaining nine - which will be transported by sea - to allow for trials, driver training and performance checks so that the other locomotives can go into service immediately after their arrival in Ireland.

The new locomotives with 100 mph capacity are the fastest and the most powerful ever to operate in Ireland and are being built at the General Motors Electro Motive division's manufacturing plant at London, Ontario, in Canada.

Historic Flight

The historic flight, which will attract the attention of rail and air enthusiasts everywhere, left London Ontario at 18:20 Irish time on June 8 and stopped for refuelling at Montreal (Canada), Gander (Newfoundland) and Reykjavik (Iceland), arriving at Dublin Airport at 0729hrs on Thursday, June 9.

To airlift the locomotive, the Antonov 124 aircraft had train tracks installed for loading and unloading which was carried out through the giant cargo door in the nose of the plane.

This loading operation was co-ordinated by UK based Air Foyle, Antonov's Worldwide General Sales Agent, who also ensured that one of their flight managers, Kevin Creighton, accompanied the flight from Ontario.

It will be unloaded onto a multi-wheeled 12 axle truck, which will remain at the airport until late Thursday night and will then travel to Inchicore Works - a journey of over eight miles.

The truck will have a Garda escort and ESB and Telecom will clear any wires obstructing the route.

The 112 tonne locomotive is the second heaviest air cargo in the history of aviation. The world record for the heaviest single load ever transported by air was a 135.2 tonne generator from Siemens, Düsseldorf to New Delhi, India on September 22, 1993. This load was also carried by the Antonov 124.

The locomotive is to be used for high-speed InterCity and freight services planned for the Irish rail network during the 1990s. It will take eight hours to unload from the Antonov and will not be transported to Inchicore until after midnight, to avoid disrupting traffic on the Airport road.

Assignment 7

1. Why do you think the headline to this news story would make a reader curious to read the entire report?

2. State five separate facts about the locomotive that can be found in the article.

3. (i) How many locomotives were ordered?
   (ii) How will they all be delivered?

4. What will be done before the locomotive goes into service?

5. (i) How long did the total air journey take?
   (ii) How many stops were made for refuelling?

6. What person is named in the article? Explain why this person is named.

7. Why are the Gardaí, ESB and Telecom mentioned in the report?

8. Why is the journey to Inchicore taking place after midnight?

9. What fact in the report could be included in the *Guinness Book of Records*?

10. Look at the two photographs accompanying this story.
    (i) Write a sentence describing each one.
    (ii) If you were a newspaper editor, which photograph would you use to go with the report? Give a reason for your answer.

travel

UK

hot
Scotch

From purple-headed mountains to crystal clear lochs, Scotland offers great walks on the wild side as well as grand, cultured cities

Glamis castle

The delights of Dundee

'We arrived by train, catching our first view of Dundee across the spectacularly wide River Tay,' says Louise Johnson who, with husband Barry and children John, six, and Lizzie, four, made the city their base for a week's holiday.

'As Dundee is a former ship-building town, many of its sights are connected with the sea. Our favourite family outing was to the Discovery Point museum on the waterfront, where Captain Scott's polar research ship, *Discovery*, is berthed. The interior of the ship has been kept as it was during Scott's voyages to the Antarctic at the beginning of the century, complete with all the crew's cabins and galleys.

'Of course, we couldn't resist a trip to Shaw's Dundee Sweet Factory. Here, the Shaw family are still turning out ten tonnes of boiled sweets, humbugs and fudge a week, all made to traditional recipes. A visit to the factory shop on the way out was a must!

'We hired a car for a few days because the beautiful Angus Glens and the Perthshire lochs are only a 1½ hour drive away. If you're keen on golf, you'll be in paradise here: Dundee is

Glencoe Gorge

surrounded by more than 40 golf courses – including the famous St Andrew's and Gleneagles – all within an hour's drive away.

'Also near is Glamis Castle, near Forfar, famous as both the Queen Mother's childhood home and the setting for Shakespeare's *Macbeth*. You can see the enormous dining rooms and surprisingly cosy living rooms, as well as the elegant gardens with an ornate sundial more than 21 feet high. Our stay passed all too quickly, but we returned refreshed from our breath of fresh Scottish air.'

Louise and family stayed at the four-star Angus Thistle Hotel (tel: 01382 226874). Prices start at £32.50 per person per night for b&b. Family rooms are also available.

Assignment **8**

1. (i) How did the Johnson family travel to Dundee?
    (ii) How long did they spend there?

2. What do we learn from the report about the Discovery Point Museum?

3. Explain how the Shaws make money from the visitors to their factory.

4. What places did the family visit outside Dundee?

5. What does the report say about golf facilities in the area?

6. What features of Glamis Castle did the Johnson family find interesting?

7. Is there evidence in the report that they enjoyed the holiday? Explain.

8. Describe each of the photographs accompanying the report and explain how they are connected with the report.

9. Study the caption in the top photograph and say what four attractions are mentioned.

10. Select a town or village in Ireland with which you are familiar and write a similar style report on a week's holiday you have spent there.

Cold Snap Set To 'March' On

WINTER continues to hold the country in its icy grip with severe frost plunging temperatures to some of their lowest levels of the year.

The west and south of the country once again bore the brunt with heavy snowfalls causing chaos.

The Met. Office said there was more to come, with bitterly cold conditions and snowshowers forecast for tomorrow and Monday.

With the east coast expected to finally get a taste of snow this weekend, there were fears of more flooding in some parts of the country when the thaw starts.

Temperatures were expected to plummet overnight to as low as minus five degrees celsius in some areas.

Donegal, Sligo, Leitrim, Roscommon, Monaghan, Galway, Limerick, Tipperary and Cork were worst hit by the weather.

Barring blizzard conditions, today's Five Nations rugby clash between Ireland and France will go ahead at Dublin's Lansdowne Road.

A Met. Office spokesman said the cold snap was expected to last for the next few days and the indications were that it would be well into the week before temperatures rise.

Assignment 9

1. (i)   In what month of the year do you think this report was published? Explain your answer.
    (ii) On what day of the week was this report published? Explain your answer.

2. Explain the phrases *'bore the brunt'*, *'causing chaos'*, *'plummet'*.

3. What, according to the report, is likely to cause more flooding?

4. What event may be affected by the bad weather?

Where is Jabbar Rashid Shifki?

In Iraq, children 'disappear' … or are tortured … or are executed. Sometimes without even a trial. They have been shot dead on demonstrations, or dragged from school, lined up against a wall and shot in public.

15-year old Jabbar Rashid Shifki was one of 315 Kurdish children arrested by the Iraqi army in August 1983. None of them was ever seen again. The authorities refuse to tell us what they've done with them. They get angry when we ask.

Saddam Hussein knows though. A month after the arrests, he said *"Those people were severely punished and went to hell"*.

Let's keep asking. Add your voice to ours - **join us**.

☐ **I wish to join Amnesty International**

I enclose   ☐ £18 Individual   ☐ £6 Unwaged

                 ☐ 25 Family/Household   ☐ £9 Unwaged Household

I wish to donate ☐ £100   ☐ £50   ☐ £25   ☐ £10   Other £_____

Total payment £_____   ☐ I enclose a cheque/postal order

Name(s) [BLOCK CAPS] _____

Address _____

_____

Tel.: _____ (home) _____ (work)

AMNESTY INTERNATIONAL
Dept. IT Z/94, 8 Shaw St. FREEPOST, Dublin 2.
To join or donate instantly by credit card, please phone (01) 6776361 or fax (01) 6776392.

Assignment   10

1. *'Where is Jabbar Rashid Shifki?'* Why might this headline make a reader cusious to read the remainder of the advertisement?
2. What do we learn about him from the advertisement?
3. *'Sometimes without even a trial.'* Explain clearly what this means.
4. *'The authorities …'* Who, in this case, are the authorities?
5. What does the advertisement want the reader to do?
6. How much would it cost an unwaged family to join Amnesty International?
7. Can you explain the symbol for Amnesty International shown in the bottom left-hand corner of the advertisment?
8. What are your feelings after reading the advertisement?

DESCRIBING PHOTOGRAPHS AND PICTURES

General Description

- Begin with a **general description** of the subject of the photograph e.g. *This is a photograph of ... a crowded street ... a bridge ... a family ... an old house ... a group of people watching a street musician ... etc.*

- Next describe, in more detail, the **main subject** of the picture. You must decide what details to include here. Give the most important ones. Bear in mind such things as size, number (of windows, people, trees etc.), material from which it is made, weather conditions etc.

Background Details

- Describe briefly the **background details.** *(Indoors, countryside, street).*

- If you are asked to describe a colour photograph then you will need to give details of the colours of the main elements in the picture.

- If possible state the location of the picture. Sometimes this will be obvious, sometimes impossible to tell. Make a guess by studying the picture carefully.

Describing People in Pictures

- Begin by stating the obvious details — Sex, approximate age, race, noticeable or striking features, hairstyle, clothing.

- Describe the expression on the face — amused, angry, sad, worried, puzzled, surprised, contented, frightened etc.

- Perhaps there is evidence in the background of the picture which may tell you more about the person or why she or he appears to be in a certain mood.

Purpose of Picture

- Finally, state what you think is the **purpose** of the photograph e.g. *To show the beauty of nature (a lake/a river/a garden/a park) ... to capture the joy of a family gathering (a wedding/an outing) ... to show off the attractive features of a car/a motorbike/a building ... to capture the excitement of a sporting event ... to illustrate some feature of a news story (a traffic accident/a flood/a strike) ... to illustrate some kind of hardship that people may be suffering (poverty/war/homelessness)*

- These are broad guidelines only. Select only those which you think apply best to any photograph you are describing.

Assignment **11**

1. Write a complete description of the previous 2 and following 4 pictures.
2. Cut out some pictures from magazines and write a description of each one.

1. **2.** **3.**

4. **5.** **6.**

7. **8.** **9.**

10. **11.** **12.**

Assignment **12**

1. Describe the expression on each of the faces above.
2. What, in your opinion, would cause people to make each of these faces?

Assignment 13

1. Tell the story of Dicky's first trick in your own words.

2. Find suitable words to describe
   (i) Mum's expression in frame three.
   (ii) Dicky's expression in frame four.

3. What features of the cartoonist's drawings helped you choose your answers to question 2?

4. What do you think will happen after frame five when Dicky warns his dad about the frog?

Assignment 14

1. Write an accurate description of Boppo's appearance.

2. Describe what Boppo does in the first three frames and say what kind of person Boppo is?

3. In frame four Boppo is laughing. Is it a pleasant laugh? Explain.

4. What happens next?

5. Describe the expression on Boppo's face in the final frame. Why is he looking like this? What is likely to happen next?

Assignment **15**

1. Explain clearly what Danny's tranny is.

2. *'I can't mend your stilts but I can ...'*
   What else do you think Danny said to the man with the broken stilts?

3. (i) Describe the man talking to Danny in frame three.
   (ii) What did he want from Danny?

4. Write a detailed account of how Danny improved the circus.

5. In the last frame the clown says to Danny - *'... this is really pulling in the crowds'*. What do you think he meant by these words?

6. Imagine that you had a tranny like Danny's. Write an account of some of the things that you would do with it.

Assignment **16**

These are the first and the last pictures of a 'Dennis the Menace' cartoon.

1. Describe each of the pictures.

2. Tell the story of what is likely to have happened.

3. What type of boy is Dennis?

Assignment **17**

1. What product is being advertised here?
2. Why do you think there are no illustrations of men in this ad?
3. Describe the illustration and say why it is (or is not) a good illustration for selling the product.
4. What things about the product are stressed in the advertisement?
5. The advertisers use the slogan *"Take Control"* - Can you explain this?
6. Imagine that your mother won a new tumble dryer and wants to sell her old one. Compose a suitable advertisement for your local paper and for the noticeboard of your local supermarket.

Send us any butter wrapper and try

FLORA EXTRA RICH FREE!

Good news for butter nutters!

If there's a butter nutter in your family who still hasn't tried **Flora Extra Rich**, here's an offer you won't be able to resist. Just simply slip any butter wrapper into an envelope with the application form below and send it off to us. In return we'll send you a voucher for a FREE 500g pack of **Flora Extra Rich** sunflower spread.

Flora Extra Rich has a delicious butter-like taste which they'll adore but, as it's made from pure sunflower oil, it contains only a third of the saturated fat of butter. So why not use **Flora Extra Rich** as part of a healthier diet.

Simply complete this form and send it with any clean butter wrapper to
FREE FLORA EXTRA RICH, Dept 7035, Hendon Road, Sunderland, SR9 9XZ

Name: BLOCK CAPITALS PLEASE

Address:

Postcode:

Please send me a voucher which can be used at most stockists to obtain a Free 500g pack of Flora Extra Rich. Offer closes 31/7/95.

Assignment 18

1. There are two illustrations in this advertisement. Write an accurate description of each one and explain how they each help to get the message of the advertisement across.

2. Explain in detail what you must do to get some free *Flora Extra Rich*.

3. According to the advertisement, how is the product (*Flora Extra Rich*) (i) similar to butter and (ii) different from butter?

4. This advertisement is taken from a magazine on sale in Ireland. Is the advertisement aimed at Irish readers? Explain.

Assignment **19**

1. Match each picture on this and the following pages with a caption from the following list.
   (a) In Safe Hands
   (b) Water is Life
   (c) Play it Again, Sam
   (d) Transport in the Good Old Days

   (e) Enjoying Our Waterways
   (f) Defender of a New Nation
   (g) Hands off, it's Mine!
   (h) A Tempting Catch

2. Write a detailed description of each picture.

1

2

3

4

5

6

7

8